D1134276

Mobility and Integration in Urban Argentina:
Córdoba in the Liberal Era

Latin American Monographs, No. 52
Institute of Latin American Studies
The University of Texas at Austin

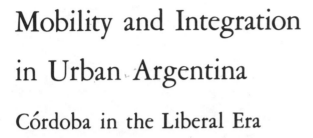

Mobility and Integration in Urban Argentina

Córdoba in the Liberal Era

by Mark D. Szuchman

University of Texas Press, Austin and London

Library of Congress Cataloging in Publication Data

Szuchman, Mark D   1948-
    Mobility and integration in urban Argentina.

    (Latin American monographs; no. 52)
    Bibliography: p.
    Includes index.
    1. Social mobility—Argentine Republic—
Córdoba—History. I. Title. II. Series: Latin
American monographs (Austin, Tex.); no. 52.
HN270.C6S95   305.5´0982´54   80-14857
ISBN 0-292-75057-9

Requests for permission to reproduce material from
this work should be sent to:
    Permissions
    University of Texas Press
    P.O. Box 7819
    Austin, Texas 78712

To Paula,
conceived at about the same time

Contents

Tables

Maps

Acknowledgments

More than my efforts went into this work. The aid, guidance, energy, and wisdom of many others went a long way toward its completion. The project was initially made possible by a fellowship from the Doherty Foundation; subsequent grants were made by the Graduate School and the Institute of Latin American Studies at The University of Texas at Austin. Córdoba is for North Americans an academic frontier, as is still much of the Argentine interior; without the help of *cordobeses* involved in historical research, mine would have floundered. Specifically, I would like to single out Dr. Aurelio Tanodi of the Escuela de Archiveros of the Instituto de Estudios Americanistas, and the director of the Instituto, Dr. Carlos Luque Colombres. Licenciado Joaquín García gave me total freedom to use the extensive newspaper collection of the Biblioteca Mayor of the Universidad Nacional de Córdoba, as well as an office; Dr. Walter Dorflinger of the Department of Economics helped with matters of sampling procedures. The archival work was made much easier by the courtesy extended by Dr. José María de Elías, associate director of the Registro Civil Municipal; Monsignor Audicio, director of the archive of the Archdiocese of Córdoba; Licenciado Moyano Aliaga, director of the Archivo Histórico de la Provincia; and Licenciado Miguel Angel Terré, director of the Archivo Municipal.

Fellow historians Edmundo Heredia, Emiliano Endrek, María Cristina Vera de Flachs, and Hector and Norma Lobos provided academic and social life. Richard Graham, Karl Schmitt, and Richard Sinkin read earlier versions of the work and provided insightful and useful comments. Tom McGann, who first proposed to me the possibility of researching a social history project in Córdoba, followed his suggestion with active interest, comments, and the best of all forms of supervision: the encouragement of independence. The effects of the exchanges I had with Gene Sofer in the course of several years are present throughout this book. Lenore T. Szuchman provided all.

Mobility and Integration in Urban Argentina:
Córdoba in the Liberal Era

Introduction

Beginning with the immigrant influx of the 1870s and lasting up to World War I, Argentine social composition and patterns of economic productivity underwent a radical alteration. The particular changes in culture, demography, and economic opportunities resulted in some degree of industrialization and lent vitality and speed to the transformation of a traditional Hispanic nation. National leaders, acting on their deep-seated beliefs in an exceptional Argentina destined for leadership among Spanish American nations, prompted their country's viability in the world's trading community. They attracted Europeans through rhetoric, claiming that Argentina offered opportunities for well-being and social mobility to all immigrants willing to take advantage of possibilities within the New World. *Hacer la América,* the label attached to the experiment of migrating to the Western Hemisphere, represented the aspirations of millions of Europeans who began to arrive in Buenos Aires in the late 1800s; to them the New World was not a mistake, as Martínez Estrada wrote, but a godsend.[1] Even ardent critics of Argentina's shortcomings, who saw little evidence of European immigrants actually becoming rich, admitted that in some areas of the country opportunities indeed existed to become unimaginably wealthy.[2] Not surprisingly, the accumulation of money and property was a constant theme in the Argentina of the late nineteenth and early twentieth centuries.

The search for immigrants who would populate the country was mandated a national goal by the ratification of the constitution in 1853. The executive branch sought ways to encourage Europeans—preferably from the north and west—to settle and work in Argentina. A massive, complex machinery was set in motion to attract immigrants to the interior, where agricultural development suffered from lack of population. The Dirección de Inmigración devoted considerable effort to attracting through propaganda, arranging for, and subsidizing the transfer of immigrants from the city of Buenos Aires to the interior

Table i.1
Immigrant Labor Placement, 1873
(N=6562)

Placed in	Number	Percent
Concordia	1,550	23.6
Córdoba	1,495	22.8
Rosario	181	2.8
Other inland areas	606	9.2
Total	3,832	58.4

Source: Wilcken, *Memoria,* Planillas Nos. 10 and 11.

of the country. Although programs designed to bring Europeans inland did not prevent their heavy concentration in Buenos Aires, the Dirección de Inmigración, at the start of its functions, placed in the interior more than half of the persons it processed.

The Office of Immigration was especially proud of its record in Córdoba and of the successes in social mobility of the immigrants. According to officials, few foreigners had failed to improve considerably their socioeconomic position. The reasons for their improvement, argued the authorities, rested on the Argentine formula for inevitable successes: low cost of living, rich soil, unexploited economic frontiers, and freedom to exercise personal choices. Moreover, immigration managers insisted that immigrants would out-perform the Creoles—natives with an Argentine lineage of considerable extent—because European cultural norms were naturally geared toward self-improvement. To Argentine leaders, the immigrant was "free from all the impediments and pains that weigh on the son of this land."[3] Although European immigrants were not as widely sought following the socialist and anarchist activities of the early 1900s, Argentines never rejected the belief that their society represented an open system of economic opportunities proven by the upwardly mobile population.

The Argentine political and economic elite at mid-century, commonly known as the Generation of '37, discussed and wrote about the course their country should take. Most of them had been victimized by the omnipotent caudillo Juan Manuel de Rosas (1829-1852); they rearranged the political system in order to avoid any recurrence of what Domingo Sarmiento, one of the leading members, called the decay of civilization. The Generation of '37 restored constitutional government with restricted participation after the fall of Rosas in 1852. It failed, however, to resolve fully the issue of whether a federal or a central form of government would prevail, until the last in a series of armed struggles resulted in the federalization of the city of Buenos Aires in 1880. The members of the ruling clique that developed had in the process formed an oligarchy which grew richer and more powerful as Argentine exports and foreign investment in Platine development increased. These oligarchs, who collectively were labeled the Generation of '80, followed many of the dicta of the earlier Generation of '37, and executed an effective program of development and commercialization of the country's primary resources. Significantly, this new leadership was composed mostly of men from the interior, determined to rectify the previous political and economic imbalance that had existed between Buenos Aires and the rest of the country.[4] The Generation of '80 also hoped to transfer the new immigrant population, along with a portion of the nation's financial and political power, to the hinterland, which they felt the Europeans could exploit fully to the material benefit of all.

The propaganda machinery employed to attract immigrants included use of the national censuses. Those volumes were translated, printed, and sent to European centers as part of the literature on economic opportunities in Argentina. The published censuses of 1869, 1895, and 1914 have also served as the evidentiary bases for modern observers of Argentine society, which showed a high degree of social mobility during the period. One of the early—and principal—writers of this genre, particularly in the 1950s and 1960s, is Gino Germani, whose work *Estructura social de la Argentina* represents the seminal study on Argentine society for the second half of the nineteenth century and first half of the twentieth. In this highly quantified study containing over one hundred tables extracted mostly from the published censuses of Argentina and Buenos Aires, Germani portrays Argentina as having historically maintained a society stratified rigidly only at its uppermost level; below it, the increases in the "secondary" and "tertiary" sectors between 1869 and 1914 prove that social mobility was viable for residents of Argentina, especially for the immigrants. Subsequent scholars, including Cortés Conde, Cornblit, Romero, and Beyhaut, have echoed some of Germani's conclusions. Their basic tools were similar: aggregate and published data, in addition to some impressionistic literature. These studies often resulted from symposia on Argentine social history held throughout the late 1950s and early 1960s. We may divide their verdicts into two general categories: on the one hand, an indictment of the liberal economic policies that resulted in a late, unsteady process of industrialization; on the other, an appraisal of Argentine social structures as having permitted rapid, successful mobility patterns.

In 1961 the literature on Argentine social structure and mobility culminated with Germani's massive research effort in Buenos Aires on mobility and migrants. Some of the results were published in 1963 as an appendix to the Argentine edition of Lipset and Bendix' *Social Mobility in Industrial Society.* Through survey techniques, Germani gathered data on migrants to the city of Buenos Aires. The levels of social mobility, in terms of occupation, education, and other variables, proved to be high. During the period of mass immigration, according to Germani, the majority of foreigners moved from unskilled and semiskilled levels of occupation to "middle-strata." Afterward, the process slowed somewhat, but social mobility remained a realistic possibility in Argentina.[5] A historical continuum has, therefore, been posited, indicating that mobility patterns in Argentina (not unlike those in the United States) resulted in an expansion of the middle class unparalleled in other Latin American nations.

This work investigates the historical intricacies of social mobility in the leading Argentine interior city of Córdoba and the setting in which such an expansion supposedly took place. One purpose is to impart both a narrower geographic focus and a historical context upon the issue of social mobility; the nation is too large an operational unit for in-depth analysis, and nearly all studies of social mobility by modern survey techniques have focused on Buenos Aires. One of the central themes of the Argentine experience has been, however, that same division between Buenos Aires and the rest of the nation; evidently, the literature on historical social stratification has followed the historical norm. The dichotomy between the nation's capital and the rest of the land and, indeed, between the city and the countryside in Latin America has been the subject of much historical literature. Yet if factors of culture, race, and entrepreneurial ethic, among others, have figured as prominent historical differentiators between urban and nonurban centers, social mobility has not. We tend to think of social mobility in present-oriented terms, but it also has a historical dynamic, which has been shaped, radically altered, or retained from the past.

But what of its historical development? If the labor of sociologists like Germani, who worked on Buenos Aires, or like that of Balán, Browning, and Jelin, who worked on Monterrey, or of T. Lynn Smith on Colombia, is of tremendous value for its empirical data and analyses, similar historical studies are difficult to find.[6] Social mobility per se has not been generally considered a subject for systematic investigation in Latin American history, despite myriad references to it or to its consequences in literature treating colonial or post-independence topics. We take for granted statements about "castes," "elites," "the poor," "merchants," or "immigrants," to name a few, without fully integrating them and their socioeconomic activities into a social continuum from the past. The relative absence of historical social-mobility studies on Latin

America is all the more striking when one considers that such studies have been made of the United States, especially its cities, for some time. The literature on historical social mobility in North American cities has mushroomed in the decade since Stephan Thernstrom's study of mobility in Newburyport during the second half of the nineteenth century broke new ground in the field of urban history.[7] The historiography of the so-called new urban history in the United States is extensive by now, much of it relying on quantitative techniques and manuscript sources. The Latin American counterpart is only just beginning. It is hoped that this work, then, provides an Argentine contribution to the growing field of urban social history.

For a variety of reasons, the Argentine historiographic tradition in general has resulted in a lacuna of social history in the purer sense—that is, unfettered by frequent references to political personalities or their consequences on the economic environment. In sum, writes Tulio Halperín Donghi,

> the search for a social clue to the ideological-political conflict has not yet resulted in totally satisfactory conclusions; either the social contentions are cast once again along ideological-political lines or the continuity between the two becomes even less evident. By the time the researcher's inquiry starts, he has already formed an image of that conflict, which will not be altered by any discoveries emanating from researching the conflict's social aspects. . . . In this fashion, even those who search in social and economic histories for the keystone to political history remain subordinate to the latter.[8]

For a study like this one, which contains little of a political nature and has as its principal thrust, local social changes, few secondary materials can be called upon for support. It is hoped that this book can be an important step in filling the void. Now that in recent years the extent and variety of social mobility patterns have come under examination in the United States, this work puts the Argentine version to some of the same tests of veracity used in the North American context by such scholars as Peter Knights, Clyde Griffen, Richard Sennett, Howard Chudacoff, and others.[9]

Method and Structure

This work traces the lives of several thousand residents of the city of Córdoba in the late nineteenth and early twentieth centuries. We selected Córdoba partly for reasons of culture and tradition: it has played a traditionally important role in the course of the Argentine political process; it has been a focus of the nation's intellectual activity; and it was a central juncture between the country's northern and western regions and the metropolis of

Buenos Aires. In addition, it has continually vied with Rosario for second
rank in extent and population among Argentine cities. Further practical advantages for the study of Córdoba lie in the facilities for research there: it offers
certain types of documentation unavailable in other cities, such as Buenos
Aires, and the informal arrangements required to use archives are simpler in a
provincial city like Córdoba, with its almost one million inhabitants, than in
Buenos Aires, which is perhaps ten times larger.

In addition, Córdoba provides a laboratory to test the nation's promise and
ideology of success. As is seen throughout this work, one could find in Córdoba the same attitudes toward material culture expressed by national leaders:
high hopes of achieving wealth; orientation toward the land as the basis for
industrial expansion; high admiration for immigrants and demand for their
labor; expectations of becoming the largest commercial and bureaucratic center in the interior; and so on. Córdoba's authorities manifested their aspirations with more than just rhetoric. Provincial agents were sent to Europe and
to Buenos Aires to recruit immigrants to settle the land, and the provincial
legislature turned over large tracts of fertile territories for colonization.[10] To
attract investments to its cities, Córdoba's municipal and provincial authorities
provided generous tax incentives to anyone who wished to open new commercial and industrial establishments.[11] Special dispensations and grants were
made to immigrants' organizations aimed at promoting and cementing relations
between local elites and the "civilizing" elements of European culture, as liberals put it.[12] Thus, if labor, demographic, and economic conditions in some
parts of Europe constituted the "push" factors aiding emigration, Córdoba had
"pull" factors of its own: propaganda, land grants, incentives, a central location, a commercial entrepôt, a railway junction linking the littoral with the
north and west, and a progressive outlook on the future.

Standing in the late 1860s in Córdoba, one could legitimately expect its
future growth and social improvement to be compatible with the promise of
opportunities found in contemporary Buenos Aires. From our current perspective it does not seem reasonable to assume that merely because Buenos
Aires possessed the main port it would necessarily monopolize social changes,
opportunities for self-improvement, and growth. Variants of *porteño* changes
could be found elsewhere in Argentina. The cities of Bogotá, Mexico, Santiago,
and Lima, as well as cities in the midwest of the United States, certainly show
that interior cities can also accrue such benefits.

Since Córdoba was the site for both in-migrants and immigrants, and since
Europeans did not settle in the large numbers that were to be found in Buenos
Aires, the city affords a site for observing the interrelationships between the
majority host culture and the newcomers from Europe. In the study of some
issues, like marriage selection and residential distribution, the high number of

migrant Argentines—non-*cordobeses*—will be compared to the immigrants. The selection of Córdoba thus permits the identification of the variables *ethnicity* and *migration* as factors which condition the complex of variables relating to mobility.

The enormous demographic growth of Buenos Aires, beginning in the second half of the nineteenth century, made the city unique in Argentina; in many ways it became less Argentine, as almost half of the annual growth rate between 1895 and 1914 came from the influx of Europeans.[13] No other Argentine city could make this claim. But if so fast a rate of growth was a source of pride for many porteño contemporaries, for the modern social observer the questions regarding a minority's assimilation and integration into a majority culture could become problematic as immigrants competed with and finally won out over the natives for the largest share of the local population. Córdoba's more tempered growth, however, retained its majority of Argentines and still witnessed a respectable growth in the number of Europeans. Here, then, is an appropriate site for testing integration: cosmopolitan and with a modern orientation, Córdoba was nevertheless not overwhelmed by either cosmopolitanism or the forces of modernization.

No single documentary source could provide data on all the questions and variables to which we wanted to address ourselves. Therefore, the people we studied comprised a number of samples and universes, gathered from different documentary sources. In this work we present the results of four such groupings. At the outset we should mention that, as is the case with other studies of individual cities, many of the statistical results are biased toward those who remained in Córdoba. The first sample was gathered from the manuscript census returns for the city of Córdoba in 1869 with the aid of a table of random numbers; it yielded 696 sample members stratified into cordobés and noncordobés categories, which include men and women above the age of fifteen. The sample size provided statistical results significant to the .05 level (unless noted otherwise in the tables), using a confidence level of 95 percent and a confidence interval of plus or minus 5 percent. This means that we could draw an infinite number of samples of the same size and the results of 95 percent of them would vary no more than 5 percent from the universe, or totality of the population. In order to verify the correct identities of sample members in the course of tracing their names into other documents, we included their families and traced them as well. This process meant that, in effect, we subjected an additional 1,583 men, women, and children to the same examinations as had been applied to the 696 sample members. We used this group to study the issues of mobility patterns in occupation, intra-urban geographic shifts, persistence in the city, university education, wealth accumulation and diversity, and vital statistics.[14]

It is important to understand the nature of systematic tracing, also known as record linkage, as a research tool in order to appreciate the validity and reliability of the data. Much of the primary material we have employed consists of several thousand notarial records, all of which were scanned in order to extract from them achievements and events in the lives of the sample members. This process entailed considerable effort, even though often it yielded no findings on sampled cases directly from the records. Our way of tracing, completely and systematically, however, does not imply wasted effort, in contrast to James Lockhart's opinion in the bibliographical section of his *Spanish Peru.* "To do the necessary notarial research for a specialized study," he wrote, "appears a sheer impossibility, not to speak of the wasted effort that would be involved, scanning so much material which would be irrelevant to the immediate purpose."[15]

By tracing specifically and systematically, however, researchers may find that if they have no trace of an individual in two or more sets of records, they have, in fact, uncovered data on that individual; in other words, "no information" can be interpreted as "information." Let us use the example of geographic persistence within the city of Córdoba as a way to illustrate this point. We shall assume that Juan Gómez is a sample member randomly selected from the manuscript census returns for the year 1869. Our goal is to find out whether he was living in Córdoba when the subsequent census was taken in 1895, or whether he had moved out of the city. We shall further suppose that tracing Juan Gómez into the manuscript census returns for 1895 yields nothing; but, the task is only half done, since there can be two reasons for his absence from the censal documentation: 1) he had actually moved out of Córdoba; or 2) he had died before the second census was taken. We must therefore go on to trace Juan Gómez through the death records of the Archdiocese and of the municipality's civil registry from 1869 through 1895. After so doing, we find his name still does not appear. Only now, after seemingly yielding no data, can we actually code Juan Gómez as not having persisted in the city between censal years.

Likewise, when we wanted to measure the educational mobility of sons at the university level, we traced the sample members to be "tested" into the enrollment books of the Universidad Nacional de Córdoba; when measuring economic mobility we traced sample members through all civil and commercial court records from 1869 through 1951, and so on. In all, the completion of the archival research involved perusing several hundred thousand documents.

Thus, we traced every individual systematically and completely through the 1895 manuscript census returns; the archive of the Archdiocese of Córdoba through 1880; the birth and death records in the municipal civil registry from 1880 through 1895; the city's notarial records from 1869 through 1882; the civil and commercial judicial proceedings from 1883 through 1951; and university enrollment records from 1869 through 1930. In addition, we employed city directories and lists of voters for municipal, provincial, and national elections.

We gathered the second sample in order to address the issue of the Argentine "melting pot." We wanted to investigate the patterns of marriage in Córdoba: how bachelor migrants chose their marriage partners, where they came from, where they lived in the city, what factors were responsible for the different levels of homogamy or exogamy, and how viable marriage was as a means of social mobility. We randomly sampled 648 unions (1 in 5) which took place between 1869 and 1909, in which the males were not natives of the city of Córdoba. The significance level of this sample was a very high .0001; the confidence level was 99 percent, and the confidence interval varied by 5 percent. We operated with such variables as occupation, ethnicity, year of marriage, age, and address in the city. The sample came from the archive of the Archdiocese, which kept a complete record of unions in which one of the partners was not cordobés. The municipal civil registry rounded out the data not included in the Archdiocesan archive.

The most vital institutions of the French and Spanish communities in Córdoba, their voluntary associations, supplied two other groups. The members' registries yielded data on 469 Frenchmen and 467 Spaniards. Since the members gathered formed the totality rather than samples of memberships during the years we are studying, we are not concerned with significance or probability figures. The personal data, together with the minutes of their meetings, provided answers to questions relating to the group members' normative values, to class differentiations within the immigrant communities, to the issues unifying and separating members, and to the differences between the constituencies of ethnic voluntary associations and the immigrants who operated outside of them. We therefore have made an effort to disassociate ourselves from the studies of immigration in Argentina which traditionally use the whole of each nationality as the operative unit; instead, we focused on the differences within each ethnic group. We did this because we assume that social behavior is not wholly a function of birthplace, but also of particular needs and limits surrounding social classes and environments. Unfortunately, the Italians' contemporary association did not preserve its records, making it impossible to study this group in similar fashion. In addition to gathering the data provided by the voluntary associations, we also traced the members through the civil registry, probate records, and the manuscript census returns.

Essentially, different sections of the work address themselves to issues and concepts of mobility and integration of one of four groups in Córdoba during the late nineteenth and early twentieth centuries: the general population, the migrants who married, the French community, and the Spaniards who belonged to the Spanish voluntary association. Our goal—to describe the social structure of the most important city in the Argentine interior—requires answers to the following questions: Who were these people? Where did they come from? Where did they live? What did they do? How long did they stay? How economically successful were they? Whom did they marry? With whom did they form social or ideological allegiances? We use different kinds of samples to bring forth the answers related to those issues. Together, the samples provide a widely encompassing social picture of Córdoba: the unskilled laborer; the European migrant; the bachelor in search of roots and identity; the merchant seeking or giving credit; the member of the elite, comprised of the oligarchs who represented perhaps 10 percent of the population, blind to some of the realities around him. The challenge that the pursuit of security in Córdoba entailed for most people and the failures of many to persist successfully make up a large part of our story.

Any study treating subjects of social mobility and integration must eventually grapple with the issue of status in the community, its definitions and parameters. To the extent that social stratification contains cultural and traditional components, status, a universal concept, takes on an even greater importance in a society with a Hispanic heritage, even if that society should be undergoing modernization.[16] Were this a contemporary sociological study, it could rely on survey techniques to delineate status attainment within cordobés society, and perhaps compare it with similar studies in the United States and Europe.[17] In fact, status has been shown to be closely linked to modern times with occupation and remuneration by sociologists Joseph Kahl, James Davis, Alex Inkeles and Peter Rossi.[18] The work of Inkeles and Rossi indicates remarkable similarity of prestige rankings accorded to the same occupations based on status hierarchy. Although invariable across space, prestige rankings pose the problem to historians of not being constant across time. Thus, while history is increasingly borrowing constructs from other disciplines, historians must avoid the use of status and occupational scales and models which are ahistorical.[19]

If the nature of historical studies prevents us from extrapolating totally from the present onto the past, such a limitation does not preclude the employment of certain sociological frameworks to observe a social stratification system, specifically its socio-occupational parameters. To this end we accept the notion that occupation and its financial remuneration are historical constants. The study of the occupational structure is thus well suited for uncovering a wide variety of social ramifications, since every occupation serves three functions. It performs as an economic differentiator, because it is an important source of income; it denotes a social role as a determinant of the general division of labor; and as a specialization of one's social function, it helps us to define prestige, class position and lifestyle. Not surprisingly, social research on Latin American occupational and social stratification has concentrated on the normative alterations in societies undergoing industrialization. Examples of this type of literature can be found in Fernando Cardoso's and José Reyna's "Industrialization, Occupational Structure, and Social Stratification in Latin America," and in Roberto Cortés Conde's "Problemas del crecimiento industrial (1870-1914)."[20]

Our study makes use of individuals' occupational and residential patterns to draw certain pictures of social status in the local community and to posit certain ideas on the role of immigrants to Argentina in terms of labor and residence. According to geographers Phillip Wagner and Marvin Mikesell, the observance of clusters of people with verifiable common characteristics allows us to classify areas according to their inhabitants.[21] Moreover, spatial models give location a cultural weighting that itself becomes an element of cultural variation. Location can thereby aid in explaining a society's cultural network, and it is also a consideration in the assignment of status.[22]

The quantitative thrust of this study is designed to give our results greater credibility at more and different levels of analysis than would be the case had we relied primarily on impressionistic literature. Dissatisfied with making general statements about the development, for example, of an Argentine middle class toward the end of the nineteenth century based upon a few examples and contemporary observations, in this work we try to go beyond to define the types and limits of "middle classness." With the computer's help, these parameters were framed in terms of where people lived in the city; or in terms of numerical distinctions of personal and real property, such as the extent of lands owned, their values, their locations, types and values of animals, and so on; or in terms of occupational levels or education. In short, with quantitative techniques we tried to add substance and limits to some frequently cited attributes of Argentine urban society.

The Argentine government itself sponsored the compilation of statistical data in the European tradition prevalent during the nineteenth and early twentieth centuries. Thus, while the volume of published aggregate data is large, the grants and facilities that the Argentine state accorded to social scientists promoted biases and had debilitating effects on research. Similar to the contemporary European case, this process caused some of the earlier historians to "become uncritical, irresponsible propagandists."[23]

At the local and regional levels the paucity of literature on social topics kept to a minimum the number of publications on social history. Enrique Martínez Paz's *La formación histórica de la Provincia de Córdoba,* written in 1941, was the first modern synthesis of Córdoba's history and became incorporated into the greater *Historia de la nación argentina* compiled by Levene.

Its focus is narrow in time (1810-1862) and in thrust (political events).[24] More recently, Efraín U. Bischoff's *Historia de la Provincia de Córdoba,* though broader in chronological perspective, provides only brief glimpses of the city's social composition, while the thrust of the work remains political in nature.[25]

Thus, the dearth of secondary materials on the city of Córdoba forces the researcher to use, in addition to primary documentation, other sources seemingly tangential to social mobility, the immediate subject at hand. The reader may note that our use of newspaper articles usually gives social pictures and opinions rather than news items. In addition, books and articles on health and sanitation prove useful in depicting lower-class living; works on the local music scene sometimes include the parlor ambiences of the rich; little-known memoirs of men who had spent their childhood years in nineteenth-century Córdoba depict scenes that add social environment to our statistical calculations; and, whenever plausible, urban and social experiences elsewhere in the nation or in cities outside of Argentina during similar periods give much-needed depth and relevance to the cordobés experience. We have aimed in this study to provide an analysis with great explanatory power, although limits of time and materials sometimes left the statistical data alone to defend the relevant points; in general, however, we have tried to provide social perspectives and theories to round out and humanize the quantitative material.

Certain of the premises and the sense of logic applied to this work are best placed in the proper context at the outset. The period under discussion in this book varies according to chapter, but it covers roughly from the late 1860s to World War I. It was an era of optimism which, despite the manifestations of modernization in major Argentine cities, obscured the uneven distribution of income and the frailty of the emerging middle groups—periodic victims of the cyclical economy. The political leadership during this period sought to integrate Argentina with trans-Atlantic economies by linking the yields of the fertile pampas to the sustenance needs of a growing European population, at the same time drawing on the surplus of that population to serve the need for manpower in an underpopulated Argentina. In order for this model of exchange to succeed, the liberal ethos claimed to contain the ingredients for the improvement and growth of both the individual and the society. Such an evolution, however, was conditioned by adherence to an economic relationship predicated on the model of comparative advantage: Europe—particularly England—would provide investment funds and durable consumer goods requiring industrial technology, while Argentina delivered grains and processed foodstuffs.

Liberalism, as applied in Argentina, was more than merely an economic approach to such issues as national integration or development. It was also an intellectual and moral force which defined what was to be proper modern human behavior; what would be the "civilized" norm in man's program of material acquisitions and exchanges; what would be the extent of an individual's activities within a restricted field of political transaction, inspired and led by a patrimonial oligarchy; and what would be the urban occupational opportunities generated by the process, first, of demographic growth resulting from immigration programs and, subsequently, of increased consumer demand deriving from revenues attendant to the export sector. Thus, an important component of the liberal ethos was the notion of individual self-realization in an environment ripe with opportunity.

Under the aura of free competition, private investment in urban commerce was encouraged for the most part philosophically, since neither private nor official lending institutions provided much credit to merchants or to small-scale industrialists. In short order, late nineteenth-century Argentine urbanization was depicted as an environment of great success, growth, and stability. However, there was large-scale population turnover, and it therefore becomes necessary to arrive at a series of explanations to account for such population mobility. I emphasize the plural quality of "explanations" not only because there is no one answer, but also because the nature of urban historical research encourages the search for a variety of factors. No single variable definitively showed absence or abundance of opportunities for material improvement. This work relies instead on a combination of indicators, including, among others, the incidence of wealth and its dimensions; the quality, size and location of an individual's home; shifts in occupational rank; and type of investments in real or personal property. The point to remember is that it is the compendium of these indicators which allows the argument that high levels of population mobility must have resulted from that population's inability to reach the levels of success they had been led to expect for themselves.

The conclusions found in this book are in fact interpretations applied to a variety of statistical and qualitative results, some of which would show only tendencies if observed individually. Yet, the accumulation of certain "soft" tendencies, when joined to a number of "hard" results, points to the need to reassess the paradigm employed to explain the Argentine—and possibly the Latin American—urban experience under liberalism.

Part I. Social Structure and Social Processes

1. Prospects of the City

The end of the 1860s promised to mark Córdoba's break with a turbulent past and its initiation into an era of peace, progress, and unity, along with the rest of Argentina. Even before the age of Juan Manuel de Rosas came to an end in 1852, the city had been at the mercy of a succession of caudillos, great and small, who had paraded triumphantly through its streets. Córdoba's social and political instability during the first fifty years of independent life may be symbolized by the installation in 1810 of the country's first gunpowder factory in the area of Pucará, adjacent to the central city.[1] As capital of the province and central juncture in the nation's commercial and military traffic, the city was captured initially by the followers of Juan Pablo Bulnes in 1816 and 1817, and later by the Army of the North under its mutinous leader, Juan Bautista Bustos, who in 1820 had led that contingent away from its campaigns in the Province of Santa Fe.

Under Bustos' direction, Córdoba struck the first blow against plans for a unified Argentina. The Provincial Assembly declared the province's own sovereignty, but agreed to maintain friendly relations with and come to the aid of the other provinces. Córdoba was not to return to the Argentine union until Justo Juan de Urquiza's victory over Rosas in 1852. In the meantime, the city and its environs continued to be the scene of encampments, armies of occupation, and battles between unitary and federal forces. After José M. Paz's defeat of Bustos in 1829, Córdoba's citizens witnessed two years of indecisive campaigns fought between Paz and Juan Facundo Quiroga, who had invaded the province in defense of his defeated ally.

Quiroga retained power in Córdoba and much of the interior until his assassination in 1835, when Manuel López, another federalist and ally of Rosas, gained control. For more than sixteen years López ruled with an iron fist over a mostly terrorized elite, a complacent legislature, and a generally supportive lower class. He was given to fits of vengeance, even against his own people.

The city underwent sporadic flares of terror after each uprising against López personally or against the federalist cause in general: victorious troops pillaged homes, and the heads of suspected dissenters sometimes appeared in the city's *paseos* as frightening reminders of the newly implanted order.

The end of the Holy Federation in 1852, and with it the end of López's rule in Córdoba, signaled only a temporary respite in the city's cyclical political upheavals. Local and regional revolutions, federal interventions, and the nation's own instability produced no less than thirteen provincial governments in the 1860s. But some sense of direction and institutional promoters of stability were already developing: a commission to improve educational facilities was resurrected; the university became part of the national system of higher learning; freedom of the press was decreed; new towns were established in the interior of the province; a new, democratic provincial constitution became law. In sum, the principal concerns revolved increasingly around social and economic issues, and less around political terrorism or violent schisms.

Despite political changes, Córdoba had retained its position as the nation's intellectual center. At the heart of this status lay the university, founded in 1613 and representing the oldest continuing center of higher education in the land. Several of Argentina's presidents and ministers graduated from the University of Córdoba—mostly with law degrees—and safeguarded its continued lead in education and thought.[2] Its program of learning, narrow and dogmatic until the 1860s, had been responsible for persuading conservative wealthy families from other provinces to send their sons to Córdoba for their degrees. In fact, the city's intellectually rigid climate was such that they considered it "closed to imported customs that might loosen the restraints [taught at] home, and [the place where] the youth could acquire . . . only the best habits of respect, sociability and culture. . . ."[3] Beginning with Urquiza's administration in 1852, the university was revitalized and brought within the national educational system. But it was not until the late 1860s, with the efforts of Sarmiento and Avellaneda (the latter was himself an alumnus), that serious restructuring took place.[4] The city's uninterrupted moral and intellectual leadership served both as a link with a traditional Creole past and as a springboard for confidence in a cosmopolitan future. Thus, among national leaders and intellectuals, Córdoba merged the traditional established Creole and the forthcoming new Argentine.

Fresh attitudes toward the buildup of the countryside, agricultural exploitation, education, and a network of roads and railways represented the new sense of nationhood. The concern with order and legality, however, was sometimes exaggerated and was manifested by seemingly perennial regulations on vagrancy and lawlessness. What the country needed, reasoned the local leadership, was a hard-working population; but, complained some, the 1853 national constitution had undermined that goal by forbidding the use of lashing as a form of punishment for the criminal element. "Congress," complained an influential daily in an article on the unstable social order in the countryside, "has taken away the only sentence capable of teaching [criminals] that they should earn their bread with the sweat of their brows."[5]   Even before the fall of López, provincial authorities had decreed regulations governing work contracts in order to prevent the flight of laborers assigned to pack trains. The law of October 5, 1850 provided a punishment of five hundred lashes to peons captured after fleeing from their employers; then the police would return them to their bosses to finish serving the terms of their labor contracts.[6]   The new liberal governments installed after the fall of Rosas and López continued the policy of trying to eradicate poverty and vagrancy by the imposition of punitive laws. The government decreed that all beggars must register with the city's medical authorities and prove their inability to work. Anyone legally certified as a pauper then received from the police "an emblem which he should wear dangled from his neck in clearly visible fashion in order to be recognized and without which he could not seek alms."[7]

Naturally, the problems that poverty created remained unsolved by such laws; only basic changes in economic conditions and an increase in the demand for labor could correct the situation. Still, provincial and municipal authorities continued to provide laws intended to curb the incidence of beggars in the cities. The provisions of an 1859 provincial law permitted the city's subchief of police and two municipal authorities to "exile" vagrants to frontier garrisons for a period of four years.[8]   Military service in the frontier, patrolling and preventing Indian attacks, meant a lonely, dangerous existence; furthermore, officers often maltreated men who had been forcibly drafted.

Then, toward the middle of the 1860s, the city's commercial and political sectors turned their attention to the area's immediate future. The railroad line, soon to be completed, represented the heart of any and all progress, according to leading cordobeses. Progress was not simply material: the nation's political survival also depended on an efficient communication network.

Alberdi recognized the fact that no other sign of advancement was as evident as the improvement in the lines of access between the littoral and the interior. "The railroad and the electric telegraph," he wrote in *Bases*, ". . . perform this wonder better than all of the world's potentates. The railroad innovates, reforms and changes the most difficult things, without decrees nor riotous crowds. It will unify the Argentine Republic better than all congresses."[9]

Córdoba was to be the terminus of the first interprovincial railway line, the Ferrocarril Central Argentino, linking the city with Rosario. President Urquiza immediately accepted the original proposal drafted by Allen Campbell for such a line in 1854. At that time, Urquiza emphasized that no other line was as

important to the nation as the projected Córdoba-Rosario route.[10] When the
contract was signed in 1863, local interests hailed the event as panacea; Córdoba's spirits were soaring and the projections were all optimistic. The speculative mentality had also been awakened: the railroad, wrote an observer, "will
raise to the skies the values of our fruits, of our fields, and of our labor. On
the day that the railroad is begun all our properties are worth ten times more
and thereby we have ten times more capital."[11] Finances and morality were
thought to be intimately connected; new work habits would be developed and
the wealth would "radiate" moral progress in a population devoid of modernizing enterprise.[12]

Thus the belief in the potential of the country, of the province, of the city,
and of the population to become rich germinated during this period. The confidence to create a new order of prosperity continued to bloom with few inter-
ruptions throughout the century. Nothing could stop hard-working men from
building up their own stations if only they were frugal and disciplined in their
savings and labor. And the more people in the country—in Córdoba—the better
for everyone. The logical place to find new people was, of course, Europe.
The confidence among leading cordobeses spilled over even to the extent of
ascribing to Europeans their desire to come to Argentina. *El Eco de Córdoba*
asserted that "the European population cannot maintain itself in its . . . impoverished territory; it needs to spread out to another . . . domain and fill . . .
European markets with the . . . goods that it would reap from the American
desert."[13]

The railroad came, of course, and so did the European immigrants; but neither the city's economic base nor the wealth distribution among its inhabitants
was significantly altered during the balance of the century. The invigorating
spirits were not able to develop the city to the expected limits, and for quite
some time Córdoba continued to be "imponderably idle, quiet and somnolent."
On the eve of the first national census in 1869, it appeared "that very few people had anything to do, and among those who worked, very few gave any im-
pression of what they did."[14]

Anyone who arrived in Córdoba at that time was struck from afar by the
attractiveness and orderly layout of the city. From the northern and eastern
hills surrounding the center viewers could see the entire urban zone of the city,
extending about five kilometers from east to west and two kilometers from
north to south.[15] The city's center rested on the bottom of the small valley in
which nearly all the 29,000 dwellings could be spotted. If Buenos Aires was
the *gran aldea* of the period, Córdoba was only a smaller version: around its
imposing cathedral and churches, nine out of ten buildings were actually just
shacks. Dirt floors and straw-thatched roofs comprised the typical shelter in
the city.[16] Only 2,500 structures were built of masonry, and this figure

included government and Church buildings. Córdoba's occupational structure reflected the urban patterns of abode and underscored the relative lack of an industrial base in the region.[17]

Residential ecology did not always reflect economic segregation, as is shown in the discussions of the population distribution among the city's various "sections" and "districts." These terms refer to the territorial divisions charted by the census enumerators: the section was similar to the ward in the North American context, while the district was a subdivision of the section. In the built-up and fully urbanized sections of the city, the district occupied an area of approximately six square blocks. We combined the original section and district boundaries of the 1869 and 1895 censuses to create Map A, which shows the resulting standardized boundaries. These new values were then used to assign addresses to every individual in this study. (The original 1869 areal boundaries shown on Map B are fully made use of only in Chapter 4.) Within every section of the center, delineated by Sections 2 (northwest), 3 (northeast), 4 (southwest), and 5 (southeast), lived the wealthy, poor, and middle-economic strata (see Map A). Through the mid-1880s, westernmost Section 1 contained only *quintas* (agricultural plots), many of which were owned by members of the upper class who resided in the center and were tilled by resident agricultural laborers; in addition, marginal groups tilled their own quintas and *chacras* in this area. Back in the center, the districts within southeastern Section 5, closest to the Plaza San Martín (6, 10, 11, and 18), remained the elite's playground throughout the nineteenth century. Within these 12 square blocks were situated the principal social and institutional foundations of Córdoba: the oligarchic families, the cathedral (and church-related buildings, including monasteries and convents), the university, and the municipal administrative offices.[18] The cathedral faced east onto the plaza; immediately north was the cabildo, which served, until the new municipal administration building was finished during the construction boom of the 1880s, as the focal point of the city's government. But even the new Palacio Municipal was erected only one block west of the old cabildo, so the governmental locus remained virtually the same. The *alta sociedad* lived in the streets to the south of the church-government complex. Here the offices of doctors, lawyers, and notaries shared the space with the private homes. The insularity of the elite extended to the small zone in which it confined its four principal activities: family-raising, work, church, and school attendance. The nearby marketplace, Mercado Sud, served the daily food needs of these families.

This area was an island surrounded on all sides by diverse poorer social groups. The commercial and financial districts lay to the north of Plaza San Martín. Districts 12, 16, and 17 comprised the principal commercial zone throughout this period: here general goods stores, shoe shops, cafés, restaurants,

Map A. Córdoba: Standardized Reference Sections and Some Metropolitan Districts.

and specialty shops catered to the tastes of the middle and upper classes. This was also the first area to receive a concentration of European merchants, who emulated the upper classes by residing on streets bordering Plaza San Martín in Sections 2, 3, and 4. The few institutional financial centers of the period, including the branch office of the Banco Nacional and the Banco de la Provincia, also bordered the plaza.

Because professionals as well as shop-owners, and sometimes their employees, resided and worked in the same building, residential and occupational patterns were closely related in the center. In a one-story building the shop was set up in the anteroom; behind it was the living space for the family. In two-story structures, the rooms upstairs also served residential needs. Bakeries, for example, reserved the front portions of their buildings for baking and retailing their products; the floors of the rest of the structure served as sleeping areas for the laborers who spent most of the day and night at work.[19] Finally, the prevalence of live-in domestic servants within these areas gave the image of limited, though clearly noticeable, residential integration between economically solvent families and their staffs; the latter would have been living in shantytowns had they not had recourse to the homes in which they served.

Until the mid-1880s any excursion beyond the area covered by less than the most central thirty square blocks would have the traveler in the midst of a variety of *ranchos,* from those built with kiln-baked bricks, adobe walls, and roofs made of zinc planks to those held together by wooden boards and straw-thatched roofs. Virtually all of them had dirt floors, but had the advantage— over most masonry structures—of letting in sunlight and air.

Such was the situation within the center; land values decreased sharply as one headed west into Section 1 and then beyond into the old Pueblito, which had traditionally been reserved for Indians, and which had only about 700 residents thinly dispersed by 1900. Immediately south of the center the terrain began to rise, and although climatic conditions were more beneficial than in the valley in which the center rested, the suburban area of Section 9 contained some of the city's poorest dwellings. The western half of Pueblo Nuevo remained a slum until recently, while the nouveaux riches did not begin to settle the eastern half until after the turn of the century. Houses there and in other marginal areas of the municipality usually had a plot of land on which truck farming and subsistence agriculture ensured the families' food supplies. A milking cow and a few pigs perhaps roamed on the land around the dwelling, and clothes invariably hung outside, for through washing and ironing clothes females of these families supplemented their meager incomes. All available resources—land, animals, people—were thus employed to maintain the survival of the home. Likewise, the heights north of the river (Section 6) contained the shacks of the laboring poor, in Villa Cabrera, San Martín, and Alta Córdoba.

Table 1.1

Residential Distribution of Cordobeses by Occupational Category, 1869

(Percentage)

Occupational Classification	Section									Total
	1	2	3	4	5	6	7	8	9	
Unskilled	25.0	38.5	25.6	21.9	17.1	0.0	0.0	16.0	21.9	21.1 (78)
Semiskilled	50.0	19.2	19.5	37.5	36.8	60.7	0.0	44.0	37.5	35.5 (131)
Skilled	16.7	7.7	12.2	12.5	6.6	3.6	0.0	16.0	12.5	10.8 (40)
Nonmanual	7.9	7.7	15.9	3.1	14.5	0.0	0.0	8.0	3.1	9.2 (24)
Professional	0.0	3.8	1.2	0.0	1.3	0.0	0.0	0.0	0.0	0.8 (3)
Miscellaneous	0.0	23.1	25.6	25.0	23.7	35.7	0.0	16.0	25.0	22.5 (83)
Total	9.8 (36)	7.0 (26)	22.2 (82)	8.7 (32)	20.6 (76)	7.6 (28)	0.0 (0)	6.8 (25)	17.3 (64)	100.0 (369)

Source: Sample data.
Note: N shown in parentheses.

Table 1.2
Residential Distribution of Migrants by Occupational Category, 1869
(Percentage)

Occupational Classification	Section									Total
	1	2	3	4	5	6	7	8	9	
Unskilled	0.0	8.7	13.3	11.9	12.4	0.0	0.0	0.0	0.0	10.7 (34)
Semiskilled	44.4	21.7	17.5	7.1	18.0	40.0	0.0	31.8	14.3	18.6 (59)
Skilled	33.3	26.1	15.8	14.3	4.5	0.0	0.0	31.8	28.6	14.8 (47)
Nonmanual	11.1	13.0	25.0	11.9	18.0	20.0	0.0	22.7	28.6	19.9 (63)
Professional	0.0	8.7	5.8	16.7	10.1	0.0	0.0	4.5	14.3	8.5 (27)
Miscellaneous	11.1	21.7	22.5	38.1	37.1	40.0	0.0	9.1	14.3	27.4 (87)
Total	2.8 (9)	7.3 (23)	37.9 (120)	13.2 (42)	28.1 (89)	1.6 (5)	0.0 (0)	6.9 (22)	2.2 (7)	100.0 (317)

Source: Sample data.
Note: N shown in parentheses.

To the east, poor *chacareros* of suburban Sections 8 and 7 shared the living space with the nascent skilled laborers and the managerial elite who worked in the railroad yards in the suburb of General Paz, and with the cash-crops farmers who resided in San Vicente. In addition, a considerable level of commercial activity had developed in the center of General Paz by the 1880s, although San Vicente's commercial growth was thwarted by financial crises. General Paz contained a great mixture of rancho and masonry dwellings; the economic integration of the area was more genuine and evident than the superficial blend of the central zones, especially of the easternmost central Sections 3 and 5.

The distribution of occupational groups among the city's sections for both cordobeses and migrants is shown in Tables 1.1 and 1.2. Sections 3 and 5, located in the city's center, were the most heavily populated areas and contained the largest proportions of all workers. Cordobés holders of nonmanual occupations also prevailed in these two sections, while the migrant counterparts were dispersed throughout all the city except the easternmost Section 7, representing suburban San Vicente. The wider geographic representation of nonmanual migrants may have resulted in part from the fact that while less than 10 percent of cordobeses held nonmanual occupations, the proportion among migrants was 20 percent. Nonmanual occupations invariably represented commerce-related enterprises. Cordobés commercial houses, by virtue of having been established for a longer period may have warded off some of the more recently arrived migrant competition; the newcomers settled instead in other parts of the city where commerce was not concentrated. In addition, the migrant merchants, simply due to their large numbers, dispersed in order to avoid glutting the same area.

Among the low-level occupational groups, cordobeses and migrants varied sharply as to their central and suburban residential patterns. Approximately 65 percent of unskilled cordobeses and 94 percent of the migrant cohort lived in central zones; among the semiskilled cordobeses, who included members of the service sector, more than half lived in suburbs, compared to only 29 percent of migrants in similar occupations.[20] These figures verify statistically the social picture that is painted further ahead: the prevalence of both single and married female cordobeses employed in domestic chores and piecework in their homes, including washing, ironing, and sewing clothes. Migrant women, on the other hand, were rarely found in the service of others, although further into the liberal era, the tenets of conspicuous consumption placed great value on European domestic staffs and private tutors, especially from France. Skilled cordobeses were evenly divided between central and suburban locations; migrants, however, were much more inclined toward central dwellings. Only as one ascended the occupational structure did similarities between natives and migrants occur, and these naturally included a predilection for the downtown area.

Principally as the results of the greater presence of cordobeses in the suburbs and of the service occupations held by poor and socially marginalized native women, the overall picture among cordobeses was of similar, though not even, proportions of downtowners and suburbanites. Migrants, on the other hand, preferred central residences.

A relationship existed in the Argentine system of social status between sub-urban residence and low socioeconomic position. This notion is illustrated by the fact that nearly 52 percent of the unskilled suburban cordobeses lived in Pueblo Nuevo (Section 9), the slums on the south side of the city; likewise, approximately 42 percent of all suburban cordobeses lived in these glutted eye-sores. Suburban migrants tended to concentrate instead in the eastern out-skirts, where railroad building was already taking place, while the rest were dis-tributed throughout other locations.

In 1870, Córdoba ranked ahead of all other provinces in the number of bakers, seamstresses, hawkers, beggars, and trail bosses. It placed among the top three provinces in merchants, accountants, secondary and university stu-dents, sculptors, blacksmiths, doctors, military personnel, millers, major-domos, nuns, professors, tailors, servants, priests, shoemakers and repairers.[21] Thus, the pattern of Córdoba's economic activities reflected a region sharply strati-fied among a few professionals and clerics, a considerable number of petty merchants and vendors, and an extremely large sector of the population either marginally or menially employed.

2. On Being Poor and Moving On

Life in Córdoba was a struggle for most of the population, including adolescents. Men, women, and children served dual roles at homes in their capacities as family members and breadwinners. In this period before the full development of agricultural exploitation, the labor market faced the frustration of a growing number of hands but scarce opportunities for employment.[1] The social dislocations that had begun with the struggle for independence continued in particular to disturb the countryside; there lawlessness guaranteed sustenance better than seasonal employment (if the latter was available). Moreover, if the leadership's plans for economic development were to be fulfilled, then the socioeconomic positions of many people would have to be improved—a goal which the strength and potential of nearly 17,000 young people between the ages of eleven and thirty, constituting almost half of the city's population,[2] might further.

The 1869 census schedules reveal that a considerable number of these young people (and some older ones) were attached to families as *conchabos* (forcibly contracted domestics), who had been put in service sometimes by their parents and sometimes by the public authorities. Córdoba's 1856 juridical code required that parents who could not provide for their children's support must hand them over to families which would be responsible for their upbringing and education. This forced separation, to begin at the age of six, was not intended to benefit the youngsters; instead, it put in service without fee thousands of young cordobeses, usually as domestic servants and menial laborers.[3] Because adults could also voluntarily put themselves in service as, for example, domestics, muleteers, or peons, conchabos of either sex and of all ages could be found throughout the city. In May 1874, under pressure from the city's well-to-do families, the police made public an edict that required all women without sufficient means of support "to be put in service or go to jail."[4] Thus, the system of forced servitude extended the households of middle and upper strata beyond blood relationships and led to an assimilated cohort that provided cheap labor. In turn, these conchabos received better living conditions than they could have expected under contracts entered into freely.[5] Censal compilations and publications, however, make no mention of this type of servitude, even though several residents reported themselves as conchabos to the census enumerators.

Many worked in the quintas along the western half of the metropolitan area. This zone, appropriately named Las Quintas, lay to the west of a canal (La Cañada) that ran directly south from the Río Primero. The soil, irrigated by waters from La Cañada, provided the city with an ample variety of flowers, fruits, and legumes. The owners of many of these quintas came from the ranks of the rich and escaped the oppressive summer heat hovering over the city center for the less congested, cooler green-belt.[6] Las Quintas also became a refuge for whole families seeking to stay united in order to weather financial difficulties; such was the case of Francisca Rincón, who was married to Andrés Mercado. He was a reaper in a quinta owned by a wealthy family in the center, while she put herself in service performing menial and domestic chores around the house on the same quinta.

Being put into service did not always require residence on another's property, however, nor did it bind the conchabo to a trapped existence. Moreover, cordobés tradition customarily safeguarded the unity of conchabo families, not through perpetuity or transference of service but merely as a result of the patronage afforded to loyal household staff members. Social castes were an undeniable reality: since colonial times, Córdoba's privileged class had defended its social position on the bases of racial purity, legitimacy of offspring, and educational levels. Many of the poor were, in fact, mestizos who could find the upper limits of their economic opportunities in domestic service and in some apprenticeships. Long after the legal barriers separating castes came down under republican rule, Córdoba's elite continued to sustain their social privileges on the basis of such factors.[7] Yet the *familias de sociedad* also continued to respect the tradition of treating their servants as wards who in some ways formed part of the family.[8] Some of those in service during the second half of the nineteenth century were the sons and daughters of freed slaves who had opted to stay on with their former masters and take their names as their own.[9] Thus social distances did not preclude warm social interactions between neighboring poor and rich. Children of elite families like del Viso, Escuti, Centeno, or Rueda played daily with children of their own and others' domestics.[10]

The lives of Matilde Moreno and her children help to illustrate more concretely what life was like among the conchabos and lower class. In 1870 Matilde Moreno was in her mid-twenties and in well over her twelfth year of service at a quinta on Santa Rosa Street. Having married José Angel Toranzo, a cordobés carpenter, at a very early age, she had had five children by him. Cordobés tradition enabled the Toranzo children to stay on as day-laborers and domestics at the same quinta as their parents. Usually, the chances for significant social mobility among such people were nil; indeed, the oldest Toranzo son, Teodoro, was still only a day-laborer at the age of twenty-five.[11] Matilde's oldest daughter, Amelia, stayed on in Córdoba but fared no better than her mother: in 1891 she lost her nine-month-old child, whom she had conceived out of wedlock with a Creole; in 1895 she reported her occupation as *lavandera* or washerwoman. By then, she had moved back to the same area of Las Quintas where she had grown up, taking along her three children, also born out of wedlock, though this time by an Italian named Barsoldi. Carolina, her eldest, already was a servant at the age of thirteen. By this time Amelia was only thirty-five.[12]

Neither did two other Toranzo children fare well. Juana died in 1877 at the age of fifteen, and Mercedes moved out of Córdoba, presumably in search of a better existence.[13] But Manuela, the youngest of all the children, proved to be the exception. Like her older sister, she lived with an Italian immigrant, Juan del Zotto, whom she finally married after eight years of cohabitation and six illegitimate children. For at least twenty years they struggled as Juan del Zotto labored as a journeyman mason while Manuela washed and ironed clothes at home. They lived first in a shack with a packed-dirt floor and a straw roof on the western extreme of Las Quintas. Eventually, the couple saved and borrowed enough money to purchase some real estate in the suburbs outside the city.[14]

The many years of privation of the del Zotto family were typical of Córdoba's poor; yet the family's accomplishments were rare in certain aspects. First, it was unusual during this period for a cordobesa to marry an immigrant; second, the data indicate the rarity of economic mobility after marriage; third, it was unusual, save for some members of the elite, to remain in Córdoba for such a long period of time. (See Chapter 8 for a close look at the role of marriage in mobility and social integration.) An aspect of their lives, however, did typify one of Córdoba's occupational norms: whatever their socioeconomic position, cordobeses of the nineteenth and early twentieth centuries gleaned their incomes from more than one occupational activity. Without straddling occupational levels, dual or even triple occupations were not unusual. It was a practice condemned by the press, which considered it an obstacle to the creation of a full-time, truly professional industrial elite.[15]

Just as practicing lawyers invested in land-holdings, so did Juan del Zotto invest five thousand pesos in the purchase of a house in the center of San Vicente in 1915 in order to derive income through rentals, while the family moved from its cottage in Las Quintas to a rented masonry dwelling in the center across from the university. The previous year Juan del Zotto had made his biggest purchase: ten hectares of land for agricultural use next to the train station at Pueblo Ferreyra, a small town of less than five hundred people, situated eleven kilometers southeast of Córdoba.[16] Further related to this success story are two unusual aspects: the source of his funds and the abbreviated occupational pattern that facilitated these improvements. Del Zotto made excellent financial contracts; he owed on private loans of 2,080 pesos and on a bank mortgage of 1,560 pesos from the Banco Hipotecario Nacional (National Mortgage Bank). It was an exceptional achievement in an era when the average Argentine was unable to secure loans from institutional sources to purchase either urban or rural property. Credit remained a perquisite of the rich, and even for them represented an expensive commodity. Structural changes, intended to liberalize loans and to expand the credit facilities of the national mortgage bank, did not significantly alter the prevailing system.[17]

Lower social classes were also thwarted in their attempts to own agricultural lands by the exclusive clientele to which large lending institutions catered. By the beginning of World War I, the Banco de la Nación was directly responsible for approximately half of all Argentine banking business. Yet that source of money was never meant to be tapped by anyone with less than the finest credit; moreover, the bank's charter permitted the granting of loans for only 90, 180, or occasionally 270 days.[18] Thus the Argentine credit system funneled the bulk of its financial benefits into one bank which favored the large commercial and export grain and meat concerns. Meanwhile, the Banco Hipotecario Nacional, founded in 1886, was so unable or so unwilling to lend to small farmers and laborers that the administration of Sáenz Peña characterized it as too clumsy to handle short- and medium-term loans.[19] When news arrived that a branch office of the Banco Hipotecario de Buenos Aires was to be opened in Córdoba, many cheered the event—short-sightedly, it turned out—as resulting in clearing the lines of credit. "God is finally remembering the poor," wrote an observer, "who are victims of the tyranny of present-day credit distributors."[20] The bank turned out to be no such panacea. Fortunately, however, Juan del Zotto had been able to circumvent all obstacles to receive this loan for purchasing land in Pueblo Ferreyra.

Another uncharacteristic aspect of del Zotto's mobility in Córdoba was that he did not use commerce as a stepping stone toward financial solvency. Whatever he accomplished in masonry or other skilled labor, he did so only as a self-employed contract worker. His absence from the city's commercial registers during the first twenty years of the present century indicates his desire to settle as a farmer, or at least as an absentee landlord in his own right.[21] He made improvements on his property, including fencing and irrigation, and built a small house. He devoted all his land to growing alfalfa and even owned his own reaper. Since virtually all real and personal properties had been acquired after their marriage, Manuela Toranzo del Zotto legally enjoyed half of their possessions, which by 1917 totalled 6,800 pesos after repayments of loans.

Raised with only the clothes on her back, Manuela had managed to lift herself out of her station to become a member of the city's lowest rung of the petite bourgeiosie. Ten hectares of alfalfa and a small suburban house did not represent in absolute terms a great economic achievement after a lifetime of toil; but relative to the average Córdoba resident, this couple improved their economic situation significantly.

To name a few among the cases of extreme poverty in our sample, conchabos like José Antúnez, Juana Figueroa, Miguel Andreete, Felipa Garay, Felisa Gómez, Severo and Carolina Ríos, and Plácida Moyano displayed great variety in their respective vital records but unanimity in their continued poverty. José Antúnez had been taken as a child into a wealthy home and had adopted as his own the name of the head of the household, the businessman Fabriciano Antúnez. José died in 1870 at the age of nineteen, while still a servant in the same house.[22] Miguel Andreete was working for an Italian family in 1869 as a domestic; he subsequently moved out of the city never to return. Likewise, Juana Figueroa became a servant after having been taken in by two sisters, who were doubtlessly helped in their home work as seamstresses. Unlike Miguel Andreete, however, she remained in Córdoba, where in 1895 she was sharing a rancho with thirteen other people (unrelated to her) in the center's principal red-light district. She had not married, she had never learned to read or write, and she now eked out a living as a washerwoman. Finally, the other conchabos, Miguel Andreete, Felipa Garay, Felisa Gómez, Severo and Carolina Ríos, and Plácida Moyano elected to follow in the footsteps of all the thousands of residents who, unable to continue living under the same harsh conditions, pulled up what roots they had and left the city.[23]

Why should menial laborers have found it so difficult to provide for their own and their families' sustenance? Reasons given by contemporaries are themselves confusing and contradictory. On the one hand, most members of the press condemned the "idleness" of poor Creoles, or native-born, and contrasted it to the "industriousness" of the immigrants; on the other, they blamed the government for not providing the economic inputs to stimulate the work force. Until the turn of the century, conservatives and liberals alike denigrated the natives' capabilities for work and frugality; unemployment and underemployment among Creoles seemed to them to manifest cultural imperfections of the "Argentine race." For example, in an article on the "frightful rise" of illegitimate births in the city, a conservative Catholic daily pronounced the two causes of the phenomenon: the relaxation of religious fervor, and the idleness and poverty of the indigent class. The poor, wrote the editors, receive "no encouragement to work, do not wish to work . . . . With such a rich soil we only see an increase of beggars and a decrease of the crop yields. On the other hand, the European finds a ready field for all types of production. . . ."[24] More than a decade later the liberal daily, *El Porvenir,* editorialized in the same vein and indicated its suspicion that beggary and vagrancy had no real causes but continued as a part of urban life thanks largely to the many who naïvely responded to the calls of the alms seekers.[25]

Governmental authorities received much of the blame for the state of affairs because of their ineffectual measures against vagrants and their failure to place in shelters the poor who were truly unable to work. Actually, part of the problem lay with the provincial and federal governments' inability to promote the full exploitation of rural lands. The rhetoric of governors' promises and plans for growth far exceeded their realization and led to extensive frustration.[26]

Despite complaints, neither the municipal nor the provincial authorities gathered the necessary financial or human resources to evacuate the poor from the streets and fields, nor was the public motivated to organize in order to help in this matter. Bureaucrats did not consider public welfare and means for securing employment as responsibilities of the state; public welfare was more often confused with charity, while the notion of shelters did not imply programs of rehabilitation and training. Funds from the city and the province fell notably short of even the minimal needs of the *asilos* and hospitals, and only the private charity of the "comfortable classes" kept afloat these institutions. The government itself did not found charitable or welfare institutions, nor did it operate them directly, even when the private responsible groups had proven themselves inept in their management. Córdoba's municipal budget for 1869, for example, provided only 4,420 pesos for charitable subventions.[27]

In the following year the province allowed the creation of a shelter for the poor.[28] The provincial government agreed to pay a monthly subvention of 50 gold pesos.[29] By 1891, thanks primarily to the exigencies that resulted from the previous year's financial collapse, the province had increased its monthly aid to 350 pesos. Still, the Asilo de Mendigos operated on a total yearly account of less than 10,000 pesos, which included one-tenth of the provincial budget.[30] Private donations and funds bequeathed in last wills and testaments equaled almost half of the funds donated by the state.[31] On the average, the poorhouse sheltered one hundred people, most of them women, and according to its usual budgets, it would spend no more than 100 pesos yearly on each of its residents. This figure amounted to merely one-fifth of the yearly income which local law prescribed as the upper limit of pauperism. Most of the money was spent on food, and little else was left for other necessities. After the crisis had abated in 1894, the asilo's administrator still reported on the difficulties created by the "exiguous subvention from the government" and on the

necessity for continued reliance on private charity. Furthermore, funds allo-
cated by the government were not always delivered; for example, in 1893 the
asilo did not receive the full monthly subvention of 75.50 pesos from the city.
In sum, noted its administrator, "the Asylum for the Poor . . . could not sustain itself . . . if the public's philanthropic charity did not favor it with numerous donations."[32]

Spokesmen unconnected with the state bureaucracy decried the unwillingness of the government to become efficiently involved in the administration
of public welfare, while the grants which fell short of needs by 25 to 90 percent highlighted the continued official attitude.[33]   The Ladies of Providence
established a home for foundlings in the mid-1880s, and received, at first, between 50 and 60 pesos monthly from the province.[34] By 1887, the home was
in such critical financial difficulties that the governor decreed an increase in
the amount of aid to 350 pesos monthly. The institution had become a death
trap for most of the children it received, noted the governor's report; out of
eighty-eight children for whom the Casa de Expósitos cared, fifty-seven had
perished. While at a similar establishment in Buenos Aires 18.1 percent of the
children died in 1886, the mortality rate in Córdoba's reached nearly 65 percent. "This unfortunate situation," concluded the report, "results from the
poor feeding of the children and the lack of careful attention. . . ."[35]

Strangely enough, what surely would have been an unbearable strain on the
welfare system—such as it was—was prevented by a serious lack of officers
available to gather the poor. The provincial minister of the treasury sent out
a memorandum in 1886 to every *jefe político* throughout Córdoba; in it he
warned that the disregard for the laws on vagrancy and beggary could no longer
be tolerated and demanded that their officers comply with the legal disposi-
tions requiring incarceration and forced labor in ongoing public works.[36] The
expenditures for those public works, prevalent during the late 1880s and 1890s,
caused concern among some who did not approve of the subjugation of the
needy for the sake of the city's beautification projects. The token donations
given to relieve the lot of the poor, some argued, indicated misplaced interests.[37]

What options, then, could the poor of Córdoba follow? As we saw in the
earlier examples involving conchabos and domestic servants, they could stay
and try to share in the opportunities which the elite described as viable.

The sample members together with their households yielded 1,131 persons
who listed their occupations in categories ranging from the unskilled and menial level to the professional. Of these, 193 people, representing 17 percent,
worked in unskilled occupations; and 474 or 42 percent formed the semiskilled and service sector, including agricultural laborers. Here we will discuss
the sample cases only.[38] Table 2.1 shows that 68 percent of the unskilled laborers moved out—probably in several stages of movements that would

Table 2.1
Persistence of Low-Status Groups, 1869-1895
(Percentage and Absolute Numbers)
(N=305)

Occupational Classification	Did Not Persist to 1895			Persisted to 1895		
	Cordobeses	Migrants	Total	Cordobeses	Migrants	Total
Unskilled	57.1	91.7	68.1	42.9	8.3	31.9
	(44)	(33)	(77)	(33)	(3)	(36)
Semiskilled	66.4	88.5	73.4	33.6	11.5	26.6
	(87)	(54)	(141)	(44)	(7)	(51)

Source: Sample data.

eventually get them to the littoral regions. Figures for geographic persistence among the semiskilled workers are similar: 73 percent of them had moved out by 1895. Local economic conditions forced these people out; the city of Córdoba could not retain its low-level work force.

Impermanence in the city among the occupationally lowly reflected the insecurity of their employment. In the slow urban development of the 1870s, unskilled men secured jobs by going through the city streets in search of people who would contract their work in home repairs, building new houses, and agricultural tasks. As the number and volume of retail businesses grew, job opportunities increased; *peones* and *jornaleros* (day-laborers) were found in small workshops carting, making deliveries, and being used as all-purpose help. Last, the advent of the railroad increased the demand for labor in the yards, while the nascent industries which simultaneously were developing—primarily shoe manufacture—followed similar employment patterns.

The increase in the city's permanent labor force came slowly. Production of goods did not increase significantly until after the 1870s; little business expansion occurred, as evidenced by drops in the volume of railroad freight carried in and out of the city.[39] Consequently, the rate of new building in the commercial center remained almost at a standstill. The composition of Córdoba's industrial output had not yet altered significantly since the start of the nineteenth century: leather tanning, wool, shoes, and lime processing—still employing a minimum of machinery—led all other types of production. Moreover, most of these industrial activities, performed by petty entrepreneurs, served only local and regional needs. The great difficulties in obtaining loans for business expansion or modernization also limited the use of machinery in work-shops.[40]

Still, the population of Córdoba grew, encouraged by two migratory currents that merged from opposite directions: from the poorer and less developed north and west came in-migrants, while immigrants from Europe made their way inland from Buenos Aires. Both groups competed for jobs and stability. The greater number, composed of the in-migrants, joined their Creole cohorts and populated the suburbs where they often built their homes on the empty lots that surrounded the city. The construction of a modest home was not usually a difficult undertaking: some planks of wood, straw or corrugated zinc formed the basic structure. Sod-built ranchos were not uncommon. It is, therefore, not strange to find contradictory reports on new building for the same time period. While the center received little impetus in the 1870s, observers reported a substantial number of new construction in the suburbs and in the areas with quintas.[41] The suburbs also received many of the peones involved in railroad work and canalizing the Río Primero, which cut through the city; approximately two hundred laborers found jobs on these two projects.[42] The boom of the 1880s presented the unskilled and semiskilled with the best opportunities: new boulevards were paved, new government buildings and railroad stations went up, and some speculative urban expansion and development took place. Commentaries on the extensive construction along Deán Funes Street, for example, alluded to the westward urbanization trend that took place within the metropolitan area toward the end of the decade.[43]

The suburbs, too, benefited from urban development. Governmental authorities did not initiate all public works programs; private enterprise, often with financial support from the official circles, planned the development of certain areas of the city, such as San Vicente's market, theater, and racetrack, and the suburb of Nueva Córdoba.[44] At the time of San Vicente's apogee in the late 1870s, nearly one thousand laborers worked on its various construction projects.[45]

The city witnessed its greatest increase in new construction during the 1880s. Permits for building sites awarded in 1880 amounted to only 47; the figure jumped the following year to 74; at mid-decade the municipality awarded 129 permits, and by the end of the decade 208 permits were granted.[46] We do not know what purposes the buildings were to serve, nor the number actually completed. They certainly were not intended to relieve the housing shortage among migrant laborers, which resulted in increments of rents and the proliferation of *conventillos* (tenements) to accommodate the laboring class. In fact, municipal authorities did little about the lack of housing until, on the eve of the Baring Crisis of 1890, the first few inexpensive quarters for workers were initiated. Even these, however, did not adhere to the minimum health standards, nor were they designed to blend with the surrounding architecture. These first attempts at municipally supported housing developed in the western quarters of the city starting in Section 1, where quintas were now giving way to small commercial concerns, and reaching into Pueblito, still further to the west. If these first initiatives came slowly and half-heartedly, the responsible officials did even less when it came to the upkeep. By the turn of the century, some city housing was already in a state of decay, and revealed "the neglect and careless attitude of the Municipal Authority."[47]   At that time, new low-rent housing intended for workers was once again being built though in small numbers and meeting only the bare essentials of the health code. No effort was made, however, to shift such housing closer to the city's center of activity.[48]

The suburbs were composed primarily of neighborhoods of poor cordobeses, who comprised nearly 75 percent of the suburbanites; General Paz offered the major exception. The farther one lived from the center, the less one received of municipal services such as running water, street lighting, sewage lines and garbage collection. In Table 2.2 we can see the sample members' sectional distribution in 1869. Section 8 (General Paz), of all suburban zones, contained similar proportions of migrants and cordobeses working in the area's railroad shops. Most of the migrants were actually Europeans who worked for the railroad and who continued to settle in that area; by the turn of the century it would have the largest number of foreigners in the city.[49]   All other suburban sections in our sample—1, 6, 7 and 9—were populated overwhelmingly by Creoles, most of whom were cordobeses. Among all persons who in 1869 had resided in suburbs, two-thirds of cordobeses and one-half of migrants remained there toward century's end. The relationship between a resident's central or suburban location and his persistence in Córdoba is shown in Table 2.3. Two-thirds of suburbanite cordobeses out-migrated; the figure among migrants stood at more than 86 percent. The phenomenon of large-scale out-migration pervaded all levels of the city's life and society; thus, we notice very low persistence figures also among central residents. The clearest differentiator of persistence rates was birthplace; significantly greater percentages of migrants than cordobeses left Córdoba. Migrants into Córdoba did not find that for which they searched; moving remained the theme of their lives. One of the repercussions of high out-migration rates was that few children who were present in the households of 1869 remained in Córdoba. Although infant mortality rates affected the depletion of the nonadult population from one period to another, the prevalence of out-migration was the principal cause of the lack of subsequent generations of residents of Córdoba. In addition, the index of intergenerational mobility was per force very low. Also as a result of the low persistence trend, nearly all members of the different occupational groups that had

Table 2.2
Residential Distribution by Migratory Status, 1869
(Percentage)

Migratory Status	Section									Total
	1	2	3	4	5	6	7	8	9	
Cordobeses	80.0	53.1	40.6	43.2	46.1	84.8	0.0	53.2	90.1	53.8 (369)
Migrants	20.0	46.9	59.4	56.8	53.9	15.2	0.0	46.8	9.9	46.2 (317)
Total	6.6 (45)	7.1 (49)	29.4 (202)	10.8 (74)	24.1 (165)	4.8 (33)	0.0 (0)	6.9 (47)	10.3 (71)	100.0 (686)

Source: Sample data.
Note: N shown in parentheses.

Table 2.3
Persistence 1869-1895 as a Function of Central/Peripheral Residence
(Percentage)
(N=688)

	Present in 1869	Persisted to 1895	Did Not Persist to 1895
Cordobeses:			
Suburban residence	41.7	34.0	66.0
Central residence	58.3	38.3	61.7
Total	100.0	36.5	63.5
	(367)	(134)	(233)
Migrants:			
Suburban residence	15.9	13.7	86.3
Central residence	84.1	17.8	82.2
Total	100.0	17.1	82.9
	(321)	(55)	(266)

Source: Sample data.

Note: N shown in parentheses.

previously resided there in 1869 simply vanished by the end of the century.

Suburban residents were subjected to two factors that made their existence precarious: criminals and infectious diseases. A piped water system was begun in 1883 but remained highly inefficient and inadequate to demand until improved at the turn of the century. The pipes reached out from the center only to Pueblo Nuevo in the south and to General Paz in the east; the rest of the population used water from wells or from the Río Primero. Sewage lines were not installed until the late 1880s, but again most suburbs did not benefit from them; not until the early 1900s did the construction of sewage lines commence in those areas.[50] Municipal officials were not unaware of the situation in the suburbs. In 1888, a report noted "the development of a high number of cases of measles and of scarlet fever which victimized quite a few people among residents of the outlying slums."[51]

Between 1882 and 1889, the municipal Civil Registry kept the death certificates of suburbanites separate from those who lived in the center. We can therefore compare the deaths caused by disease alone in the suburbs with the city's total mortality figures. Death caused by disease in the suburbs accounted for an average of 26 percent of Córdoba's mortality rate during these years.[52] Not surprisingly, an average of only 23 percent of migrants—composed mostly of Europeans—lived in areas out of the city's center; if we exclude General Paz from the calculations, only 10.5 percent resided in the suburbs. Eight out of ten residents on the quintas of Section 1 were cordobeses; they also represented 85 to 90 percent of suburbanites to the north and the south, respectively. Europeans, perhaps accustomed to more modern sanitary facilities and already conditioned by their travels through large European cities and Buenos Aires, would not settle in poorly urbanized zones; instead, they concentrated in the center, especially in Sections 3, 4, and 5. Table 2.4 gives the relationship between birthplace and residential sections of sample members in 1869. Foreigners settled principally in the blocks with concentrated commercial activity within Sections 3 and 5. Nearly 55 percent of immigrants lived in these two divisions. Section 5 contained fewer Europeans because of the higher cost of housing in that area, where most of the city's doctors, lawyers, and professors lived.

Roadway and railway construction also created a demand for labor outside of the city. Officials of large corporations such as railroads or colonizing companies advertised employment opportunities in local newspapers; these corporations tended, however, to favor immigrants over Creoles. For example, an advertisement in 1888 exhorted only foreigners in need of jobs to apply for employment digging a tunnel sixty miles from Córdoba.[53] This favoritism notwithstanding, Argentine antinativists continued to assail Creoles for their underemployment. The cycle, in short, became a self-fulfilling prophecy. In the hinterland of the city of Córdoba, for example, railroad field officers discriminated against Creoles. In the repair shops of the Córdoba-Rosario line, Argentine employees protested against the favoritism shown to "certain people to the great detriment of the [native] operatives, who are treated in unwarranted fashion."[54] Yet leading voices typically decried the way in which Creoles shunned "honest labor": "It is lamentable that in our country all the tasks that can provide honest livelihoods are in the hands of the foreigners, who employ them to good use. The Argentine does not wish to work . . . he is ashamed that sweat might moisten his brow . . . never will he *lower himself* to have a vocation with which to earn a living honorably. . . . Argentines! Let us observe the foreigner, who gives us an exemplary lesson in how to earn a living without losing any . . . dignity. . . ."[55]

The living conditions, the impermanence of jobs, and the call for labor in other parts of the country all served to drain the number of people living in the city at any one time. We gathered data on the intra-urban geographic mobility patterns of the 102 sample members who remained through 1895; the figure represents an overall persistence rate of only 15 percent. Nearly two-thirds

Table 2.4
Birthplace and Residential Distribution, 1869
(Percentage)

Birthplace	Section									Total
	1	2	3	4	5	6	7	8	9	
Córdoba	9.7	7.3	22.1	8.6	20.5	7.5	0.0	7.0	17.3	54.1 (371)
Other Argentina	2.0	7.6	35.9	13.6	31.3	1.5	0.0	5.6	2.5	28.9 (198)
Foreign	4.3	6.0	41.9	12.8	23.1	1.7	0.0	8.5	1.7	17.1 (117)
Total	6.6 (45)	7.1 (49)	29.4 (202)	10.8 (74)	24.1 (165)	4.8 (33)	0.0 (0)	6.9 (47)	10.3 (71)	100.0 (686)

Source: Sample data.
Note: N shown in parentheses.

of the cordobeses remained in homes within western Section 1, while the original population that had resided in the north of the center (Section 6) had completely out-migrated. Cordobeses of General Paz, perhaps because of the predilection that railroad authorities showed for hiring immigrants, moved west to the neighboring Section 3. Last, a considerable number of rural residents left the southern suburbs within Section 9, particularly those who had been concentrated in Pueblo Nuevo, one of the city's oldest slums. A percentage equal to those who remained in Pueblo Nuevo moved to other poor fringes of the metropolitan zone: Sections 1, 6, and the decaying San Vicente (Section 7). The rest moved into the center, especially into Section 5, where most professionals resided. The move northeast to Section 5 leads to the suspicion that many of these people, by working as domestics, had traded their low residential status but had not climbed out of their low occupational levels.

Cordobeses who had lived in the center in 1869 displayed greater stability in their mobility rates. Sections 3 and 4 each contained in 1895 over 40 percent of the persisters. One-fourth of those who had resided in Section 2 moved to Section 5, while half of them moved to suburban regions. The rates of out-migration from Section 5 to suburban sections indicate that an outward push was taking place simultaneously with an inward pull from those same outlying regions. This appears to have been the result of generational translocations as the young within families entered the domestic labor market while the older ones were retired from it. Overall, one-third of the persisters remained in the center, together with the nearly 18 percent who stayed within Section 5.

The most striking factor among non-cordobeses is their massive out-migration rate. Yet if they stayed in Córdoba they remained in their original sections with greater consistency than their native cohorts. Their occupational successes obviously played important roles in both their high out-migration rates and their intra-urban stability.

Residential stability did not imply, however, persistence among migrants; instead, if people who migrated through greater distances—interprovincially or intercontinentally—remained in the city, they tended to stay in the same area in greater proportions than natives or than shorter-distance, intraprovincial travelers. The occupational dimensions underlying residential equilibrium are discussed in the next chapter.

Summary

The city of Córdoba acted as a figurative turnstile, attracting people from the opposite directions of the Argentine interior and European countries, only to subsequently push them out and on. Usually they exited empty-handed. The propaganda sponsored by the government and the rhetoric of self-importance in which the local elite engaged promised a mythical well-being, however, which continued to attract thousands more, especially of immigrant stock, nearly every year until well into the twentieth century. The slow process of industrialization worked in conjunction with suddenly shifting economic cycles to maintain in flux the population pool. Non-cordobeses were particularly quick to react to the few available opportunities for economic success by out-migrating in greater proportions than local people. The lack of significant vertical occupational mobility lay at the heart of the problem. Although there was plenty of status mobility for European merchants, it did not, however, entail financial security.

The phenomenon of large scale interurban migration is not at all unique to Argentina; it may, in fact, be an American experience among Western Hemisphere nations which underwent both urban growth and an influx of immigrants. As Stephan Thernstrom notes, urban population fluidity in the United States during the late nineteenth century was even more extreme than in the rural zones. While much evidence points to a close relationship between socioeconomic success and spatial mobility, the situation was very different in the late nineteenth and early twentieth centuries. The poor were geographically more experienced than their social superiors. Thernstrom concluded that "if there was anything like a 'culture of poverty' in the [North] American city, it lacked deep local roots, for most people exposed to it were incessantly on the move from place to place."[56] High residential mobility was the trend in the United States as a whole during the late nineteenth century. Data from Omaha show that residential mobility contained a slight differential based on class and ethnicity: blue-collar workers and foreigners moved more often than white-collar workers and natives. The main point remains, however, that impermanence was a basic element of urban society in North America during the same time period covered in this study.[57] More comparative and systematic work must still be done, but it appears that material progress, as the *idée fixe* of nations in the Americas which attracted immigrants, propelled their populations onto a widespread movement in search of the fantasy.

3. On Being Rich and on Getting By

Although obviously not belonging to the same class, the wealthy and the middle levels of Córdoba's society shared certain common traits, which together served to distinguish the two groups from the third—the poor—discussed in the previous chapter. In terms of worldly possessions, the rich were far in advance of the middle class, but in terms of outer, visible characteristics the two groups were closer. Both groups lived in the city's center, in similar types of structures and with similar family sizes. Although workshop proprietors were represented in the middle classes the merchant (*comerciante*) and white-collar employee constituted such a substantial element that nonmanual labor set apart the poor from the rest of society.

It becomes evident upon closer observation that, unlike the wealthy, Córdoba's middle classes led utterly precarious lives. The margin for error left to most of them was minimal; the family often worked together, unlike the rich, and the low volume of assets left behind upon the death of someone who had appeared to be a solid member of the middle class betrayed the economic facade he had erected while alive. Finally, for those many who were simply getting by, the solution was to leave town. But as this chapter shows, even if the climb up the economic ladder was very difficult, at least social distances in Córdoba could be narrowed by titular and occupational machinations and ascription.

The Wealthy

The lifestyles of Córdoba's wealthy families can be divided according to generations: those who had gathered their acquisitions before and those who had gathered them after the boom of the 1880s and late 1890s. The pattern of distribution of wealth among the oligarchs of the two generations shifted, but only in terms of conspicuous consumption and of the type of construction of their dwellings. The bases of wealth, however, remained the same: urban property in the city of Córdoba and rural estates within the province. Nor did the incidence of wealthy families increase significantly between population samples taken from the 1869 and 1895 schedules.[1]

During the first period, wealthy families lived almost solely in the districts within the southeastern Section 5. The facades of their homes suggested their austere and uncomplicated lives.[2] Sometimes, only one window faced the outside world onto the street. Following Spanish tradition, heavy iron bars covered the window; thus even a simple iron design created a break, albeit Spartan, in the otherwise grey monotonous facade. These masonry structures were limited to one story, and their floor plans invariably were rectangular, extending deep into the block's interior. On the other side of a large, heavy wooden front door opened a patio in the Moorish-Spanish style in which a few flowers and fruit trees grew. The rooms of the family members, a sitting room, and dining facilities surrounded the courtyard. A portal at the rear of the patio gave access to the living quarters of the domestic staff, to latrines, to the cooking oven, and to the grills on which the staff barbecued the traditional beef *asado*. This rear portion of the house did not usually have finished walls; rather, low-ceilinged brick structures, sometimes with dirt floors, made up the servants' quarters.

Furniture was conspicuously scant. A few wooden tables and chairs with simple details carved on their legs could be found in the living areas, while each sleeping room contained not much more than the bare essentials: an unpretentious bed and a dark chifforobe. Small social gatherings took place either in the sitting room or, in warm weather, around the patio. Ornamentation on floors and walls was also notably absent. Luxurious chandeliers did not hang from the ceilings; lacy curtains did not frame the wooden window shutters; rugs or carpets seldom covered the tile floors; and neither local nor imported art objects or paintings altered the monotonously painted walls.

In spite of sparse furnishings and drab interiors and exteriors, the homes of Córdoba's rich were distinguished from other homes by four contemporary cultural norms: the numbers of servants; the single-family masonry dwellings; the location; and, last, the sense of insularity and privacy that emanated from these structures. Thus, while the geographic distance was small between the dwellings of the elite and of the lower classes, the homes of the well-to-do, with their somber exteriors, glaringly symbolized enormous social distinctions.

An additional separator at the local level of society was skin color. Although racial references did not appear in national census, all cordobeses were not white. According to the 1832 census, the last city census in which racial categories appeared, 52 percent of the population consisted of what the enumerators labeled *pardos,* the regional term given to mestizos.[3] The euphemism employed at midcentury had been *libres,* or free ones, and their occupational and residential distributions made clear their continued social and economic subservience to the white minority.[4] Moreover, ten percent of the mestizos in 1832 were still held as slaves, in violation of the laws of 1813 that had outlawed slavery. The 1840 municipal census showed that the situation had not altered.[5]

Mestizos in Córdoba had two fundamental occupations: artisanry and truck farming. These tasks effectively kept them out of white elite residential areas. Mestizos comprised nearly 60 percent of the city's 1840 population, and, as had been the case in 1832, most of them lived in the zones around the city's green-belt in the suburbs. Within the center, the northwestern Section 2, the northeast reaches of Section 3, and the southeast portion of Section 5 housed the city's mixed bloods.[6]

The city of Córdoba did not receive the large numbers of Europeans who settled in Buenos Aires. The Europeanization of the latter, in demographic terms, made it difficult by century's end to discern Creoles of dark skin. Córdoba's geographically central position, however, made it available to migrations of putative mestizos—even if porteño standards stifled the use of the term— from the nation's northern and northwestern regions. Their continued influx maintained an unspoken though rigid racial differentiation unaltered by the presence of Europeans; in fact, the oligarchy's facile generalizations about the Europeans' superiority over low-class Creoles were internalized by the immigrants, who themselves promoted racial dimensions in class distinctions.

Nineteenth-century economic and social suppression by the elite on the basis of race is hard to document, but contemporaries did make some allusions to it.[7] The population of domestic servants, almost invariably poor Creoles, largely consisted of the *pardos* or mestizos who ministered to the needs of the elite whites and the foreign and native merchants in the nascent middle strata. An anonymous cordobés made the following observation: "Respectable ladies send maids, because of light infractions, to the house of correction . . . after they were perfectly served by them for a year or more. The maid wishes to leave to take another job where she could be treated as a human being and before she knows it, she is sent to the house of correction. . . . No sir, for people of color there is only defamation. It seems that it is not crime that vilifies people, but their dark skin color."[8]

In sum, the distinctive characteristics of Córdoba's upper class encompassed social ecology, lifestyle, and race. Naturally, the amount and nature of wealth was essential to social position; but how rigidly maintained was this class and what were the parameters of its wealth?

The avenues for becoming wealthy were limited in the city of Córdoba. The infrastructure necessary for industrialization required a pool of skilled labor not yet present in the 1870s.[9] In the 1880s acquisitions of large areas of real property were becoming profitable in the province's southeastern departments bordering the province of Buenos Aires: Marcos Juárez, Unión, Juárez Celman, and others, which formed the western extensions of the fertile pampas. Yet the land values of these agricultural areas rendered them virtually inaccessible to the limited funds with which migrants arrived in the city.[10] For enterprising migrants commerce represented the most viable and easily accessible occupation. This does not imply, however, that commercial activities were necessarily the most profitable or stable. On the contrary, from a total of 211 merchants we gathered from the 1869 census, 49, or less than one-quarter of them, remained in Córdoba.[11]

Success stories were few among immigrants in Córdoba, and none signified rags-to-riches situations: the people who owned large sums of money or achieved great success by the end of their lives had operated solid foundations developed earlier by their ancestors. For example, the course of events in the lives of Carlos Dellaperriere and his wife, Ana Benza, are typical of the "exemplary actions" of Europeans about which contemporary Argentine liberals boasted. Dellaperriere had arrived in Córdoba with his family in the late 1860s from Buenos Aires, where he had met his wife, born to Italian parents. By the time they arrived in Córdoba they already owned 22,000 pesos' worth of real estate in the city of Rosario.[12] As a French pharmacist, and probably with the help of his in-laws who had been living in Buenos Aires during the previous thirty years, Dellaperriere commanded status, respect, and evidently sufficient funds for undertaking speculative ventures into the real estate market at the young age of thirty. In Córdoba, Dellaperriere continued his acquisition of real property without interruption.

Moreover, he was one of the few members of our sample to have experimented with a virtually untapped source of wealth in the province: mining. To the degree that Dellaperriere invested in the mining industry—gold, silver, copper, and nickel—we can label him an industrial pioneer among the immigrants residing in the city. Most of Córdoba's population was "completely ignorant of the province's mineral riches" at the time that he invested, even though several treatises on its mineral potential had already been written.[13] Mining, in fact, remained a virtually unexploited industry through the turn of the century, yet Dellaperriere owned many mines, the total worth of which was 10,000 pesos by 1885.[14]

Dellaperriere concentrated his investments, however, on urban real estate. After the census enumerator knocked on Dellaperriere's door in September 1869, he probably entered the Frenchman's newly acquired two-story house in the heart of the city on Deán Funes Street. Bought for 15,000 pesos, the large house was the first of several purchases of property he made in Córdoba which eventually added to a value of 50,000 pesos. In a mode that emulated the Creole elite's multifaceted acquisitive patterns, Dellaperriere's holdings included urban real properties leased for both commercial and residential purposes, quintas in the periphery, especially in Section 1 near the river, and rural estates. His ownership of land in the city of Río Cuarto in 1872, approximately 280 kilometers south of Córdoba, made him an absentee landlord in the truest sense. Impressively, his assets at the time of his death in 1886 amounted to more than 130,000 pesos. Two-thirds of his property was real estate, almost entirely devoted to agriculture, while one-fifth of his assets were liquid.[15] Status, and sometimes wealth acquisition, meant that professionals such as Dellaperriere stood a much better chance of persisting in Córdoba than did merchants. Out of the total of forty-five professionals we gathered from the 1869 census, twenty-one persisted to 1895.[16]

Table 3.1 provides an overall view of persistence in Córdoba across the occupational spectrum, from which we can make some general observations. Migrants were much quicker to move on in search of their dreams than were cordobeses, although both groups exhibited extremely low persistence figures. None of the unskilled migrants remained in Córdoba. The less than 12 percent of the semiskilled and skilled laborers who stayed represented the highest persistence rates, followed by the 11.1 percent figure of the professionals. That mercantile endeavors did not ensure financial success is evidenced by the mere 6.3 percent of migrant nonmanual workers who remained in Córdoba. The situation among cordobeses was similar in direction, but varied in degrees. While none of the unskilled migrants remained to the end of the century, 11.5 percent of cordobeses did. The conchabo system and its informal aftereffects, once it had become obsolete, had much to do with the difference between the two groups. It was not unusual for conchabos of the 1870s to remain in their chores as domestics through subsequent years or for younger members of their families to stay on and receive the benefit of certain food and shelter.

The cordobés and migrant figures of persistence were similar at the semiskilled and nonmanual levels, but significantly differed in the skilled and professional categories. Though economically divergent, the members of these two occupational categories were more deeply rooted than migrants in the traditional social and labor structure of Córdoba. The skilled workers represented traditional regional artisanry, such as *alpargateros* (hemp sandal makers), *curtidores* (tanners), *lomilleros* (saddle makers), and *zapateros* (shoemakers). All of the professionals among the cordobeses and a relatively high proportion of the ones among migrants had remained in the city until 1895. Representing traditional established families of the region, professionals were not dependent upon their putative occupations for their economic well-being, but upon their financially speculative enterprises.

As in the case of a European like Dellaperriere, most of the Creoles who died rich had come from wealthy homes. Wealth meant enormous sums, often in

Table 3.1
Occupational Persistence, 1869-1895
(N=696)

Occupational Classification	Cordobeses			Migrants		
	Distribution 1869	Distribution 1895	Persistence Rate	Distribution 1869	Distribution 1895	Persistence Rate
Unskilled	21.1 (78)	12.5 (9)	11.5	11.3 (37)	0.0 (0)	0.0
Semiskilled	35.5 (131)	23.6 (17)	13.0	19.3 (63)	7.1 (2)	11.8
Skilled	10.8 (40)	13.9 (10)	25.0	14.7 (48)	7.1 (2)	11.8
Nonmanual	9.2 (34)	2.8 (2)	5.9	19.3 (63)	14.3 (4)	6.3
Professional	0.8 (3)	4.2 (3)	100.0	8.3 (27)	10.7 (3)	11.1
Miscellaneous	22.5 (83)	43.1 (31)	37.3	27.2 (89)	60.7 (17)	19.1
Total	100.0% (369)	100.0% (72)	19.5%	100.0% (327)	100.0% (28)	8.6%

Source: Sample data.
Note: N shown in parentheses.

the range of hundreds of thousands of pesos, usually invested in urban real
property and agricultural estates. For example, Adela Alcorta, a sample member from the province of Santiago, owned in partnership with her husband,
José de la Quintana, over ninety thousand pesos. She was the aunt of José
Figueroa Alcorta, who assumed the nation's presidency in 1906.[17] José de la
Quintana and his wife owned an estancia in the Department of Santa María,
sixty kilometers from Córdoba, worth over fifty thousand pesos. On it they
maintained an active production schedule that centered on raising cattle valued
in 1898 at ten thousand pesos; in addition, they owned almost 200 sheep and
over 120 horses. The good upkeep of the buildings, the orchards, and the forests indicate the active exploitation that the family gave the estancia.[18] This
estate also served as the springboard for subsequent purchases of urban properties in Córdoba during the 1890s, some of which served residential needs
while others were meant for agricultural uses. The purchases of homes in Córdoba reflect the urbanization process and buildup of elite houses within the
center's southeast corner toward the end of the century. Houses bought on
Junín, Corrientes, and Chacabuco streets signaled the genesis of an area of nouveaux riches' homes that would culminate in the 1920s.

Similar patterns of landholding appear in the records of oligarchs like Simeón
Aliaga. A twenty-two-year-old student at the Universidad Nacional de Córdoba
in 1869,[19] he graduated the following year as a *maestro* in philosophy and with
a bachelor's degree in canon law.[20] Later, he received his law degree in Córdoba.[21] Before Aliaga's death in the city in 1909, he had amassed a fortune worth
over 330,000 pesos. Most of his wealth depended on his investments in real
property, yet much of his initial capital came from his family and that of his
wife—another member of the local elite.

The Aliagas' acquisitive career encompasses some of the patterns found in
most contemporary probates. First, no holding extended beyond the boundaries of the province: his agricultural estates were in Río Ceballos in the Department of Colón, and in the Department of Tercero Arriba, while his urban holdings, both central and peripheral, were all located in the city of Córdoba. Second, the urban properties purchased after the Baring Crisis of 1890 had subsided reflected, as did the Quintana Alcorta's case earlier, a pattern of urbanization in turn creating a new speculative drive toward the southeast and northwest areas of the center. For example, Aliaga purchased his home, located to
the west on 358 Colón Street, at an auction in 1896. The location would not
have been selected in previous years, when quintas for truck farming and vacationing dotted the area. By the mid-1890s, however, the movement of professionals away from the central district of Sections 3 and 5, which had begun
during Juárez Celman's last years in the presidency, regained strength. Thus,
we found residential properties belonging to the Aliaga family in Districts 22,

23, and 27 and in the area of Nueva Córdoba to the south of Section 5. Last, the amount of Aliaga money invested in urban property rivaled that spent in rural agricultural holdings: nearly 96,000 pesos were tied up in rural estates, while urban property in Córdoba amounted to 105,000 pesos. Each cluster of properties in Córdoba city and province accounted for one-third of the total value of the estate; the rest was in cash.[22]   This distribution of assets was exceptional among the probates of Córdoba's residents. Only a few of the oligarchs had much cash; in fact, personal property, including jewelry and furniture did not receive much attention from most people in the city during the nineteenth or twentieth centuries.[23]

Ramona Cabanillas' case represents the typical distribution (not the amounts) of assets found in all social classes in the city. Although she owned a fabulous sum, once again we find that she was herself responsible for very little of its creation. The source of her capital was an estancia of 2,700 hectares bequeathed by her father. Assessed at 54,000 pesos in 1903, it had become the prized possession of the total estate, valued at nearly 95,000 pesos. Quickly available liquid assets, however, were limited to less than 1,800 pesos, or only 2 percent of the estate's worth.[24]   The Cabanillas' estate typified the deprecation with which oligarchs treated liquid assets, including stocks and bonds, in a nineteenth-century society that placed real property speculation and primary production above all other forms of capitalization.

The large gap between the possession of liquid assets and real property assets among cordobeses reflected an old tradition. Even before the revolution for independence, notes Tulio Halperín Donghi, Córdoba's elite had been characterized by such a trait. When the Jesuits departed in the late 1760s they left behind a vacuum of liquid resources and an elite that was both wealthy and poor: wealthy in lands, poor in money. This phenomenon, which spread throughout the Argentina of the late nineteenth century, had its basic outlines in old Córdoba.[25]   H. S. Ferns observed the same phenomenon when he wrote that "the revolution which overthrew Spanish power produced a quite exceptional community in Argentina. The exceptional element in the community was its domination by a class of poor rich, of men rich in land but poor in capital. With the progress of time this class became both richer and poorer: they acquired more and more land or their holdings became smaller in size but more and more productive, but at the same time they became more and more dependent on the import of capital."[26]

We do not have data on the forms of agricultural exploitation; ours is not a study of the region's economic history. The data set, however, indicates that land, above all else, had been reenforced as the sine qua non of wealth and status; neither industrial nor commercial enterprises sufficed, if at all involved, in maintaining economic stability or in achieving financial solvency. The disinclination to invest seriously in industry followed the dictates of a propaganda system geared toward convincing people of the need for the full exploitation of primary resources. Reference to *industria* meant the processing of primary products: wheat mills, meat-packing houses, foods. "The best savings bank in the world," boasted a local publication, "is the land of the Argentine Republic." Seemingly in contradiction, the same observer complained of the lack of industrialists in Córdoba "because nobody was fond of industries."[27]

But lack of interest was in itself caused by other factors. Investments in the agricultural sector were supported by powerful European houses which limited their geographic scope to the littoral, while their economic interests rested on the export of primary materials. Simultaneously, the lack of governmental support and virtually nonexistent bank loans for industrial promotion, coupled with a general apathy toward the idea of a national program of industrialization of manufactured consumer goods, aborted the Argentine industrial potential and permitted the continued competition of imported manufactured articles of consumption. Not until that flow was cut in 1914 did Argentine industrialization move beyond the complementary and alimentary levels.[28] Even the immense growth of Argentine industries between 1895 and 1914 (the number of industrial establishments grew by 102 percent) was limited to subsidiary and food processing activities, while the increase in manufacturing industries was very small.[29] Further, whatever the level of industrial production, it remained stubbornly centered in and around the city of Buenos Aires.

The unfavorable position of Córdoba's industry is reflected in the volume of its railroad freight traffic. Between 1873 and 1885, the province imported nine million kilograms (nine thousand tons) of goods from the more industrialized littoral zones than it exported to that region. From the north of the country—including the provinces of Tucumán, Salta, Santiago del Estero, and Catamarca—Córdoba imported nearly forty million kilograms more than it exported. Most of the imports, especially from the littoral, were manufactured goods: iron, building materials, and "commodity goods."[30] The fact that the province still imported manufactured products at the end of the 1880s had not been significantly altered more than a decade later. By 1900, Córdoba's "industries still remained in an embryonic state, with some exceptions, such as the manufacture of lime, charcoal, wood, flour, noodles, shoes, calcium carbide, and a few others. . . ."[31]

The Middle Class

If the rich in Córdoba did not generally subscribe to the notion of economic growth through manufacturing, neither did the middle levels of local society. Surplus proceeds from daily commercial activities, especially among Europeans, were used to purchase real property in the hope of securing comfort in the future. Business expansion was ignored whenever speculation in real property appeared a lucrative alternative. As Córdoba grew, land utilization changed and the ownership of property by suburbanite cordobeses increased; here we are not making any implications on size or type of real property, so we may not assume that a redistribution of wealth had taken place during the second half of the nineteenth century. In fact, the continued large gap between rich and poor was manifested in that the two most prevalent types of holdings were either subsistence agriculture plots or *latifundios.* According to the data in Table 3.2, the number of property owners among the centrally located cordobés persisters in 1895 fell by 10 percentage points; at the same time, real-estate-owning suburbanites increased from nearly 26 percent to 40 percent. The changes among migrants were less sharp; virtually the same proportions of central residents in both periods owned real property in 1895, but an increase of 10 percentage points took place also among suburbanites. The indications here are that most migrants—composed increasingly of foreign stock—did not acquire the cheaper agricultural plots in the city's outskirts; they settled principally in central areas where the cost of property was dearer and devoted themselves to urban occupations. Instead, cordobeses were the ones who became vegetable gardeners, for example, around the city's green-belt.

The relative lack of growth of Córdoba's industrial base was reflected in the relative absence of occupational mobility among individuals and in the continuation of certain preindustrial norms, such as the rapid rate of turnover in the laboring population and its specific job obligations at any one time. The rate of turnover within the working class is evidenced by all the previous discussion of out-migration rates and is manifested as well in Table 3.3, where we could only find one hundred persisters. The increasing rigidity of an occupational structure attendant on industrial growth was absent; here the large proportions of laborers within the miscellaneous category comes into play. Taken from an Argentine occupational classification, the specific responses in the censuses and notarial records which went into "miscellaneous" included: unknown, with his children, provincial deputy, student, sick, men of letters, disabled, retired, prisoner, landlord, unemployed, and lives on earnings. Of course, there were not enough provincial deputies, students, men of letters, prisoners, or wealthy retirees to account for all the people in the category. But there were enough people in the sample who labored at different tasks continuously and whose membership in the labor force was always temporary. These two groups, women and occasional laborers, took in laundry, cleaned houses, carted packages, paved streets, acted as messengers, worked on someone else's land, baked, and sold pastry, and otherwise conducted their chores all the while with an underlying temporary quality to each period of employment. Thus, most members of cordobés society lacked job security. The relationship between the

Table 3.2
Central/Peripheral Residence and Real-Property Ownership by Persisters, 1869-1895
(Percentage and Absolute Numbers)
(N=90)

	Distribution 1869	Owned Property, 1895		Distribution 1895	Owned Property, 1895	
		No	Yes		No	Yes
Cordobés Persisters:						
Central Residence	60.3 (41)	68.3 (28)	31.7 (13)	55.2 (37)	78.4 (29)	21.6 (8)
Suburban Residence	39.7 (27)	74.1 (20)	25.9 (7)	44.8 (30)	60.0 (18)	40.0 (12)
Total	100.0% (68)	70.6% (48)	29.4% (20)	100.0% (67)*	70.1% (47)	29.9% (20)
Migrant Persisters:						
Central Residence	90.9 (20)	35.0 (7)	65.0 (13)	54.5 (12)	33.3 (4)	66.7 (8)
Suburban Residence	9.1 (2)	50.0 (1)	50.0 (1)	45.5 (10)	40.0 (4)	60.0 (6)
Total	100.0% (22)	36.4% (8)	63.6% (14)	100.0% (22)	36.4% (8)	63.6% (14)

Source: Sample data.
Note: Not significant at the .05 level.
* Address not reported in one case.

Table 3.3
Occupational Mobility, 1869-1895
(Percentage)
(N=100)

Cordobeses

1869 \ 1895	Unskilled	Semiskilled	Skilled	Nonmanual	Professional	Misc.	Total
Unskilled	33.3	22.2	11.1	0.0	5.6	27.8	25.0 (18)
Semiskilled	8.3	29.2	8.3	4.2	0.0	50.0	33.3 (24)
Skilled	0.0	10.0	60.0	10.0	0.0	20.0	13.9 (10)
Nonmanual	0.0	50.0	0.0	0.0	0.0	50.0	5.6 (4)
Professional	0.0	0.0	0.0	0.0	100.0	0.0	1.4 (1)
Miscellaneous	6.7	20.0	0.0	0.0	13.3	60.0	20.8 (15)
Total	12.5 (9)	23.6 (17)	13.9 (10)	2.8 (2)	5.6 (4)	41.7 (30)	100.0 (72)

Table 3.3–Continued

Migrants

1869 \ 1895	Unskilled	Semiskilled	Skilled	Nonmanual	Professional	Misc.	Total
Unskilled	0.0	0.0	0.0	0.0	0.0	100.0	3.6 (1)
Semiskilled	0.0	0.0	33.3	0.0	0.0	66.7	10.7 (3)
Skilled	0.0	0.0	33.3	33.3	0.0	33.3	10.7 (3)
Nonmanual	0.0	0.0	0.0	60.0	20.0	20.0	17.8 (5)
Professional	0.0	0.0	0.0	0.0	100.0	0.0	3.6 (1)
Miscellaneous	0.0	13.3	0.0	0.0	6.7	80.0	53.6 (15)
Total	0.0 (0)	7.1 (2)	7.1 (2)	14.3 (4)	10.7 (3)	60.7 (17)	100.0 (28)

Source: Sample data.
Note: Not significant at the .05 level.
N shown in parentheses.

occupations (or lack thereof) within the miscellaneous category with low-level jobs and with few positions of *ilustrados* can be discerned from Table 3.3. Following across the line of "Miscellaneous" we can see that 60 percent of the cordobeses and 80 percent of the migrants originally in such a category remained so, and the rest were spread out through the low levels of the unskilled and semiskilled or service groups.

If for most people an occupational level meant, in fact, constantly varying jobs—not in nature but in patrons—the remainder of the population which held steadier jobs at the start in 1869 did not prove highly mobile by 1895. Among the cordobeses, the largest proportion had been unskilled, and one-third remained so; their next largest proportion shifted into the amorphous miscellaneous classification, which we know to have been comprised of low-level jobs. Over 20 percent of the unskilled cordobeses rose to the semiskilled level, over 10 percent to the skilled category, and 5.6 percent to the professional group. Among the semiskilled cordobeses, nearly one-third remained so; as in other cases, a sizeable 50 percent ended up among the miscellaneous, 8.3 percent dropped to the unskilled and another 4.2 percent entered the nonmanual level. The general picture of low-level cordobeses traced by the statistical shifts over time is of a group unable to break out of their class situation after more than twenty-five years.

Again within the cordobés group nearly two-thirds of skilled laborers retained their position, one-fifth went into the miscellaneous group, and one-tenth rose to the level of nonmanual. At the same time, half of the cordobeses who had held nonmanual occupations in 1869 dropped to the semiskilled, and the rest into miscellaneous jobs. Despite its small size, the group in the nonmanual level—comprised primarily of merchants—illustrates the case in which one could drop out of the commercial community. Last, the one professional who persisted into 1895 remained at the same level.

Within the migrant community, two data are particularly striking, though they merely represent statistically matters already discussed and illustrated earlier: the small number of persisters, and their preponderance in the miscellaneous category. Otherwise, their patterns are similar to the ones noted for cordobeses. Though virtually absent from the unskilled group, their proportions from the original semiskilled level are retained mostly by the miscellaneous group. Skilled migrants remained so, moved up to nonmanual, and into the miscellaneous levels in equal proportions. Nearly two-thirds of the nonmanual individuals remained as such, the balance being evenly split into the professional and miscellaneous groups. Precisely as was the case among cordobeses, only one professional among the migrants persisted into 1895 and he retained his professional rank until then as well.

The data in Table 3.3 help to explain an important motive force underlying large-scale out-migration: significant vertical occupational mobility in Córdoba, even among the few persisters, was rare. Few rags-to-riches stories—implied in the immigration publicity programs—are shown by the data here. Specifically, most shifts in occupational levels occurred between immediately proximate ranks, or between one rank and the miscellaneous category. This did not necessarily indicate occupational mobility, however, since most holders of the unskilled and semiskilled occupations changed jobs with great frequency. Thus, it was normal to hold a series of temporary jobs which for the moment required some skill, only to follow with a job where less or no technical knowledge was required. The same process also resulted in a great incidence of temporary unemployment or underemployment, which is why the miscellaneous category contains sizeable percentages. Moreover, within the observed shifts between the skilled and nonmanual levels are masked the cases of lateral-only occupational mobility, which did not imply any improvements in economic base, as shown by other indicators, including a review of all their probates. Worker-proprietors of *talleres* (workshops) for example, did not have their financial stability improved merely by their status within the mercantile sector. Nor were retailers assured of financial success; usually the comerciantes' only surplus was of the status ascribed to them by a society that sought mercantilistic aggrandizement and that could proudly point to its local wholesalers and retailers for evidence of such achievement.

Yet businessmen often ran greater economic risks than members of some lower-level occupational groups, and the vicissitudes of the economy increased the uncertainty of success in business ventures. Financial support was almost totally unavailable from established lending institutions; instead, merchants had to secure loans from private sources. Thus they often depended for their success more on personal contacts and the accidents of informal arrangements than on the solidity of the business ventures. So prevalent was the use of private loans among Córdoba's merchants that the usual 1 to 1.5 percent monthly interest rates charged by lending parties was no higher than those of the banks, had the latter been willing to make commercial credit available.

To understand fully the complexity of the Argentine social structure we need more than just statistical representations of movement along an occupational scale. In fact, even though occupational mobility in nineteenth-century Argentina signified social improvement, it did not necessarily indicate financial solvency. Few among the sample or their household members depended solely on their occupations for economic security—only for status and acceptance within the community. Lawyers and notaries lived in the districts of the wealthy but did not necessarily belong to the landed gentry; families of day-laborers usually lived in squalor, with limited intergenerational mobility, but a handful managed to save enough to own respectable parcels of land. Most of these rural day-laborers—invariably cordobeses—had not shifted their location or habitat: they continued to comprise the majority of the rancho-dwelling population, while 80 percent of non-cordobeses lived in the well-constructed masonry buildings in the center.[32] Of the nearly 30 percent of the persisters who lived in ranchos, 80 percent were cordobeses, who thus represented one-third of their ethnic cohort. The 20 percent of rancho-dwelling migrants, however, represented only 20 percent of the migrant persisters. Such data again indicate the urban nature of migrants and the rural preponderance of poverty-stricken cordobeses.

In between the lawyers and the few successful day-laborers were other occupations, ranging from the petty entrepreneur to the comerciante of unspecified mercantile dimensions, or to the *industrial,* who was usually a simple artisan, not an "industrialist." The room for positioning oneself within a "middle class," therefore, was ample. But here again, occupational titles categorized social, not financial, distances. A skilled worker, for example, might live in the center, near the wealthy and among the established commercial houses, but not have much more to his name than his tools. Juan Muzzio represented such a case. He was among the few non-cordobeses to persist in the city from the first to the second census. As one of the early Italian arrivals, he preceded his thousand other conationals, and in 1869 worked as a carpenter in Section 3, closest to the heart of the center. Most of his Italian, Spanish, and French neighbors were skilled entrepreneurs like himself—that is, shop-owners or artisans; in fact, he was one of four European carpenters who in 1869 were concentrated in four blocks.[33] Italian sculptors, Spanish shoemakers, French blacksmiths, even an Italian organ-grinder lived and worked in the area, trying to realize the dreams of comfort with which they had set out to America. Most of them failed, not because of lack of enterprise but because all the economic frontiers touted by promoters of development required funds and organization beyond the remunerations gathered by skilled entrepreneurs.

In the generation after the 1869 census, Juan Muzzio moved a number of times. In 1895 he lived one block from the train station of the Ferrocarril Central Argentino, a westward move that was probably to less expensive quarters as the stronger corporate commercial houses, which could better afford the rent increases, began to settle in the downtown area in greater numbers. Muzzio again listed himself as a carpenter in the second census. He now lived alone in his apartment, next door to other European and Creole skilled and semiskilled workers. He owned no real property, little personal property, and could not have been under any delusions of increasing his assets now that he was seventy-five years old. Three years later he moved in with his son and filed an affidavit with the judge of the First District Civil Court in which, seeking privileges accorded to paupers, he proved his total lack of resources and his inability to continue working; his son now "tended to his sustenance."[34]   The economic status of this European carpenter was not unusual in nineteenth-century Córdoba; only the fact that he stayed for so long proved exceptional. Most of his skilled cohorts had left for other parts, probably to return to the littoral or to Europe in search of greater economic opportunities.

Evidence that skilled occupational status and economic improvement had separate and often unrelated dimension is provided by the Murúas' family history.   In 1869 José Murúa was a skilled shoemaker. His household consisted of himself, his wife, his four brothers and sisters and his one-year-old daughter. They all lived in what the census enumerators then called the "Arrabales del Pueblo," the slum area at the southern edge of the city in the 1869 Section 5 (see Map B). Everyone in that rancho worked at odd jobs except the baby, of course, and José's wife, who took care of the house. Helping José was his fourteen-year-old brother Andrónico; twenty-one-year-old Manuela was a servant; twenty-three-year-old María was a seamstress; and Pabla, the eldest, worked as a washerwoman.[35]   For the next twenty-five years the family experienced no social improvement; instead, the individual members continued to display signs of poverty. José's daughter died at the age of eight.[36] Andrónico, his brother, married a Creole and moved westward to the slum of Pueblo Nuevo, where his own five-year-old daughter died of smallpox in 1891.[37] The vicissitudes of Córdoba's labor market kept Andrónico as a day-laborer picking up odd jobs wherever possible; he remained at this low occupational level and still resided within Pueblo Nuevo until his death in 1918.[38] By that time he had no family in Córdoba, except an illegitimate daughter to whom he bequeathed the insignificant legacy of his personal belongings.

His sister Manuela moved out of the city and no further record exists of her in Córdoba. María and Pabla Murúa did stay in the city. Pabla died of tuberculosis in her rancho, situated on the shores of the canal that snaked through Pueblo Nuevo, where she had continued to take in clothes to wash and mend.[39] María remained in Córdoba long enough for the 1895 census. By this time she had been married for twenty-five years and had given birth to ten children, six of whom were still living at home.[40] The listing of her husband, Pedro Ontiveros, as an *industrial* in the census schedules exemplifies the misrepresentation of Argentine census officials' categorization of occupations and the results of their compilations. Ontiveros was not an industrialist by any definition other than the enumerator's own. Only two of his six children could read and write; the girls worked with their mother washing clothes and the oldest son was a carpenter, probably helping his father in his "industrial establishment." All lived in a rancho at the southern edge of the Pueblito, the site of an old Indian settlement west of the center which later became the accepted location for the poor and for some members of the working class. In this area lived fewer than

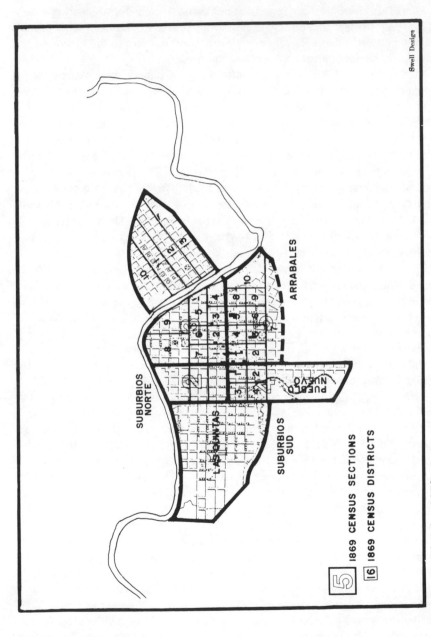

Map B. Córdoba, 1870s.

seven hundred people in 1895, and fewer than nine hundred in 1906.[41] The vast majority of rented residential dwellings in the Pueblito cost less than ten pesos monthly and comprised three rooms or fewer.[42]

What kind of an industrialist was Pedro Ontiveros, that he and his family would live in such miserable surroundings? According to the census enumerator, he labeled as an industrialist any "cutter of material or maker of bricks. All the people," he noted, "who figure in the schedules with the profession of industrialist should be considered in this manner."[43] The important fact is that, even though María Murúa was born poor, she grew in status and acquired relative financial stability, even if dependent on the continued miserably hard work of all family members. Her brother José and his wife had moved away during the intervening years, but María now owned some property that, though limited to the home, the surrounding plot, and the handmade kiln where the family baked and cut the bricks, was sufficient to place her in a position of relative economic security.

Something similar occurred to her old neighbor in the arrabales, Eulogia Moreno. The Moreno nuclear family consisted in 1869 of ten members, sustained by the father, who worked as a teamster, by the two oldest sons, Asencio and Gregorio, who were shoemakers, and by the mother, Juana Montenegro, a seamstress. Most of the family had out-migrated from Córdoba in the course of the years. Eulogia stayed, however, and in 1883, in a fashion similar to María Murúa, married a cordobés with enough property to get by. Her husband, Donato Garay, was a petty merchant who dealt in general goods. They moved to Ayacucho Street within District 9 in Section 4, a definite improvement over her previous neighborhood in the arrabales; lived in a rented one-story masonry dwelling, a promotion from a dirt-floor rancho; and even enjoyed the status of maintaining a domestic servant of their own.[44] Yet even Donato Garay's achievements were not of his own making. While they lived in the center of Section 4, Garay inherited from his father a plot in Alta Córdoba to the north which measured 550 square meters and which was situated in an area of sparse population, composed mostly of laboring class members living in the slum neighborhoods known as rancheríos.

By the early 1900s, Eulogia had become a widow and had moved out of the center to the less expensive zone of Alta Córdoba. Her only possession was that parcel of land which her father-in-law had bequeathed to them. Her difficult financial situation at the turn of the century is indicated not only by her move out of the center for reasons of economy, but also by her mortgage of the property. When she died in 1911, Eulogia's sole inheritor was her sister, Luisa Margarita. To her she left the mortgaged property, which was then auctioned at its original assessed value of 4,000 pesos. After the payment of the mortgage loan and interest, the net worth of Eulogia Moreno de Garay's estate amounted to a respectable 2,155 pesos.[45]

By contemporary local standards people like María Murúa and Eulogia Moreno, who had given clear indications of poverty in the 1870s and had subsequently acquired some property, belonged to that vast middle ground that in Córdoba separated dire poverty from great wealth. They did not represent success stories of frugality and hard work; in fact, frugality and hard work had done little for Juan Muzzio, the Italian carpenter who died with no possessions. María Murúa had exchanged her poverty-striken life, devoid of any financial security, in one poor zone of the city for a similar life in another area, but with the confidence of being the owner of her shack and small plot. Her "industrialist" husband and all able-bodied members of the family worked to keep themselves alive. Eulogia Moreno's childhood background had been similar and she, too, received some security from real property thanks to her husband's family. Neither of the two, on the other hand, benefited from the financial perquisites normally associated with the status ascribed to families of comerciantes and industriales.

However, even many professionals failed to gather the wealth normally associated with the status of their occupational rank. Thus Mizael Páez, who came from a respected family in the province of Catamarca, had migrated to practice in Córdoba as a *procurador,* or solicitor. He had already traveled extensively in the country and had also lived in Buenos Aires for some time.[46] In addition, he had served in the armed forces during the war against Paraguay in the late 1860s and as reward for his services had received grants of fiscal lands, an acceptable form of payment by the Argentine state to its veterans during or after times of war. Páez received an unusually large grant in the Department of Tercero Abajo, south of Córdoba, although the actual transfer did not take place until 1875. His approximately 1,200 hectares, assessed at 5,000 pesos by 1888, was the foundation that served as collateral for subsequent purchases within the Páez estate. His only prior purchase of real property, in 1866, had been a share in a lot within the city north of the Río Primero, which was assessed at only 110 pesos. For payment in an inheritance case he had handled, Páez received a share worth 200 pesos in a property totaling over 200 hectares. His own subsequent purchases from the time of the provincial grant amounted to no more than 300 pesos, and he had borrowed so heavily against his estate through private sources that half of his inventory was composed of unliquidated debts. Still, toward the end of his life in 1887, Mizael Páez had all the trappings of a truly wealthy man: he practiced as a solicitor; he had moved from Section 4 to a rented house in a prestigious portion of Independencia Street in the District 11 (Section 5); and he owned a considerable area of land.[47] Yet his net worth of only 6,300 pesos was a figure far distant from the truly rich, and belied his lifestyle.

On the whole, few members of this disparate middle class attempted to invest cash or to apply their properties as collateral in the industrial ventures upon which—according to contemporary progressive voices—solid futures depended. Real estate and the consequences of attendant speculation continued to form the end-all of nearly all financial activities in Córdoba. The industrial speculator was the exception; so, too, was the commercial empire-builder. An owner's real property (whenever available) and his daily occupation were joined in a symbiotic relationship; commercial sales volumes were second in value and importance to the properties which they served to bankroll and which the culture demanded as collateral. Law practice, likewise, served to maintain a family in an urban setting while land exploitation and speculation remained the basic source of wealth, whether real or fictional.

The economic status of members of Argentine society was measured almost entirely by the quality and extent of their real property. Perhaps the paradox inherent in the existence, on the one hand, of so great an agricultural area which produced so richly, and of the limited number of owners, on the other, caused real property to attain its cherished value. Land and buildings became increasingly synonymous with political and economic power as Argentina became one of the world's breadbaskets. The relationship, therefore, between the nation's political leaders and its foremost producers of staple exports remained an intimate, albeit sometimes dissonant, one. The *unicato,* or elite of political power holders who monopolized federal and provincial elected and appointed posts until 1916, ordained the participation of the economic elite.

Naturally, the latifundio system that was responsible for propping up the elite limited the number of participants in agricultural exploitation in Córdoba. Rental of land by many, rather than outright ownership, served to keep numerous men, women, and children in agricultural tasks. In tracing through all the probates adjudicated in Córdoba, we found only ten cordobés and six migrant sample members who met the two necessary (though not sufficient) conditions to leave real or personal properties after their deaths; that is, persistence and acquisition. Not surprisingly, a close relationship existed between the small numbers of propertied and persistence cases. For greater breadth in our discussion of economic ascent, we counted all occurrences of propertied people, including the members of the sampled persons' households who persisted into 1895. Less than 38 percent had acquired some form of real estate; of these, approximately 60 percent were cordobeses (less than 30 percent of cordobés persisters) and 40 percent were migrants (who, in turn, represented 64 percent of migrant persisters).

By analyzing the various properties we can observe their extent and the utility given to them by property-owners who resided in Córdoba. To a large extent, Table 3.4 reflects the state of agricultural classes in Argentina by

Table 3.4
Size of Real Properties Owned by Persisters, 1869-1895
(Percentage)

Size of landholdings (in square meters and hectares)	Cordobés Persisters (N=41)	Migrant Persisters (N=75)
1-500	24.4	22.7
501-1,000 (.1h)	17.1	8.0
1,001-5,000 (.5h)	9.8	12.0
5,001-10,000 (1h)	0.0	12.0
10,001-50,000 (5hs)	7.3	10.7
50,001-100,000 (10hs)	2.4	6.7
100,001-500,000 (50hs)	4.9	5.3
500,001-1,000,000 (100hs)	0.0	5.3
Over 1,000,000 (>100hs)	34.2	17.3
Total	100.0	100.0

Source: Sample data.

showing the prevalence of holdings of less than five hundred square meters, in which only subsistence agriculture could be practiced, and at the uppermost levels, large-scale holdings greater than one million square meters. The first significant judgment we can make from the data is that at no level of land-holding size were migrants, including European immigrants, excluded from the process of ownership any more than were the cordobeses. Later we discuss in greater detail the example of the Spaniards' equal participation with Argentines in land ownership, but for now we submit that the unavailability of land alone does not suffice to explain the preponderantly urban radication of immigrants in Argentina. Small agricultural units, exploited in the periphery of Córdoba mostly by a growing proportion of cordobeses, indicate an availability of land for small and medium-level agriculturalists. We suspect that, while many Europeans came in search of land, most of them immigrated with general hopes of fulfilling economic achievements in only vaguely defined modes. There existed little moral or folk commitment to the land; men who had been lowly peasants in Italy, Spain, France, or Russia were as easily enticed into staking their futures on an urban commercial environment as they had been attracted earlier by literature and propaganda about the potential riches they could reap from the soil of the Argentine frontier.

Urban and suburban property prevailed in the probates left behind in the late nineteenth and early twentieth centuries; thus, over half of the properties owned by cordobeses and one-third of the ones owned by migrants were located in and around the city of Córdoba. An equal proportion of the migrants' properties were situated in the western portions of the province, where land was less productive and, consequently, less expensive. Many of these migrants came to Córdoba already owners from that area, which included the departments of Pocho, Calamuchita, and Cruz del Eje, among others; many purchased lots or country houses there after their urban migration, in the hope of spending their last few years in their native western hills. Evidence of the geographically parochial nature of land ownership among both cordobeses and migrants is the fact that more than 85 percent of the properties owned by each group were located within Córdoba province. Few of the inventories of even oligarchs contained possessions of land or urban property in adjacent provinces like Buenos Aires and Santa Fe. When established families of cordobeses moved out of the city, they usually settled in the Federal District, where they would speculate in its hinterland and in porteño real estate.

Our observations on the worth of all real properties permit two general conclusions. First, the overwhelming number of properties were valued at five hundred pesos or less; the next preferred property values ranged from ten thousand to twenty thousand pesos, and here migrants owned more such properties. Second, the poorly valued properties were not all owned by poor people who could not afford better; members of the middle and wealthy classes, too, owned cheap properties that were in turn rented to others. The land-holdings valued at ten thousand to twenty thousand pesos, on the other hand, included the urban residences of the wealthy as well as large rural expanses devoted to agriculture and cattle raising. Cordobeses tended to prefer rural properties more than did the migrants, evidence of which coincides with previously presented quantitative data regarding the urban predilection among the latter. Finally, ownership of only one property was the norm, followed by the possession of more than ten properties. With few exceptions, the multipropertied cases were better represented by cordobeses than by migrants—the effect of oligarchic activity in the primary production sector of the economy.

Summary

Migrants generally tended to settle in the city's central areas. This fact was particularly applicable to Europeans, who favored zones where viable commercial opportunities existed away from rural areas; there cordobeses joined with

in-migrants to form the majority of the produce growers who fed the city's
population.

   Commercial activity, however, did not imply the funding necessary for the
greatest provider of status and the best potential for wealth: land. A few comerciantes succeeded in acquiring real properties, as did a few skilled laborers
and, of course, the few members of the elite. Throughout most of the nineteenth century, property ownership meant a small vegetable garden or a somewhat larger plot that could accommodate a milking cow. By the turn of the
century, Argentine and foreigner alike turned to urban real estate as the most
viable form of property ownership during the evident process of demographic
and economic growth. The number of propertied people, while increasing only
10 percent between 1895 and 1951, nevertheless reflected a sharp turn away
from agricultural estates and instead toward urban lots, office buildings, and
suburban residential housing. Through 1925, cordobeses preferred rural land
ownership, while migrants had already been seeking out speculative ventures in
urban properties. Still, the processes of massive immigration and an increased
volume of exports did not alter significantly the social stratification system.
A budding middle class was in fact developing, albeit without possessing much
marginal savings; its extent and financial base of support were more products
of ascription and wishful expectations than the factual results of a basic alteration in the system of wealth distribution.

Part II. Ethnicity in the Formation of Modern Society

4. Urbanism, Racism, and Social Differentiation: Frenchmen among Creoles

How does an immigrant group establish its social position among its hosts? What are the dynamics whereby newcomers gain their reputations as social builders or disrupters of the cities in which they settle? Are social allegiances the same for every member of a given immigrant group? Conventional histories of immigration into Argentina have often failed to ask these questions, or have unconvincingly used national aggregate data to formulate their interpretations.

Prevalent theoretical formulations have dictated that European immigrants, especially those who came before 1890, were low-status, often displaced, agricultural laborers.[1] These laborers had been unable to cope with the economic fluctuations caused by the European industrialization processes and—so goes the accepted truth—seeking better opportunities for socioeconomic improvements they crossed the ocean to settle in Argentina. The stresses which migrants from rural areas underwent in urban environments is a theme treated in both theoretical and operational terms by Argentine and American sociologists.[2] Under their premises, the processes of immigrant integration reflect and, in turn, affect the receiving country's willingness to provide opportunities for socioeconomic improvement among immigrants. Immigrants into Argentina have been described as having been overwhelmingly successful in climbing the occupational scale and in integrating in such a manner as to result in a "synthesis that created a new cultural type."[3] Thus, the Argentine system must have been so open that it not only permitted wide margins of occupational success, but also proved amenable to an amalgamation of cultures rather than merely absorbing immigrants into the majority group.

Three problems are connected with these theoretical frameworks. One is that dissatisfaction with evolving European industrialization has been viewed as a rational impulse for migration; further, an implied constant states that motivations for improving one's socioeconomic situation took place at the level of the individual. Indications exist, however, that even though the creation of industrial systems in Europe did not significantly improve the opportunities for mobility among the unskilled and semiskilled workers, their European persistence rates remained high.[4] Furthermore, low expectations of individual mobility for these low-status men often indicated their difficulties in identifying themselves as individuals: group identity took precedence over individual identity. Given such indications, it would appear that a sense of community allayed the frustrations stemming from their inability to improve their situations.[5] Thus, the prevalent theories dealing with European emigration—based on the push-pull paradigm—have been limited to the use of noncausal frameworks to explain the dynamics of migration while ignoring the dynamics of group *mentalités*.

The second problem with the literature on the success of immigrants into Argentina lies with the data and sources employed. Although authors often recognize the ambiguities of the aggregate official quantitative data, they usually ignore the conceptual difficulties of that data. While admitting to essential differences between the Argentine and European industrial technologies, the authors gloss over the matter to return to jargon closely associated with highly modern societies. The nonquantitative contemporary materials supporting the view of the immigrants' successful transition—the press or official publications—present the difficulties of working with what was essentially propagandist information. The use of these sources to show nonconflictual integration ignores the differences between history and inspirational or propagandist material.[6] Moreover, in the closed political system of nineteenth-century Argentina, newspapers and public policies were products and instruments of the elite—the unskilled and even the artisans had little role in shaping events. Lack of challenge to the elite, however, did not necessarily imply consensus by the remainder of the population, except perhaps in the choices of the governing personalities.[7]

Finally, the prevalent historical writings on immigration to Argentina posit a working relationship between the traditional and the modern, although occasionally, natives and immigrants reverse their roles as projected in the North American scene. The result is a paradigm in which the least that could occur is no influence on either group; the most, an interaction resulting in a hybrid nation. Instead of supporting this dichotomy, we hold the view that subgroups of immigrant communities were flexible enough to use alternatives within the existing social order to promote their own well-being without having seriously amended their social structure or that of the majority culture.[8]

Rather than generalize that the immigrants' success was a function of the openness of the Argentine system, we propose here to look specifically at the particularities of the process and at the degrees of success of the Frenchmen who resided in the city of Córdoba and belonged to the French voluntary association during the second half of the nineteenth century. In this manner, we add a "theater of operations" to the dialogue on immigration, for conventional explanations usually possess no internal geography, but only the anonymous boundaries of the national economy's indices of productivity. By investigating certain social variables of the men under study we have opportunities to clarify and differentiate their individual positions, while observing the flexibility of the group at the municipal level.

We argue that nineteenth-century Argentine views on immigrants were shaped at the local level by an ongoing mutual cultivation of informal and institutionalized contacts between the Creole elite and certain social groups from within the immigrant community; that the action of these immigrants was not communal, but societal, in that it stemmed from a rationally motivated adjustment of interests without coupling widely divergent classes;[9] and that the Creole elite's myopic view of a sector of the total community resulted in self-serving, exaggerated interpretations of its immigrant programs.

Liberals and Urban Growth

After a period of dictatorial rule and some cultural stagnation ended in 1852, the oligarchy ruled with a revitalized liberalism tempered by the tragic political experiences of the past. Its goal was to replace what it considered the innate barbarism of the countryside with the civilizing factors inherent in the European and Argentine urban centers. The liberal intellectuals who formed the Generation of '37 argued that the countryside presented the ecological factors responsible for promoting lawlessness and for continuing the course of social stagnation. Still, midnineteenth-century Argentina depended on the countryside for its existence; the riches of the soil served the needs of the cities, albeit in disparate fashion. While the hinterland of Buenos Aires provided the necessities for the coastal areas, the central region did the same for the city of Córdoba; on a national scale, the wealth depended on wheat, leather, mutton, and beef exports. The liberals' formula for constructive change called for populating the countryside and posed an equation linking population growth with progress. The liberals also created a subtle equation of northern European immigrants with "civilization."

Domingo Sarmiento, the leading liberal spokesman, presented at some length the Argentine disjunction caused by what he labeled the "barbarism" of the countryside and the "civilization" of the city:

> The cities of Buenos Ayres and Córdova have succeeded better than others in establishing about them subordinate towns to serve as new foci of civilization and municipal interests; a fact which deserves notice. The inhabitants of the city wear the European dress, live in civilized manner, and possess laws, ideas of progress, means of instruction, some municipal organization,

regular forms of government, etc. Beyond the precincts of the city every-
thing assumes a new aspect; the country people wear a different dress . . . ,
their habits of life are different, their wants peculiar and limited. The people
composing these two distinct forms of society do not seem to belong to the
same nation.[10]

The wild cattle roaming over the unfenced plains formed the greater part of
the nation's wealth. The mixed-blood cowboys—the gauchos—who tended the
herds represented stagnation. Progress was impossible under such circumstances,
argued Sarmiento, "because there can be no progress without permanent possession of the soil, or without cities, which are the means of developing the
capacity of man for the processes of industry, and which enable him to extend
his acquisitions."[11] The intelligentsia strongly wished to emulate European
ways by simply superimposing them on the national realities.

Left aside were the complex and less enchanting problems of the European
industrial and revolutionary experiences—a striking attitude since European
growth and stability were no longer guided by an unquestioned rigidity of government and ruling class. The economic fluctuations and depressions of the
late 1840s shed some doubts on the desirability of those "processes of industry" to which Sarmiento had referred so invitingly. The political and social unrest in central and western Europe were giving clear indications of what would
follow; in fact, it became almost routine to find predictions of revolution toward the end of the decade.[12] The Argentine oligarchs ignored these agitations,
however, and rested their arguments on the surface qualities of European urban
life and the ability of cities to shape attitudes.

The liberals saw the city as the setting where the individual could best exert
his talents, where he could best develop his potential for work, frugality, and
savings, and where he would become industrious. If for Weber the city, through
its social structures, was the instrument of social change, for the Argentine liberals it was the potential urbanite population which would create centers of
human activity in previously deserted areas. The division of labor could be best
effected in the city; by allowing man to do what he can do best, the city freed
him from the shackles of nature and permitted him to rise above the primitive.[13]

The intellectuals' solution to the problem of their anarchic, underpopulated
country represented an experiment in human fusion. Attracting certain types
of immigrants and placing them in the interior, they reasoned, would change
the attitudes of working class Argentines. While the immigrants would be free
from the fetters of Europe's limitations on man's freedom, the Argentines
would break out of the social imperfections conditioned by that area of the
Americas. Working, saving, and judiciously spending together in the atmos-
phere of unlimited possibilities afforded by the laissez-faire system, Creoles

and immigrants from western and northern Europe would mold Argentina into
a rich, powerful nation. The members of the Commission of Immigration,
therefore, made efforts initially to attract western and northern Europeans.[14]

If Sarmiento presented in *Civilización y barbarie* a savage countryside ruled
by the whim of rural caudillos, in *Conflicto y armonías de las razas de América*
he sought the reasons for Argentina's social and economic plight. He saw the
answers within a framework that compared the heritages of Latin America and
the United States. The differences in wealth between Spain and England, he
contended, were transferred to their colonies in the New World.[15] Moreover,
Sarmiento believed in moral superiority of the Protestant world over the
Catholic domains.[16] Several authors continued to echo Sarmiento's words on
race and culture during the nineteenth and into the twentieth centuries.[17] They
espoused the idea of cleansing the native genetic pool by means of a new Argentine culture created by European immigration, thereby changing the Creole
from an indolent, rebellious spirit into an agent of progress.[18]

Locally, the mestizos of Córdoba were described in similar fashion. Argentine literature paid close attention to the countryside version, the gaucho; less
was written, however, about the urban mestizo, the *chino*. Described as arro-
gant and impudent by the local representatives of the white oligarchy, he embodied the bastardized results of miscegenation; in him "the pride of the Spanish father had degenerated into insolence; intelligence into malice, enterprising
genius into audacity."[19]

The program for populating the countryside did not succeed, however, because Creole oligarchs already owned most of the fertile areas. Large numbers
of immigrants arrived, but they settled mostly in the main urban areas, especially Buenos Aires, Córdoba, and Rosario. Prevailing intellectual currents concerning immigrants could deeply affect public opinion in Argentina. Moreover,
mid- and late-nineteenth-century Argentine intellectuals performed a central
function in planning public policy. Their role, in fact, conflicts with observations which would later be made in Europe, such as Stanislav Andreski's that
"intellectuals cannot avoid being marginal," that their specialization and unusual intelligence naturally keep them away from the centers of power, thereby
relegating them to another powerless minority.[20] But then after the fall of
Rosas the Argentine intelligentsia was not only prestigious, since it formed a
well-to-do minority, but because it had succeeded in bringing down the pre-
1852 political order it also commanded access to the subsequent governments.
Thus when we speak of the Generation of '37 or the Generation of '80 we are
alluding to the complement of political execution of power and intellectual
underpinning of developing programs, often acted out by the same *gobernadores-
letrados*. These men had spent a good part of their lives thinking and writing
out new formulas and would spend the rest of the nineteenth century, at least,

experimenting with them. This does not preclude differences of thought and action within the ruling intelligentsia, but its members were committed on the whole to the creation and preservation of stability and material growth: agreements and disagreements alike were the results of this singular commitment. At the local level, elites also manifested a variety of views, yet these differences were subsumed under the drive to gather immigrants. The clearest manifestation of this general agreement can be found in the city's newspapers. Catholic and traditionalist publications like *El Eco de Córdoba* and later *Los Principios* welcomed immigrants to the city as much as did the specifically pro-immigrant *El Progreso,* the oligarchic *La Patria,* or the muckraking *La Carcajada* and *El Oráculo.* Even if the Catholics did not celebrate the fall of the Bastille alongside the liberal Frenchmen, no one doubted the essential contribution of the French community to Córdoba's progress.

One factor aiding the near unanimity of opinion regarding immigrants in the nineteenth century was that the external qualities of Europeans prior to about 1900 resembled the ideal desired by the liberals: they appeared to have come from cosmopolitan backgrounds, to be literate, to have skills and mercantile abilities, and to be family men. After 1900 the general character of immigration to Argentina became more diffuse. Now the immigrant contingent also represented new areas, especially some which had larger peasant economies, like Spain, eastern Europe and the Ottoman Empire. Twentieth-century immigration—and its representation in Córdoba—thus tended to contain illiterate, unskilled and semiskilled elements as well as an increase in the population of single men with no fixed direction given to their future. This general picture of incipient anomie and the breakdown of the simple optimistic spirit that had characterized the nineteenth century were reenforced partly by the increasing difficulties encountered by immigrants trying to move into the middle class from their working-class origins.[21]

The level of interest in and recruitment of immigrants to Argentina by the state was never matched by its willingness to aid directly in the welfare of those who settled in cities.[22] No governmental organization, federal or local, had the finances or the disposition to provide social benefits other than lodging for a limited period to a limited number of Europeans. Most of the immigrants had to find their own housing, their own employment, and their own transportation; most of them had also to find medical and burial facilities without the aid of government authorities. The relative absence of state welfare measures was largely responsible for the growth of voluntarism in Argentina, and voluntary associations spread throughout the more heavily populated zones and the areas where immigrants had settled. Voluntary associations served two principal functions for Europeans. The more immediate and concrete services included medical and burial benefits. Each association hired a local doctor and contracted a pharmacy for the needs of all its members, who were entitled to such services for little or no money. Associations bought or leased land from the municipality's cemetery grounds to bury its deceased members; occasionally, associations' revenues also paid some benefits to widows or ailing members.

The second function of immigrant voluntary associations was social, involving a wide range of mechanisms for the mutual social adaptation of both immigrants and natives. Voluntary associations, more than individual immigrants, symbolized many of the ideals of the immigration program, effected social control within the foreign community, and served the ideological premises of the oligarchy. These associations served as artifices to structure a rapidly changing local society of increasing numbers of Europeans who, even though they had arrived in a presumably egalitarian and individualistic society, were themselves responsible for the creation of alternative systems of stratification. Thus, the same process that developed among voluntary associations in the United States during the same period took place in Córdoba: "these associations substituted for an aristocracy (or a system of inherited status) a new system for sorting people out and assigning status on the basis of their achievement within the local community. Membership itself conferred a certain status . . . ."[23] Yet because the bourgeois norms of various voluntary associations depended greatly on their own process of membership selection, sometimes class position above all else served to identify potential members. In such cases, nonmembers remained social outcasts in their own communities.

By maintaining a strict code of ethics and expecting appropriate moral behavior from the members, voluntary associations offered opportunities for social mobility, particularly in building private contacts with a view toward securing private commercial credit. In the virtual absence of bank loans, private creditors provided the wherewithal of Córdoba's position as a commercial entrepôt linking the nation's three principal agrocommercial zones of the north, west, and east. The private, informal arrangements required a network to inform lenders as to who in the community were credible risks and upstanding citizens. Voluntary associations thus were essential not only for connections with influential community members but also for certification, in effect, that their members were respectable, sober, progressive, and business-oriented.

The Société Française

The Europeans who congregated in the cities found avenues of communication with their cohorts through the voluntary associations which they organized during the second half of the nineteenth century. Municipal and provincial government officials perceived the leaders of the Europeans' voluntary associations as spokesmen for the foreign communities. The immigrants' voluntary associations served as foci of attention which shaped communal attitudes toward immigrants at large. The Frenchmen's association, the Société Française de Secours Mutuels du Córdoba, reflected the social behavior of its members, and influenced the oligarchy's response to them during the period under discussion.

The population of the city of Córdoba in 1869 was approximately 34,000. Included were 120 adult Frenchmen, yet only sixteen of them joined the Société at its founding in 1875. It appears that any enthusiasm for erecting institutional bonds of fraternity was weak among these men.[24] What made the difference for those who chose the institutional path to socialize, as compared to those who went their own individual ways? First, a common factor among the initial members was that in 1869 they had lived within the city's most highly urbanized districts. The 1869 census divided the city into five major sections, and the district within the third and fifth sections formed the center of the city (areal references in this chapter are to Map B). The center of Córdoba denoted more than just a concentrated area of commercial and financial activities; within a nine-block area beat the cultural, religious, educational, and commercial pulse of Córdoba. The city as a whole boasted over nine hundred square kilometers in area, yet much of this territory was rural and populated by marginal socio-occupational groups: small tenant farmers, peons, and mestizos. Córdoba had hardly changed its social ecology since the time of its founding in 1573.[25]

Only two Frenchmen of the sixteen who joined the association in 1875 had previously resided in the city's rural areas, and one of them had by then moved into the urban confines and had changed occupations. Those who joined the association at its inception reflected a tendency of the French immigrants toward the city center, for the city's western sections (1, 2, and 4) had no representation in the original membership, while sections lying within and bordering the center (3 and 5) gained in representation. Only one member moved to an area tangential to the city; he had been one of the organizers, however, and continued to be active in the institution he had helped to create. Clearly, this urban mentality was a function of the overall residential preferences of Frenchmen, who, as shown in Table 4.1, lived primarily in Sections 3 and 5. It is significant, however, that there was no representation from the sizeable geographic area encompassed by the entire western half of the city. None of the Frenchmen living within the Sections 1, 2, and 4, with the two exceptions already noted, and none living in the suburban districts within the Sections 3 and 5 joined their centrally located cohorts.

The length of the urbanizing experience was partly responsible for a centripetal attraction. Members more recently arrived in Córdoba were more widely dispersed, in part because of their general marginality, which was expressed by a high incidence of transience and by their agricultural labors within the

Table 4.1

Residential Distribution of French, Cordobés, and Total Adult Male Population, 1869

	Section					Suburbios Norte	Suburbios Misc.	Total
	1	2	3	4	5			
French	8	7	51	5	49	0	0	120
Cordobeses	1,551	1,669	4,817	1,894	5,381	1,321	1,294	17,927
Total Population	3,571	3,124	8,920	3,741	10,167	2,489	2,355	34,367

Source: Argentine Republic, *Primer Censo (1869)*, legs. 156-163.

Note: This table includes the populations of some suburban districts which the census commissioners did not consider as belonging to the municipality of Córdoba and were not included in the official results. Once these suburbs are removed, the figures in the table vary less than 0.03 percent from the official statistics.

predominantly rural Section 1. Those in the 1869 census—equipped with a longer urban experience—realized the importance and status of being located by residing in Sections 3 (56.3 percent) and 5 (31.3 percent). The Société Française acted as a filtering mechanism in which the low-status Frenchmen measured in terms of geographic marginalism, never figured prominently while the more stable sector maintained its representation.

The censused Frenchmen who never joined the Société Française also preferred to live within the most populous sections, Sections 3 (43.3 percent) and 5 (41.3 percent). The similarity of residence patterns between members and nonmembers is superficial, however, since the membership of the association showed a marked segregation at the district level. One-third of the French who stayed out lived in districts in Section 3 farthest from the center of the city. Only 11 percent of those who entered the Société Française lived in those districts, and none within the farthest districts of Section 5.

A second factor set apart those who joined from those who did not: the occupational structure. According to Table 4.2, the French who joined the Société Française had shown movement upward along the occupational scale.

Table 4.2
Occupational Distribution of Frenchmen Censused in 1869 and Société Française Membership
(Percentage)

| | Members Société Française 1875 (N=16) | | Nonmembers Société Française 1875 (N=104) |
Occupational Classification	In 1869	In 1875	In 1869
Unskilled	0.0	0.0	10.6
Semiskilled	12.5	6.2	19.2
Skilled	50.0	43.8	44.2
Nonmanual	31.3	37.5	16.4
Professional	6.2	12.5	6.7
Miscellaneous and Unknown	0.0	0.0	2.9
Total	100.0	100.0	100.0

Sources: Société Française, *Livre des societaires,* vol. 1; Argentine Republic, *Primer Censo (1869),* legs. 156-163.

Between the time of the census and the formation of the association, there were increases of those in nonmanual and professional jobs while the semiskilled and skilled workers decreased in representation. No comparisons can be made with the censused Frenchmen who did not join the Société Française at the time of its initiation, since no listing exists for them, but we can make observations about them and draw some inferences. In 1869, these men displayed a solidly middle-level occupational position; there were, however, unskilled and menial laborers (10.6 percent), a larger percentage of the semiskilled (19.2 percent), an equal proportion of skilled (44.2 percent), and fewer nonmanual workers (16.4 percent) than among those who did join the association. Among the professionals, those who remained outside the Société Française formed a higher proportion (6.7 percent) than those who joined it.[26]

The Frenchmen residing in Córdoba who stayed out of the association were socially marginal even within their own community. They remained anonymous drifters: only 9 of those 104 remained in the city and became members in the years following 1875. The length of their urban experience proved beneficial to the members who had resided in Córdoba at least since 1869. Longer experience in the city affected not merely the geographic distribution; the censused members also manifested higher occupational levels than their less experienced cohorts, as shown in Table 4.3. Once again, there were no unskilled laborers present, while the transients continued to drift in and out of the city. Over one-quarter of the 1875 membership had left within a year.

Why this reluctance to join with one's compatriots? The original regulations of the Société Française mention no qualifications for membership except those dealing with birthplace, age, moral behavior, and health. The institution was meant to "bring together in fraternal relationships the Frenchmen in . . . . [Córdoba] . . . , to come to the aid of its members in cases of illnesses . . . and to aid, by means of the relief funds, the Frenchmen not belonging to the Society and whose needs are recognized."[27] Originally, two types of membership were available: active and honorary; later, in 1881, a third type, that of *protecteur,* was added.[28] Honorary members did not pay fees or monthly dues while protectors were exempt only from the membership fee, but neither drew benefits from the association. No restrictions were placed on the age or nationality of honorary members or protectors. Only Frenchmen, Belgians, or their sons, between eighteen and fifty years of age, in good health as certified by a doctor, and who presented "sufficient guarantees of morality," could become members.[29] In addition, the applicant had to be sponsored by two members who would vouch for his good standing in the community. The final step toward admission was a vote by the full membership on whether to accept the applicant into the association. Members could be expelled from the Société for the following reasons: keeping secret an illness or abusing the privileges

Table 4.3
Occupational Distribution of Société Française Members, 1875
(Percentage)

Occupational Classification 1875	Members Not Resident in 1869 (N=49)	Members Resident in 1869 (N=16)	Total Membership (N=65)
Unskilled	0.0	0.0	0.0
Semiskilled	8.2	6.2	7.7
Skilled	32.6	43.8	35.4
Nonmanual	18.4	37.5	23.1
Professional	6.1	12.5	7.7
Miscellaneous and Unknown*	34.7	0.0	26.1
Total	100.0	100.0	100.0

Sources: Société Française, *Livre des societaires*, vol. 1; Argentine Republic, *Primer Censo (1869)*, legs. 156-163.
* Most left the city shortly after 1875.

accorded by the association; blocking the association's general progress; habitually addressing meetings on politics or religion; and committing "inflammatory, scandalous, or dishonorable" acts.

The reason for an exclusionary membership ritual despite a putatively inclusionary program was that many immigrants' mutual-aid societies in nineteenth-century Argentina were not simply gathering places for the socialization of foreigners. Subtle qualifications and unwritten restrictions altered the socioeconomic composition of their constituencies. As shown by the overall geographic and occupational distribution of the original members, only the relatively stable and elitist elements of the French community constituted the Société Française. The association maintained its social composition through requiring that two members introduce and sponsor the applicant; thus social limits were automatically placed on the persons who were presented for membership.

Fully aware of their status as foreigners, members assumed that the Société Française would be looked upon as the representative institution of the entire French community, whether or not it comprised the numerical majority or the majority views of Córdoba's Frenchmen. Occasionally, members created embarrassments, causing swift institutional responses. For example, the leaders expelled three members for operating a house of prostitution, while taking pains not to announce the matter or lecture publicly to the community on the dangers of such a profession. Instead, the Société's leadership ran the culprits out of town and swiftly laid the issue to rest.[30] The members' private financial matters also came under scrutiny of the leadership, once again in order to insure the continued respectability of members in the city's commercial and lending circles. In the executive council meeting of February 14, 1876, one member was expelled from the association for defrauding his creditors.[31] In a commercial center like Córdoba this issue was especially delicate.

The rules inhibiting any activities which might have been considered controversial, such as political or religious debates, reflected the French leaders' sense of their tenuous position as foreigners. They were unwilling to behave contrary to the Creoles' expectations of them, as expressed during a heated debate over the one hundred pesos the executive council had voted to donate in response to a call to help the poor Creoles of La Rioja and Catamarca provinces. The executive council members confessed to the protestors of the move that they had known the donation went against the association's rules, yet they had felt unable to deny help since the Argentines had shown themselves sympathetic toward indigent Frenchmen.[32] On another occasion, the Société's membership was reluctant to make public the honorary membership awarded to a French doctor for his outstanding service during the devastating cholera epidemic which swept through the city in 1886, because the members of the city's Health Council had been subjecting him to "persecution" over his questionable credentials.[33]

The constituents of the Société Française, not unlike those of other immigrant benevolent associations, shaped Creoles' attitudes by promoting a biased view of the total foreign community. They did so by maintaining a membership of upwardly mobile individuals through the end of the century; as shown in Table 4.4, the skilled and nonmanual occupations formed nearly two-thirds of the membership.[34] Even in voluntary associations which contained important working-class components the orientation of the leaders was directed toward bourgeois norms which met the authorities' approval. Whenever it came to a choice between members' ethnic values versus the nation's interests, the leadership of each organization defined its interests synonymously with the ruling class.[35]

By the time of the second national census in 1895, the Société Française had not only failed to open its doors to lower social groups, but had closed ranks (Table 4.5). The 1875 membership had contained larger numbers of the semi-skilled and a large proportion of the skilled workers. In the following twenty years, however, the membership came to be recruited increasingly from the

Table 4.4
Occupational Distribution of Members at Entry into
Société Française, 1875-1900
(Percentage)
(N=525)

Unskilled	0.0
Semiskilled	13.7
Skilled	36.8
Nonmanual	24.2
Professional	9.3
Miscellaneous and Unknown	16.0
Total	100.0

Source: Société Française, *Livres des societaires,* vols. 1-4.

Table 4.5
Occupational Distribution of Société Française Members,
1875 and 1895
(Percentage)

Occupational Classification	Membership 1875 (N=65)	Membership 1895 (N=80)
Unskilled	0.0	0.0
Semiskilled	7.7	6.2
Skilled	35.4	30.0
Nonmanual	23.1	60.0
Professional	7.7	3.8
Miscellaneous and Unknown*	26.1	0.0
Total	100.0	100.0

Sources: Société Française, *Livre des societaires,* vols. 1-4; Argentine
    Republic, *Segundo censo (1895),* legs. 883-894; Córdoba (City),
    Guía de Córdoba, 1901.
* Most left the city shortly after 1875.

Table 4.6
Membership in Société Française, 1895, and Occupational Distribution
(Percentage)

Occupational Classification	Total French Population (394)	Nonmembers of Société (314)	Members of Société (80)
Unskilled	5.1 (20)	100.0	0.0
Semiskilled	15.2 (60)	91.7	8.3
Skilled	39.1 (154)	84.4	15.6
Nonmanual	29.4 (116)	58.6	41.4
Professional	7.6 (30)*	90.0	10.0
Miscellaneous and Unknown	3.6 (14)	100.0	0.0

Sources: Société Française, *Livre des societaires,* vols. 1-4; Argentine Republic, *Segundo Censo (1895),* legs. 883-894; Córdoba (City), *Guía,* 1901.

Note: N shown in parentheses.

* The high number of professionals derives in part from the fact that those who listed themselves as *contadores* were often simply self-ascribed accountants without formal training; some of them simply kept the books of the family store.

upper social levels of the French community despite appeals from the leadership to enlarge the group without reference to specific social directions. On Bastille Day, 1878, the president of the association noted that it was "regrettable to see in a colony so numerous as ours such a small number of Frenchmen participating as members of the Société." He exhorted the members to seek applicants and got their pledges to do so.[36]

How representative were the Société Française of Córdoba's Frenchmen in 1895? Table 4.6 indicates that the 1895 occupational distribution of the adult male French population of Córdoba and the proportions of those within each occupational category who remained outside the association. Not one of the unskilled French laborers—who presumably most needed the association's services—became a member. Relatively few of the professionals, who through their informal contacts and processes of emulation mingled more with the Creole oligarchy, joined the association. The semiskilled and skilled workers continued to be underrepresented. Together, these laborers, composed primarily of men who worked in the city's four railroad stations and repair shops, formed the French community's largest census group. Most of them lived near their places of work in the suburbs. They exercised informal contacts within their own occupational groups and neighborhoods, while the Société's members continued to orient their activities to the commercial sector and the Creole authorities.

French Integration, French Segregation

In an era severely lacking public social welfare services, the immigrants' benevolent associations filled some of the gaps. The utility of the provincial building program begun in the 1880s was often only cosmetic: boulevards, parks, plazas, and theaters did not benefit Córdoba's sick, poor, aged, and orphaned. Although private charities received some aid from the provincial government, the amount of assistance had been declining for some time before the financial crisis in 1890 virtually ended it.[37] Not surprisingly, the plan of the immigrant associations to build a private hospital, which would also serve the public, received widespread support among influential Creole groups in Córdoba and Buenos Aires.[38]

These associations also helped in the field of education. The provincial government often subsidized such private efforts without burdening itself with their administration. The French, German, Italian, and Spanish communities hired their respective countrymen to establish schools where their children would learn about their European heritage as well as about Argentine culture. Sometimes the government granted them funds in exchange for free education for a number of students. The subsidies, however, served to provide education to the immigrant sector of the population, which already had a much higher literacy rate than the Creoles.[39]

Members of the Société Française received perquisites granted by the oligarchy to merchants in exchange for training Argentine apprentices. Sometimes, as in the case of Henri A. Pellici, the conditions took the form of a business arrangement. In 1894, Córdoba's Ministry of the Treasury exempted Pellici's proposed statue workshop from the annual license taxes for a period of ten years, on the condition that he undertake to train two Creole youths as artisans.[40] Such attempts at facilitating occupational mobility through learning outside the formal classroom had only limited success, since they were infrequently tried and their accomplishments depended upon the suceess of the exempted enterprises. In the case of Henri Pellici the results were nil: his small operation did not yield him enough money to purchase any real property. Moreover, his personal property, like that of most cordobeses, was limited to some furniture and the tools of his trade.[41] He finally had to sell his business and leave the city. Still, as one of the many European merchants in Córdoba and as a member of the Société Française, he held some responsibility for the credit which official sources, and much of the press, gave to immigrants for uplifting Córdoba's status and for providing the "example of habits introduced from other, more civilized countries."[42] Thus the mercantile elements of the immigrant community of Córdoba joined together during the second half of the nineteenth century, primarily to socialize informally within their own group as well as to enjoy the medical and funeral benefits which formal avenues could not adequately provide. More important to their image was the fact that the members represented the literate, the businessman, the urbanite, and the "self-made man," whose activities expressed a distinct personality and who acquired a middle-level status which was not widespread among Creoles.

The mutual aid society enlisted the help of the press, which in turn used the associations as proof of Argentina's progress and to reinforce the values ascribed to immigrants; usually, this arrangement was made without considering the countless indigent Creoles who were struggling for their own livelihoods. The press also coopted the desired image of these successful immigrants to further the view that Argentina was indeed a land of opportunity where anyone able to work could improve his lot. The press, however, failed to examine closely the thousands of immigrants in Córdoba province alone whose lot had not changed radically, who still worked in low-level occupations, who enjoyed hardly any economic improvement, and who remained unaided by any official or private self-improvement programs.

The Société performed functions essential to the maintenance of the members' social position by acting as a "booster" society and by stressing the value of acculturation through the cooperative efforts of its leaders and the influential natives. By virtue of belonging to the Société, the members enjoyed the status and perquisites associated with a thriving social group which had been partly responsible for the city's progress. The institutional contacts between the ethnic voluntary associations and the government led to informal connections among members and Creole oligarchs. These relationships served the interests of the associations' constituents by bringing them to the attention of groups within the Creole establishment. Since so much of one's socioeconomic success depended on local personal contact and informal exchange, the awareness of the groups' existence in itself improved members' opportunities for material well-being. We have seen in Pellici's case one result of such dynamics: the province's generous commercial tax exemptions which benefitted immigrant merchants, many of whom had cultivated their contacts at the local level through the efforts of the voluntary association.

Members of the nineteenth-century Société Française operated in a milieu of growing urbanism in which "the larger the number of persons in a state of interaction with one another the lower is the level of communication . . . on an elementary level, i.e., on the basis of those things which are assumed to be common or to be of interest to all."[43] The result was that members monopolized what benefits were given in recognition of the French contribution to Córdoba's progress, to the exclusion of the majority of Frenchmen. A symbiotic relationship existed between the immigrant and the Creole establishments of Córdoba which few nationalists perceived at the time. Moreover, the city's immigrant institutions, having been promoted by the government and having been publicized by the local Creole press, served to shape community attitudes toward immigration. These attitudes would remain largely intact until shaken by urban protests in Buenos Aires and labor strikes in industrial areas at the turn of the century. In the meantime, the picture painted by the French membership represented the fulfillment of the expectations of the Generation of '37 and the satisfaction of the contemporary Generation of '80 by showing a group of prosperous and law-abiding Europeans who, through their customs, were helping to "civilize" the nation. The Société Française received the best wishes of the Creole leaders, who hoped it could soon reach the "heights which it merited."[44] The membership proved to the liberals the validity of their theory that Europeans would be more likely to take advantage of "a world less hostile toward individual endeavor and more receptive toward human enterprise," as they characterized Argentina.[45]

Not surprisingly, Córdoba's newspaper advertisements could often be found announcing: "Day-laborers needed. Foreigners preferred, with or without families."[46] The Creole elite of Córdoba applied almost indiscriminately what it saw in the Société Française and other immigrant associations to all Europeans who settled in Argentina until the turn of the century. The Société Française thereby became an integral part of a self-fulfilling prophecy which the oligarchy had created and through which it attempted to continue the flow of European immigrants into Argentina.

5. Class Formation and Cultural Pluralism:
The Spanish Voluntary Association

Spaniards, like other immigrant groups, joined together in voluntary associations to promote integration within their own local communities, to cushion the initial emotional and cultural shocks of migration, and to provide environments conducive to mutual aid because of the lack of public medical and burial assistance. The social composition of the Spanish voluntary association in Córdoba affords a view into a microcosm of Spanish society in Argentina. More specifically, we can study its structure, its aspirations, and the degree to which it represented the promises of socioeconomic improvement that the country had held out to the Spaniards before emigrating. This chapter and the next analyze some aspects of the lives of 467 members of the Asociación Española de Socorros Mútuos de Córdoba. The list of names was compiled from the available registries of members for the years 1872, 1883, 1889, and 1902. All members who joined during one of those years were traced through a number of documentary sources, including: the subsequent registries of the Asociación through 1927; the death records of the Archdiocese and municipality; the 1869 and 1895 manuscript census returns; and the notarial records contained in probates executed in Córdoba. In addition, the minutes of the general meetings and of the association's executive council from 1872 through 1902 provide an account of the interests and concerns of the most important and well-respected Spanish organization in Córdoba.

The intent of this chapter is to portray the normative values of one of the principal sectors of the immigrant community and to investigate the members' social attributes and degrees of social mobility. Residential location, occupational structure, geographic persistence, and occupational and economic improvements are the principal social variables measured. Afterward, we conclude with some appraisals of immigrant society and class structure in Argentina.[1]

By the start of 1870, the city of Córdoba contained approximately two hundred Spanish men, putting the city's Iberian population in third place after the Italians and the French.[2] From the start of the European migration to Córdoba, Spanish men filled all occupational strata, from lowly jornaleros like Miguel Balls to pianists like his neighbor Jaime Romeu.[3]

Good diplomatic relations between Spain and Argentina reenforced the traditional affinity between the two peoples. A shared language and similar customs enhanced Argentina's appeal to those Spaniards thinking of emigrating to the Americas. As usual in situations in which ethnic minorities coexist with a majority culture, Spaniards occasionally protested against what they considered slander and other anti-Spanish behavior by Argentines. Nevertheless, the struggle for independence had left no latent anti-Spanish sentiment in the Platine area, where residents remembered the liberating campaigns only as a receding part of their historical consciousness. For example, in March, 1882, Spaniards in Buenos Aires protested against an art exhibit in which one artist depicted the Argentine Republic stepping on the Iberian lion. In Córdoba, as in Buenos Aires, the press requested that the Spanish population remain calm. The editors of *La Carcajada* suggested that Spaniards not view the exhibit as a personal affront since there was no conscious plan in the occurrence; moreover, the militant confrontation between Spaniards and Argentines, the editorial continued, "was all . . . in the past."[4] Spaniards, as well as northern Europeans and Italians, received the admiration of Argentine intellectuals.[5] In turn, Argentina exerted a powerful attraction for Spanish families. Emigration to Argentina served as the topic of dicussion in many homes in Spain, according to an observer: "During the meal, the widow's entire conversation was about Argentina and Paraguay, where she had been with her [late] husband . . . During every meal it was the same thing: Argentina this, Paraguay that, and all because she was intent on convincing her new husband to go . . . ."[6]

Thus by the 1860s a steadily growing Spanish colony lived in Córdoba. The Spanish men in the 1869 census displayed the usual residential distribution found among the city's immigrants: they tended to live in central sections and in central districts within those sections. The numbers of Spanish men living in the 1869 censal Sections 3 and 5 (Map B) were virtually the same: 37.9 percent lived in Section 3, while 39.1 percent lived in Section 5. Moreover, these Spaniards distributed themselves more centrally than their French cohorts: in 1869 only 3.4 percent of the Spaniards lived in peripheral districts of Section 3 (Districts 8-13), while none lived in similar areas within Section 5 (Districts 7-10). The small number of Spaniards in rural zones signified their predominantly urban mentality, one result of which was the preponderance of urban-based occupations among them, especially those in the nonmanual and professional categories (see Table 5.1).

Only 4.7 percent of the Spaniards, compared to 10.6 percent of the Frenchmen, labored as menial and unskilled workers. Over two-thirds of the total

Table 5.1
Occupational Distribution of Spanish Men
Sixteen and Over, 1869
(Percentage)
(N=87)

Unskilled	4.7
Semiskilled	5.9
Skilled	12.6
Nonmanual	60.8
Professional	10.3
Miscellaneous and Unknown	5.7
Total	100.0

Source: Group data.

male Spanish population in 1869 devoted themselves to commercial and professional enterprises. The 12.6 percent who represented the skilled laborers actually included some worker-proprietors, so that we should consider the nonmanual representation as being conservative.[7] Thus the overall picture of the Spaniards, by 1870, was of a well-to-do, centrally located population thriving on the economic opportunities that Córdoba afforded it.

In addition, the supposedly fervent Catholicism of Spaniards was welcomed in Córdoba, a city that some people characterized as having the largest number of church steeples in the nation. Liberals, however, sometimes taunted Spanish religious orthodoxy, as in the case of a Spanish merchant who, according to a local reporter, never even turned on the lights inside his business until after the cathedral bells signaled the end of the morning mass.[8] Such teasing was to be expected when two different nationalities met; the immigrants' ways often differed from the habits of the Creoles. In time, styles of living merged, and a new generation was formed "in the melting pot of an understanding which was nearly always arrived at through the sentimental track."[9] Moreover, Spaniards and cordobeses were especially cognizant of their sentimental and religious affinities. "The Spanish nation," editorialized *Los Principios*, "was born, lived, and reached the highest peaks of the universal dominion under Religion . . . . The Spaniards' blood is our blood, their glories our glories, their hopes our hopes . . . ."[10]

La Asociación Española

A number of Spanish men joined together to form the Spanish Choral Society in 1872. Such informal associations of immigrants for the purposes of dancing and singing native tunes were not unusual either in Argentina or in the United States.[11] Córdoba witnessed the development of a number of societies organized by Germans, Swiss, and Italians. In June 1872, thirty-three members of the Spanish Choral Society formed the nation's third Spanish voluntary association: the Asociación Española de Socorros Mútuos de Córdoba, which followed the general pattern of its predecessors in the cities of Buenos Aires and Rosario. The principal founder of the association, Enrique López Valtodano, was a newcomer to the city of Córdoba, but he quickly commanded the respect of his conationals because of his literary abilities. He founded the newspaper *El Ferrocarril* in 1870; through its pages he became one of the leading spokesmen of the Spanish community and well connected with the Creole intellectual and elite circles.[12] As the symbol of Spanish economic and social success, López Valtodano soon gave his place to Manuel Méndez y López, the first president of the association. Méndez y López embodied all the positive characteristics of the Spanish community: a forty-two-year-old, respected professor who had devoted most of his unassuming and honest life to intellectual activities.[13]

The purpose of the association was to bring together the city's Spaniards not only to help the needy among them but also to perpetuate a feeling of ethnic consciousness in a new and strange environment. Sentimental attachment for the mother country was the bond keeping all Spaniards together in the face of external pressures, or so it would have appeared from the initial proceedings that established the association on June 2, 1872. The principal result of that first meeting called for action on the following resolution: "To convoke, by the most able and expeditious means, the Spaniards residing in [the] city to a meeting or general assembly with the objective of . . . carrying out a general membership drive, and, lastly, to lay down the foundations of the planned association."[14] At this planning stage no one mentioned any restrictions on membership; on the contrary, to any observer the energy and emotion of these men could only symbolize the fraternal spirit of all Spaniards in the city. Yet almost immediately an air of jealous guardianship of their benefits enveloped the original group, resulting in a series of restrictions on membership. Some of the changes in the bylaws of the association stemmed from the desire of the members to display moral and ethical leadership; for example, no medical aid was to be rendered to victims of duels, fights, "immoral accidents," or venereal disease.[15]

While the Spaniards of the Asociación initially concerned themselves with their public image, subsequent regulations indicate a retreat from the original goal of conducting fraternal relations with all Spaniards. In 1881, a distinguished member suggested that the Asociación Española accord burial benefits only to those who had maintained their memberships for one year, but whose poverty levels had subsequently prevented them from paying their dues. Others followed the lead by suggesting that nonmembers, such as Spanish ministers, consuls, and military personnel, also be accorded burial privileges in the association's mausoleum. A lengthy debate followed when several members opposed the moves because such "charitable acts showed lack of planning by favoring some, thereby possibly harming all." Opponents pointed to the provision in the association's contract that only members would be buried in the limited plot of land awarded the group by the municipal council. After a lengthy debate, the motion was defeated.[16]

The following year, the members approved an amendment limiting the geographic reach of the Asociación Española: to the east, as far as the streetcar line reached into General Paz; to the west, as far as the streetcar lines extended into the semirural Quintas. The shores of the Río Primero and the start of the hills around San Juan and Junín streets bounded the area to the north and south, respectively. These limits excluded Spanish residents of San Vicente, Pueblo Nuevo, Alta Córdoba, Pueblito and most of General Paz. Even though membership was not de jure limited on the basis of residence, no reimbursements or aid for doctors, medicine, or disability was forthcoming until the potential victims moved within the Asociación's radius of operations.[17]

The leaders of the association could perhaps defend these moves on the basis of the institution's limited resources; yet other regulations also served to isolate the Asociación Española from low-status Spanish immigrants. For example, applicants for membership had to be employed fulltime, and no assistance would be rendered for the initial three months of membership. Even though poor Spaniards could be found in the center, the exclusion of residents of Pueblo Nuevo, Alta Córdoba, and Pueblito guaranteed that transient agricultural skilled and unskilled workers would not participate in the affairs of the association.

During the first two decades after the Asociación Española was organized, an almost immediate series of institutional changes sufficiently altered the composition of its membership to limit participants almost exclusively to the socio-occupational types who had joined in 1872. Although less than three years had elapsed between the first national census and the formation of the association, only ten of the eighty-seven Spanish men present in the city at the end of 1869 joined in 1872. The ten included seven well-established businessmen, one pianist, one professor, and one university student. The social attributes of those ten men characterized the general membership of the Asociación Española de Córdoba. No unskilled laborers joined or were recruited: in fact, two *agricultores* formed the lowest socio-occupational stratum in that year's membership. Sixty percent of the 1872 membership worked in non-manual occupations; of these 48.2 percent depended on their own businesses for their livelihoods.[18]

Surprisingly, most of the founders and early members of the society were recent arrivals, the great majority of the seventy-one members who joined in 1872 had been in the city of Córdoba for two years or less. Residents of longer standing remained outside the association. Low persistence rates and nationalistic partisanship among Galicians, Asturians, Catalans, and Basques depressed what could have been a very large enrollment figure. It should be noted that Catalans in Córdoba had also formed an association of their own. A number of times, leaders of the Asociación Española exhorted their Catalan counterparts to merge with their association. The minutes of a special meeting of the executive council of the Asociación Española attest to the deep emotional divisions within Córdoba's Spanish population.

A "state of dissidence" had existed for some time between Catalans and the rest of the Spanish population before the leaders of the Asociación Española voted in 1876 to form a commission in an attempt to bring Catalans into the fold of the Spanish association.[19] When the two groups met, the president of the Asociación Española appealed

> to the patriotism of the members of [the] . . . sister *Sociedad Catalana* . . . so that by dissolving that association completely, only the Española would remain functioning; he explained that damage was being done to the reputation of the entire [Spanish] colony to its own discredit as a result of those divisions, thus providing those who only wish[ed] to find opportunities to criticize it with a basis for their sarcasm; that this division [was] unjustified here where all should remain closely tied by the bonds of patriotism. . . .[20]

In response, the Catalans pointed out the way the Spaniards mocked them for speaking in their own language or for being unable to speak Spanish correctly. Other Catalans accused the Asociación Española of having favored "privileged members," none of whom had been Catalans. Spaniards, in turn, accused the Catalans of being overly sensitive. At the end, in spite of guarantees of good and cordial treatment, the Spaniards were unable to absorb the Catalans into the Asociación Española. In time, the Catalan association disintegrated —too few Iberians lived in Córdoba at the time to accommodate two associations. Many Catalans, however, continued their refusal to join the Asociación Española, Subsequently, members of the Asociación worried over its low enrollment and attendance figures.[21]

Social Structure

What was the social composition of the Asociación Española? During the thirty years which our study encompasses, the average age of the members was 29.69 years old, while 28 years of age was the modal category. The youngest member entered at the age of 11; the oldest was 65. Single men formed a slight majority, and 41.2 percent of the members were already married. Between 1872 and 1902, only nine Spanish men holding menial occupations entered the Asociación Española, representing only 2.2 percent of the entire membership; likewise, the semiskilled representation was minimal at 5.5 percent. Businessmen and business dependents were in the majority with 50.7 percent, while skilled laborers represented over one-third of the membership. Spanish professionals, few of whom existed in Córdoba, constituted 4.7 percent of the total membership.[22]

The data on the members' residential patterns yield a general picture similar to that of the Frenchmen. The regulations limiting the geographic reach of the Asociación within the city worked most effectively to discourage rural-based and poor Spaniards from joining. Sections 2, 3, 4, and 5, which formed the city's center, contained over 90 percent of the members. Only five Spaniards lived in Sections 8 (General Paz); two resided in the suburban southern Section 9; and two in Section 1 to the west. The typical member of the Asociación Española, then, was a man in his late twenties, recently arrived in Córdoba, and already in business; he was almost as likely to be married as not, but always displayed an urbanite's orientation by living in the center, usually near his place of work.

We can observe the shifts in the social composition of this group by the use of tabular displays which focus our attention on the residential patterns over time and illuminate the issue of geographic persistence for the Spanish establishment in Córdoba. Table 5.2 shows the residential distribution of members who joined in 1872, 1883, and 1889, respectively. By the 1890s there would be some altering in the concentration of Spaniards in the high-status Section 5 and in the commercial and financial hub of Section 3. The membership now showed a drift to the west, although still remaining within the center; thus, Sections 2 and 4 increased their representation from zero to 19 and 4 percent, respectively, while Sections 3 and 5 fluctuated sharply. The residential shifts become clearer at the district level. District 2, in the northern half of Section 3, was considered to be only slightly less poor than District 1, on the river's edge. By the late 1880s, the city had filled this area and had constructed river walls in order to end the perennial flooding of these low-lying districts during the rainy season. In 1889, three new members from District 2 joined the association, and members also joined from other northern districts within the

Table 5.2

Residential Distribution of Members Entering Asociación Española, 1872, 1883, and 1889

(Percentage)

Year of Entry	Section							Total
	1	2	3	4	5	8	9	
1872	0.0	0.0	50.0	0.0	20.0	30.0	0.0	8.2 (10)
1883	0.0	9.1	63.6	0.0	9.1	18.2	0.0	9.0 (11)
1889	2.0	19.0	58.0	4.0	15.0	0.0	2.0	82.0 (100)
Total	1.6 (2)	16.5 (20)	57.9 (70)	3.3 (4)	14.9 (18)	4.1 (5)	1.6 (2)	100.0 (121)

Source: Group data.

Note: N shown in parentheses.

center, such as 14 and 15. Of course, the new areas were represented in the Asociación as a function both of the pressure on the centermost areas and of general urban growth, but they also reflected the geographic diffusion of the growing middle class among the immigrants.

Not only did members move within the city, but they also displayed the basic characteristic of local cordobés society: large-scale out-migration. Spaniards, like Frenchmen, had a remarkably low persistence rate in the city of Córdoba. On the average, from 65 to 75 percent of each year's group failed to remain within the association or in the city. Table 5.3 tabulates the results of the systematic tracing of every member in each of the designated years into the following years of registry through 1927. The figures attest to an ongoing process of migration, with its multiple social and economic repercussions.

Over time, a greater degree of participation by lower occupational groups, thanks to increased recruitment efforts, accompanied the Spaniards' geographic dispersion.[23] By the turn of the century, a number of menial and semiskilled workers had joined the Asociación Española. A considerable number of members of the "low nonmanual" category also joined, consisting almost entirely of *dependientes de comercio* (see Table 5.4). Men like Gaspar Barreras Massó from the city of Vigo, or Marcos González, born in Casarejos, found jobs as salesmen, mostly in Spanish-owned businesses.[24] Cultural familiarity and national propinquity often bridged the gap between two Spanish strangers: a shop owner and a recently arrived immigrant. Perhaps more than any other immigrant group in Córdoba, Spaniards relied on nonfamily members to help

Table 5.3
Persistence to 1927 of Asociación Española Members
Entering 1872-1902
(Percentage)

Year of	Persisted to Year				
Entry	1883	1889	1902	1916	1927
1872 (71)	33.8	22.5	8.5	2.8	2.8
1883 (34)	–	29.4	11.8	8.8	8.8
1889 (190)	–	–	14.2	7.4	5.8
1902 (172)	–	–	–	23.3	15.1

Source: Group data.
Note: N shown in parentheses.

Table 5.4
Occupational Distribution of Members Entering
Asociación Española, 1872-1902
(Percentage)

Occupational Classification	Year of Entry				Total
	1872	1883	1889	1902	
Unskilled	0.0	0.0	2.7	2.4	2.2 (9)
Semiskilled	7.4	3.8	3.8	7.1	5.5 (22)
Skilled	22.2	38.5	49.5	17.8	33.7 (136)
Low Nonmanual*	3.7	0.0	7.7	20.7	12.4 (50)
Nonmanual	44.4	34.6	31.9	45.0	38.4 (155)
Professional	11.1	7.7	3.3	4.1	4.5 (18)
Miscellaneous	11.1	15.4	1.1	3.0	3.5 (14)
Total	6.7 (27)	6.5 (26)	45.0 (182)	41.8 (169)	100.0 (404)

Source: Group data.
Note: N shown in parentheses.
* Mostly petty-business employees.

in their businesses; Syrian, Lebanese, and Jewish immigrants, on the other hand, kept close ties between commerce and family, probably because so often the family, not the individual, represented the unit of migration for them.

The Spaniards who joined the local Asociación Española in 1902, through the short time span between the dates of their arrival and their entrance into the association, reflect the widespread transiency in Argentina. Over 85 percent of the new members had not yet been present in the city at the time of the national census in 1895.[25] Although this percentage of newcomers is higher than that of the general population, it reiterates the theme of massive and ongoing internal migration throughout Argentina. An average of only 27 percent of the membership of each of the selected years persisted in the city to 1895 (see Table 5.5). Approximately 70 percent of the members who joined in 1872 and in 1883 did not persist to 1895, while the figure for the 1889 membership was over 80 percent. Reenforcing the view that the low persistence scores of the men in our study resulted from out-migration, Table 5.6 shows the proportions of members who died in Córdoba. Low persistence figures, therefore, resulted not from deaths in the city (which would also show members as having been absent from the 1895 schedules), but from actual moves out of the city. No more than one-quarter of any membership group died in the city.[26] Thus, geographic impermanence, the characteristic of Argentine rural life during the first half of the nineteenth century, also affected urbanites of the latter nineteenth and early twentieth centuries.[27]

What is striking is the rapidity with which changes took place at so many levels of the socioeconomic structure. Members joined the Asociación Española relatively soon after arriving in Córdoba, as evidenced by the short time that members of the 1872 and 1902 groups had spent in the city before joining. In addition, members displayed great ease and speed in establishing themselves in professional occupations. When Pedro González, for example, arrived in the city in the second half of the 1890s, he was in his late forties and had already had some experience in other parts of Argentina.[28] By 1900, less than four years after his arrival, he had opened a pharmacy at the corner of San Luis and Ayacucho streets, within Section 4.[29] Because of failing health he closed down his business only three years after he had opened it.[30] He did not have an opportunity to out-migrate, though; he died within a short time in Córdoba, still belonging to the Asociación Española.[31]

The case of Pedro González provides an unusual example of rapid socioeconomic integration, though not of great acquisition of wealth. He and his Spanish wife had lived and married in the province of Santa Fe. Their backgrounds were similar: their fathers had been farmers; their mothers, seamstresses. From their first home in Section 4, they had moved and established the pharmacy a few blocks to the east along San Luis street, a symbol of upward social mobility

Table 5.5
Persistence to 1895 of Members Entering
Asociación Española, 1872-1889
(Percentage)

Year of Entry	Not Present in 1895	Present in 1895
1872 (71)	69.0	31.0
1883 (34)	67.6	32.4
1889 (190)	81.6	18.4

Source: Group data.
Note: N shown in parentheses.

Table 5.6
Membership Status at Time of Death of Members Entering
Asociación Española, 1872-1902
(Percentage)

Year of Entry	Not Member at Death	Member at Death	Total*
1872	76.8	23.2	16.2 (69)
1883	83.9	16.1	7.3 (31)
1889	91.1	8.9	42.1 (179)
1902	88.4	11.6	34.4 (146)
Total	87.3 (371)	12.7 (54)	100.0 (425)

Source: Group data.
Note: N shown in parentheses.
* Missing observations: 42.

into the more prestigious Section 5. There they lived surrounded by lawyers and academicians teaching at the nearby University of Córdoba. However, the González couple did not represent the rich immigrant. They never owned real property, the index of Argentine economic status. At the time of his death in 1905, Pedro González' savings amounted to the contents of his pharmacy's cash register: 230 pesos. His other personal property consisted of the drugs on the shelves, which were valued at less than 2,000 pesos. Medicines and drugs, however, were difficult items with which to clear accounts; in short, his widow was left with almost no means of support.[32] The Asociación Española aided by providing burial privileges, but the widow still had to pay dues for the up-keep of the crypt. All in all, however, the career of Pedro González showed a remarkable economic integration, especially in view of the rigorous require-ments that the provincial law of 1890 placed on druggists before they could be certified by the Consejo de Higiene.[33]

We can learn how some of the socioeconomic factors weighed on the Span-iards' decision to move out or to stay in Córdoba by comparing the members' persistence rates with their various social attributes. Table 5.7 shows the results of a comparison between the Spaniards' occupational class at the time of their entry into the Asociación and their persistence in it. We can best analyze this relationship by looking, in order, at the persistence rates of the member-ship from year of entry by occupational sector. In this fashion we observe that for the 1872 and 1883 groups the skilled and the nonmanual occupations had the highest persistence rates to 1883 and 1889, respectively. The financial crisis of the early 1890s, which did not end in Córdoba until late in the decade, radically altered the picture: the persistence rates for the skilled and nonmanual Spaniards of the 1889 and 1902 groups fell drastically to between 14 and 23 percent. The largest occupational group, the nonmanual sector, composed pri-marily of businessmen, lost large portions of its constituency for each of the selected years. But thanks to its greater size and "durability," it continued to exert its hegemony for every year except 1889.

Thus between its founding in 1872 and the turn of the century, the Asocia-ción Española underwent two divergent processes. While lower occupational groups were able to enter the association, the business elite maintained and sometimes expanded its strong social base, thereby determining the course of the association. The relationship between occupational levels and persistence in the Asociación also had geographic ramifications. Section 1, poorer than all other central sections, and Section 3, the commercial hub, increased their pro-portional representation over the period from 1872 to 1927 at the expense of all other sections (from zero to 16.7 percent and from 57.1 percent to 83.3 percent, respectively).

The highest persistence rates in the association were those of the merchant

Table 5.7
Membership Persistence by Occupational Classification, Asociación Española, 1872-1927
(Percentage)
(N=390)

Year of Entry	Occupational Classification	Persisted to Year				
		1883	1889	1902	1916	1927
1872	Unskilled (0)	—	—	—	—	—
	Semiskilled (2)	50.0 (1)	50.0 (1)	0.0 (0)	—	—
	Skilled (6)	100.0 (6)	100.0 (6)	33.3 (3)	0.0 (0)	—
	Nonmanual (13)	69.2 (9)	30.8 (4)	15.4 (2)	7.7 (1)	7.7 (1)
	Professional (3)	66.7 (2)	66.7 (2)	33.3 (1)	0.0 (0)	—
1883	Unskilled (0)	—	—	—	—	—
	Semiskilled (1)	—	0.0 (0)	—	—	—
	Skilled (10)	—	30.0 (3)	0.0 (0)	—	—
	Nonmanual (9)	—	55.6 (5)	33.3 (3)	22.2 (2)	22.2 (2)
	Professional (2)	—	0.0 (0)	—	—	—

Table 5.7–Continued

Year of Entry	Occupational Classification	Persisted to Year				
		1883	1889	1902	1916	1927
1889	Unskilled (5)	—	—	0.0 (0)	—	—
	Semiskilled (7)	—	—	0.0 (0)	—	—
	Skilled (90)	—	—	14.4 (13)	7.8 (7)	7.8 (7)
	Nonmanual (72)	—	—	15.3 (11)	8.3 (6)	4.2 (3)
	Professional (6)	—	—	33.3 (2)	16.7 (1)	16.7 (1)
1902	Unskilled (4)	—	—	—	25.0 (1)	0.0 (0)
	Semiskilled (12)	—	—	—	16.7 (2)	16.7 (2)
	Skilled (30)	—	—	—	23.3 (7)	13.3 (4)
	Nonmanual (111)	—	—	—	20.7 (23)	14.4 (16)
	Professional (7)	—	—	—	42.9 (3)	28.6 (2)

Source: Group data.   Note: N shown in parentheses.

and professional groups who resided in the heart of the commercial and financial area of Córdoba, and of the skilled workers who lived and labored in the small operations that sprang up, as the old area of Las Quintas became increasingly urbanized, in the western part of the center. Tanneries, storage sheds, tin shops, and other low-status businesses situated themselves in Section 1 and in the area of suburban Section 9 immediately to the west.[34]

While the nonmanual sector had numerical control of the Asociación Española, the extreme apathy of most of its members served to balance the skilled workers and the nonmanual group as forces controlling the actual assemblies. The record of members present at the meetings held in even-numbered years illustrates the concern of the Spanish community leaders that lack of participation in the Asociación was working against the interests of all members. During one meeting in 1886, a member began by praising the Spanish community for the "sociability" that distinguished it, "and for its proverbial greatness, elevating it above the moral level of the other [foreign communities]." He decried, however, the "noticeable absenteeism of members, which offered a pathetic contrast that needed to be eradicated by a greater display of interest on the part of all members . . . ."[35] Despite the fact that the size of the membership kept increasing, the apathy of the members continued to plague the Asociación throughout the years.[36] Because any amendment to the regulations of the association had to be requested and approved by more than half of the membership, some worried that such a majority would never be assembled. They argued, therefore, that an alternative course of action be taken so that in the event of an "absolutely needed" change the Asociación would not flounder for lack of participation.[37]

Apprehension over the future of the association and concern over lack of Spanish "patriotism" were well founded. Of the 467 Spaniards we are analyzing here, only 81, or less than 18 percent, ever attended any of the meetings that took place during the period of their membership, starting in 1872 and ending with 1894.[38] Nearly half of these Spaniards had an attendance record of less than 1 percent, and only 7 attended all the meetings held during their tenure. The rate of attendance of these men averaged approximately 21 percent.[39]

Commentators on the immigrants' low degree of original national identification are thus correct in suggesting that "this must be counted as an important factor in the survival of an Argentine national identity."[40] Although the rhetoric of the meetings of voluntary associations in Córdoba would have one believe in the members' strong patriotic fervor, the fact remains that identification with the country of origin was limited mostly to decorative superficialities. In the case of Spaniards, the exceptions came only during great disasters or impending wars in the mother country, and always after heated debates among the members. Generally, the Asociación's very parochial concerns did not reach beyond itself, even if they involved other Spaniards. For example, it was often the custom for foreign associations to honor their consular representatives with dinners and gifts. Therefore, in 1883 when Spaniards in Buenos Aires organized a commission to put together an album depicting the Spanish community in Argentina in order to present it to the Spanish ambassador, they requested the cooperation of major Spanish organizations throughout the country. However, after the president of the Asociación in Córdoba read to the executive council the request for funds, the members voted unanimously to take no action at all on the issue, since the matter was "completely alien to the nature of . . . [the] association . . . ."[41]

Ten years earlier, a member had requested that the Asociación organize a concert to benefit the victims of a series of Indian raids in the province of Santa Fe. The executive councilmen, though recognizing the philanthropic intent, voted down the proposal because the association should "limit itself only to exercising its charitable influence on its own members." The decision created long arguments until some of the members requested that the council vote on the appropriateness of using the name of the Spanish association for charitable purposes as long as its interests were not hurt. The councilmen refused to lend the association's name for any such acts.[42]

Whenever Argentine public officers requested their attendance at official functions, however, the Spaniards accepted much more readily than the Frenchmen, especially when the affairs celebrated joint church-state events.[43] In the fifty-seven regularly scheduled and extraordinary general meetings that took place between 1872 and 1902, members almost never discussed Spanish or Argentine politics, the fate of Spaniards outside the city of Córdoba, the Spanish-American War, or any issues other than those directly concerning their own welfare.[44]

The only time that the Asociación officially took a positive stand in matters of politics came in 1885 during Cánovas del Castillo's failing negotiations with Germany over the disputed Caroline Islands.[45] In October an emergency meeting was held to discuss a letter from the "Spanish Central Committee" in Buenos Aires, requesting that Spaniards throughout Argentina organize in support of Spain. The local groups were to gather funds for Spain's defense of "its rights over the Caroline Islands Archipelago that were threatened by the German government." Córdoba's Asociación Española responded with enthusiasm and protested any possible Spanish acceptance of the German suggestion of arbitration, labeling such an eventuality "a cowardly and indecorous act on the part of the Spanish government that [would] submit to arbitration what it [already] legally possesses."[46] At a subsequent meeting, members approved a resolution promising funds for the purchase of a warship in the event of hostilities.[47] The course of these meetings clearly violated the institution's charter, which forbade any discussions of political or religious matters during meetings.

Throughout the nineteenth century, the Asociación hardly shifted from its unwillingness to aid Spaniards who needed it the most, even when its help would have resulted in the immediate improvement of the needy. Such were the cases in which the association refused to lend money to poverty-stricken nonmembers to enable them to move to other cities where they had jobs already waiting for them. When it came to charity for other Spaniards, members of the Asociación donated rarely. One of the few exceptions occurred during the 1885 cholera epidemic in Spain, when members agreed to send contributions.[48]

Cohesion, Disparity, and Class Behavior

Apathy toward the needs of others complemented the members' disinterest in the affairs of their own association. The number of attendants per meeting between 1872 and 1902 averaged approximately thirty-three members.[49] Such a low figure adds credence to the judgment of Menéndez Pidal on the Spaniards' sense of individualism. "The Spaniard," he commented, "is inclined not to feel a sense of solidarity with the community except insofar as it will bring him immediate advantages, for he will always neglect indirect or future benefits. Hence, he is rather indifferent to the welfare of the community or its problems . . . ."[50]

Although apathy spanned all social classes, it was not manifested evenly throughout the social structure. The occupational distribution at the meetings tempered the predominance of the nonmanual sector, so that the numbers of voters among skilled workers and commerce-related persons were closer to each other than to each of their total memberships. Skilled workers comprised over 35 percent of the attending members, compared to a 45 percent score for the merchant class, so that the skilled had somewhat higher and the merchants had lower attendance records than their membership representations.[51] Attendance and occupational structure were related to the extent that the skilled laborers often joined with lower occupational groups and employees of petty commerce to insure that they retained the benefits of the association.

The low degree of participation by nonmanual elements and by skilled workers, so many of whom were themselves workshop proprietor-operators, represents a component of Sebreli's conceptualization of the petite bourgeoisie, itself a skeptical class by nature and by its economic culture.

> Negating history as a totality where each part depends on the others, and hiding social relationships behind the particularities of individual people, the *petit bourgeois* permanently balances himself between two contradictory

and equally equivocal attitudes—optimistic voluntarism and pessimistic voluntarism—without deciding, of course, to admit the consequences of either of the two and without taking sides . . . "Sadness," "indifference," "fatalism," . . . are . . . reactions . . . of a class which does not act, which does not take up measures, nor does it wish to make commitments, which does not congregate in meetings . . . ; of a class, in sum, which does not wish to participate in history, which believes it does not participate and which, therefore, participates blindly and without knowing what it does, what it wants, or where it is going.[52]

The lack of participatory fervor in both the Spanish and the French voluntary associations, the reflection of bourgeois attitudes, and the predominance of petty and established merchants within them join to detract from the accepted idea that the immigrant working-class elite provided the leadership for both the voluntary associations and for the nascent protest movements among industrial workers during turn-of-the-century Argentina.[53] It is difficult to conceive of working-class elites spending all the time and devotion required to organize protest movements that would, at best, result in some future improvement of life; the fact was that they would not give of themselves even on issues which often could have resulted in immediate rewards, such as material benefits and the quality of treatment by the host society.

The parochial quality of the normative values of the ethnic voluntary associations in Córdoba served to fuse their social constituencies into relatively narrow boundaries that easily located the members' class interests. The rhetoric extolling the unlimited opportunities for self-interested socioeconomic improvement did not prove true, since the cases of extensive mobility were dwarfed by the more usual cases of limited mobility and stationary conditions. The diversity or gap among social classes within the immigrant communities, in conjunction with large-scale migration, prevented the immigrant groups from permanently belonging to any one major working class organization. The ethnic voluntary associations in Córdoba did not facilitate the organization of institutions with proletariat concerns, even when it meant aiding their ethnic cohorts.

Even without the existence of self-imposed restrictions on the discussion of politics, members of the Spanish voluntary association would not have had different normative values. No part of the charter mentioned any specific social barriers for membership, except that applicants must be employed; and still the social structure that developed from its beginning served informally to protect itself from strongly differentiated Spanish groups: *labradores* or peones, on one hand, and intellectual radicals on the other.

The social superiority that members felt over the lower-status population surfaced over the issue of the annual Columbus Day picnic sponsored by the Asociación. Beginning in the mid-1890s, leading Spaniards had begun to lobby for a government declaration of October 12 as a national holiday. The pro-immigrant press echoed their feelings and assisted the cause by printing favorable editorials on the issue. "It is truly strange," wrote *La Patria* in 1896, "that that day has not been declared a holiday in all of the Americas, since no people could help but be susceptible to the events commemorated on [October 12]. Argentines, Spaniards, and Italians in the Argentine Republic have glories and civilizing conquests to remember on that day."[54] In 1895 as part of the general lobbying efforts the Asociación Española sponsored a public picnic, complete with music, food, and amusements, to celebrate Columbus Day. The local press responded warmly to the event. The affair grew in size during subsequent years until the crowds became unwieldy, as in 1900 when some blows were exchanged by the participants. Determined to prevent such disruptions in the future, the president of the Asociación urged members to stop the affair temporarily. The association also organized a religious celebration earlier in the day, in which the provincial authorities and "the most select group" of Córdoba's society participated. After the first few years, however, the "respectable" society members would not attend the picnic. Now members questioned the validity of holding similar outings. "For what?" asked the president. "So that the vagrant common people could invade our premises, our [social] circles, with the police unable to contain such an enormous mass of people . . . : it is sad to say . . . our outings have come down to such a low grade that last year we saw our families having to mingle with persons whose views and customs are in complete counterpoint with our morals and customs."[55]

While professing his love for the "lowly people," the president suggested that the annual picnic not take place until the Asociación could organize it on fenced property of its own. The membership accepted his suggestion.[56] Some authors have argued that the visible products of superiority are industrial; for members of the Asociación, however, one of the "products" of membership was superiority itself. Functionally, this helped to elevate members to the Creole oligarchy's plane of communication; normatively, they were rewarded with the dignity and honor which membership in an established institution could provide.[57]

Members who steered the affairs of the Asociación through their attendance and active participation were the most bourgeois: those in attendance usually came from homes in the business-dominated Section 3, and comprised an average of two-thirds of the constituents of meetings. Not only did centrally located bourgeois sectors of the Spanish association predominate in its membership registries and meeting, but also the "old guard" continued its interest, attendance, and, by inference, power in the association. Over 40 percent of members who attended the meetings belonged to the original group which had joined in 1872; 37 percent had joined in 1889, and 22 percent came from the

1883 group. The limited geographic representation in meetings, due both to the exclusion of suburbanites and the continuance through the turn of the century of many original members in the daily affairs of the Asociación, thus continued to benefit primarily Spaniards of better socioeconomic levels.[58]

6. Mobility Patterns among Spaniards

Instead of discussing social mobility in Argentina in terms of generalities, this chapter looks into the degrees of mobility of specific Spaniards. We discuss their geographic, occupational, and economic mobility to determine the parameters of "success" in Córdoba.

Table 6.1 shows the out-migration rates for the socio-occupational groups from the time of their entry until 1895. The professional sector, not surprisingly, had the highest persistence scores, while unskilled and menial laborers persisted least in the city. A striking agreement in rates occurred among the semiskilled, skilled, and nonmanual occupations, thereby indicating the similar economic pressures to which proprietor-operators of petty businesses were subjected. An average of approximately 80 percent of those three socio-occupational groups were no longer living in Córdoba by 1895.

Residentially, the highest depletion rate took place among residents of Section 5—followed by Section 2—signifying that among our Spaniards, residents of the commercial hub had somewhat greater stability, though all merchants per se did not. Of sixteen members who lived in the highly commercial Section 3 at the time of their entry, for example, over 81 percent stayed in that section through the mid-1890s.[1] Occupationally, the nonmanual sector represented fully half of the persisters. Residence and occupation of the persisters to 1895 were cross-tabulated, as shown in Table 6.2. Even with a general persistence rate of only 18 percent (Table 6.1) the nonmanual sector of the Spanish membership is shown in Table 6.2 to have been large enough to represent over half, while the skilled represented only 23 percent of the persisters. More than half of each of these two groups, as expected, lived in Section 3, together with 40 percent of the professionals.

The amount of intersectional geographic mobility, therefore, was minimal; in effect, only two choices generally existed when it came to spatial movement: to out-migrate; or to remain in the city, which meant staying in one's original

Table 6.1
Persistence to 1895 by Occupational Classification of
Asociación Española Members at Entry
(Percentage)

Occupational Classification	Did Not Persist	Persisted	Total
Unskilled	88.9	11.1	2.2 (9)
Semiskilled	77.3	22.7	5.5 (22)
Skilled	79.4	20.6	33.7 (136)
Nonmanual	81.4	18.6	50.6 (204)
Professional	55.6	44.4	4.5 (18)
Miscellaneous and Unknown	57.1	42.9	3.5 (14)
Total	78.7 (317)	21.3 (86)	100.0 (403)

Source: Group data.
Note: N shown in parentheses.

Table 6.2

Residential Distribution by Occupational Classification of Asociación Española Members Persisting to 1895

Occupational Classification	Section									Total
	1	2	3	4	5	6	7	8	9	
Unskilled	0.0	0.0	0.0	0.0	0.0	0.0	0.0	100.0	0.0	1.3 (1)
Semiskilled	0.0	16.7	0.0	0.0	0.0	66.7	0.0	0.0	16.7	7.8 (6)
Skilled	5.6	16.7	55.6	0.0	11.1	0.0	11.1	0.0	0.0	23.4 (18)
Nonmanual	2.6	2.6	51.2	2.6	23.1	5.1	2.6	7.6	2.6	50.6 (39)
Professional	0.0	20.0	40.0	20.0	0.0	20.0	0.0	0.0	0.0	6.5 (5)
Miscellaneous	25.0	0.0	25.0	0.0	12.5	0.0	25.0	12.5	0.0	10.4 (8)
Total	5.2 (4)	7.8 (6)	44.2 (34)	2.6 (2)	15.6 (12)	9.1 (7)	6.5 (5)	6.5 (5)	2.6 (2)	100.0 (77)*

Source: Group data.

Note: N shown in parentheses.

* Nine persisters did not report their address.

section. Other indicators support this view. In general, Córdoba's suburban population did not move into the center, and the central population remained within their own pockets; the Spaniards acted no differently. It made no sense, furthermore, for merchants to live too far from their places of business. Occasionally, the owner of a large suburban industry, such as a flour mill or a beer factory, lived in the center and commuted to his office in the periphery. Usually, however, merchants lived near their businesses, often within the same building. A look into the addresses of homes and businesses in the probates of Córdoba's merchants shows their tendency to live on the floor above their business places whenever possible. Some pages of the 1895 manuscript census returns show that merchants' entire households, including infants, lived in the same building with the employees of their stores.[2]

As in the case of Buenos Aires, the population concentrated in the center because most of the employment opportunities existed downtown and because of the availability of rental housing in the area.[3] Low salaries paid to employees placed even the low nonmanual Spanish groups in the same financial stress as the unskilled jornaleros, resulting in their inability to move out to the edges of the core during this period of urban expansion and speculative land pricing in the peripheral areas. Some professionals moved from Section 5 to Sections 2 and 4 at the end of the century as lawyers chose to build their offices on previously bare plots, thus paying lower construction bills by avoiding building demolition costs as was the case of Buenos Aires.[4]

The degrees of occupational mobility among Asociación members, displayed in Table 6.3, indicate the limited mobility inherent in a fluctuating economy based principally on the commercialization of primary products. None of the semiskilled improved their station. Among skilled workers, a considerable proportion opened small establishments of their own, usually in the repair, footwear, and furniture trades; some, however, fell victims to the vicissitudes of the labor market, particularly severe during the 1890s, and dropped in their occupational levels. The nonmanual sector remained mostly the same, though some dropped to the level of skilled employees. Most of the professionals were certified public accountants who lent their professional services in addition to owning their own businesses. Thus, they listed themselves variously as *contadores* or comerciantes on different records, and the proportion of professionals at the time of entry which appears in the nonmanual category in 1895 does not, therefore, reflect a drop in occupational standing. The general trend that appears from the foregoing shows a clustering over time around the commercial spheres. The consequent social attitudes of these men reenforce the notion of the increasing bourgeois quality among immigrants in the voluntary association; at the same time, radical labor activities and social unrest increased in Córdoba.

Table 6.3
Occupational Mobility of Asociación Española Members
(Percentage)
(N=73)

Occupational Classification Year of Entry	Occupational Classification, 1895					
	Unskilled	Semi-skilled	Skilled	Nonmanual	Professional	Miscel-laneous	Total
Unskilled (0)	—	—	—	—	—	—	—
Semiskilled (3)	0.0	100.0	0.0	0.0	0.0	0.0	100.0
Skilled (24)	4.2	4.2	45.8	41.6	4.2	0.0	100.0
Nonmanual (33)	0.0	3.0	15.2	69.7	3.0	9.1	100.0
Professional* (7)	0.0	0.0	0.0	42.8	42.8	14.4	100.0
Miscellaneous (6)	0.0	0.0	0.0	50.0	0.0	50.0	100.0

Source: Group data.
Note: N shown in parentheses.
* Professionals here include *contadores*, who often were not trained professional accountants, but who kept the books of their businesses.

Beginning in the 1880s, the local press worried about the increasing number of vagrants, many of whom had migrated in search of jobs. The dislocation caused by migrations and by new forms of industrial production resulted at times in a breakdown of social discipline.[5] The 1890s witnessed a notable increase in the number and militancy of labor struggles in the city.[6] One of the major labor strikes took place against the shoe factory of Pedro and Mariano Farga, Spaniards who had arrived in the city in 1880. After working as employees for one year, they opened their own workshop, facilitated by a loan from a banker and fellow Catalan. By 1884, Pedro Farga had become president of the Asociación Española. Most of the growing company's employees were Creoles, many of them females laboring at home. The Creole constituency of the employees resulted from the predilections of the Fargas, who considered them "more intelligent."[7] During the 1904 strike against the company, no Spanish members of the Asociación took sides with the laborers, who had been won over by socialist organizers. Instead, prominent wealthy Spaniards like Vicente Perea Muñoz participated as the intellectual leadership of the local Catholic Workers' Circle (*Círculo de Obreros Católicos*), organized following Pope Leo XIII's encyclical *Rerum Novarum*. At the meetings, attended by workers in addition to public and ecclesiastical authorities, the wealthy would lecture to the audience on the virtues of humility. Following a May 1 socialist rally in 1901, the president of the Circle addressed laborers at a meeting by saying that although "the worker plays an important role in society, . . . it is absurd for him to pretend to be an equal . . . There will always be rich men and poor men because there will always be those who work and those who idle . . . The poor are God's favorite . . . , why do you fret over [temporal] and fleeting goods of [this] life . . . ?"[8] The same president's favoritism toward the management of the Farga company caused the breakdown of the negotiations between strikers and owners and the protraction of the strike to four months before Pedro Farga and the labor leaders came to an accord.[9]

The working conditions of the factory became widely known in the course of the strike, and for a moment, at least, the conscience of the public was alerted to the treatment of Córdoba's laborers. The workday lasted eleven hours, including some Sundays. By midafternoon, complained a female employee, "my hips, thighs, and the upper part of the spinal column ache and by the time I leave work, I can no longer keep going, it would be impossible to continue for another hour; my eyesight becomes blurred, and I can no longer even see the thread or my stitches."[10] Her state resulted from being made to work on her feet or leaning over a counter throughout the day. The management even charged two cents for the use of the latrines. Pedro Farga's recalcitrance in dealing with the strikers and the maltreatment of his workers symbolized to many people the greedy Spanish immigrant, ever trying to get rich at someone

else's expense. The affair aided in maintaining some latent anti-Spanish sentiment, manifested by people asserting that "trying to convince a Catalan with
boots and money is a waste of time; once he has [made up his mind], it is use-
less; especially when he thinks that his rich man's vanity has been wounded."[11]

Of course not all Spaniards, in or out of the Asociación, acquired an industrial plant hiring hundreds of workers; nor did all Spaniards maintain similarly
terrible working environments for their employees; nor, finally, did all Spaniards become successful. On the contrary, the vast majority of the members of
the Spanish establishment group, the members of the Asociación Española, did
not leave behind the wealth which we would expect from merchants and professionals.

The enormous gap between the real income status and the superficial trappings of the Spanish bourgeoisie in Córdoba becomes clear as we trace these
Spaniards through the city's probate court records.[12] The high index of out-
migration between 1872 and 1895 depressed the number of Spaniards who
would otherwise have had probates had they stayed and died in the city. However, the tracing through probate records also included the 172 members who
joined in 1902, yet the process yielded only eighteen financial records left behind by members of the Asociación. Only two reasons can explain such a low
figure: the continued high rate of out-migration, and the fact that most people
conducted their lives with no marginal savings or property. In effect, most of
these people led subsistence lives, trying to exist within the limit of their
meager resources. "Comerciante" and "industrial" acted more as self-ascribed
labels than as statements of economic solidity. Tenuous finances nevertheless
did not prevent these men from taking on the values and the social behavior of
the truly rich merchants. Some, to be sure, made money and left the city with
their wealth; the great majority, however, remained petty merchants, as some
probate records show, and either left Córdoba or died there with little more
than they had possessed when they first arrived.

The inventories of the probates themselves afford us a view into the variety
and nature of wealth in Córdoba. The probates we found spanned the years
1874 through 1930. The calculation of the simple average of net economic
assets yields a total of 29,300 pesos per Asociación member. The individual
assets, however, ranged from a high of 250,000 pesos to an indebtedness of
250 pesos. Half of the men left less than 5,000 pesos to their families; two
died leaving between 5,000 and 10,000 pesos. None of the other probates contained less than 23,000 pesos. Regardless of their total assets, most of the
members of the Asociación placed their confidence primarily in real property.
(Table 6.4 shows the individual real property assets as percentages of total
assets.) Even with the inclusion of cases where the members left no net assets
at all, these men invested, on the average, over half their money in real

Table 6.4
Real Property as Percentage of Net Assets of
Asociación Española Members
(N=18)

Case No.	%	Case No.	%	Case No.	%
1	52.7	7	88.1	13	0.0
2	83.0	8	20.1	14*	0.0
3*	0.0	9	97.4	15	34.9
4	89.2	10	100.0	16	76.8
5	0.0	11	100.0	17	98.1
6	31.1	12*	0.0	18	100.0
				Mean Average: 53.9	

Source: Group data.
* Left no net assets.

property; excluding the cases of no assets, the figures comprised an average of two-thirds of the investments. Thus, while few out of the total membership remained in Córdoba and left financial assets, those who did had no difficulty purchasing both rural and urban property, in spite of the latifundist elements that supposedly drove immigrants to the cities. Moreover, the rural properties lay primarily in rich, fertile areas of the province rather than in the poorer northern or western quarters of the interior. Instead, Spaniards like Mariano Abarca Costa purchased two parcels of 1,500 square meters in the department of Río Segundo, conveniently located near a station of the Ferrocarril Central Argentino. Silverio de Lara purchased three hectares (30,000 square meters) in 1909 in the prosperous department of Colón.

Juan Pardal and Victor Petroch illustrate the land-based finances of those who could afford such purchases. Pardal had been involved in the Spanish voluntary association from the start of his Argentine experience. In the early 1880s, the Asociación in Buenos Aires had funded him on a journey to Córdoba for reasons of health.[13] When he became a member of the Asociación of Córdoba in 1883, he was already in business for himself as a kiosk-owner, selling cigarettes, lottery tickets, and fireworks for carnivals. Twelve years later, he appeared in the census as the owner of a house in San Vicente, where he lived with his wife and sixteen children.[14] He gave no occupation, however, and he probably no longer operated his kiosk. He ended his temporary retirement, if such it was, three years later when he sold his home and with the help of one son opened a new business, "Juan Pardal e hijo," on 13 Constitución Street in the heart of the city's center. There he and his family ran another cigarette, lottery, and newspaper stand.[15] The business grew rapidly: by the time of Juan Pardal's death in 1907, his inventory totaled over 15,000 pesos. To read the words of the executor of the estate, we would believe that Pardal symbolized a rags-to-riches story in ways reminiscent of Horatio Alger's rhetoric: "Since the year 1898 the business corporation of Juan Pardal and Son, founded by the deceased don Juan Pardal and his son, has operated in this capital city. Together, they devoted their labor and industriousness to the business . . . They started out with a capital of forty-odd pesos. . . . "[16] The executor betrayed a paraphrase of the prevalent philosophy of Argentine liberals, "that energy and industry are rewarded, and indolence suffers."[17]

His advanced age at the time he acquired land may indicate that real property for Pardal acted as a security for the future of his family, while his business funded their contemporary, daily needs. In 1905, the fifty-nine-year-old Pardal purchased a tract of land in Colonia Oliva, ninety kilometers southeast of the city, and through which the Ferrocarril Central Argentino passed.[18] The land measured 1,665,384 square meters and was valued at 5,000 pesos; subsequently, he bought a lot of 1,080 square meters in the town of Oliva for 200 pesos. In addition, he kept horses and had agricultural equipment to work his lands. At the time of his death, Juan Pardal's worth totaled over 25,000 pesos, one-third of which had been invested in land and the rest in his business.

Victor Petroch's case offers a different picture of economic achievement and a distinct speculative mentality. He belonged to the wave of immigrants who arrived in Córdoba after 1900. Like Pardal before him, he quickly became established in a business of his own, partly with the aid of some savings accumulated prior to his arrival in Córdoba. Unlike Pardal at the time of his start, Petroch was a young man in his mid-twenties. Even though he listed himself as a comerciante, Petroch's name did not appear in any of the commercial listings of Córdoba's city directories of the period, because in fact his business involved loans and speculative ventures. His probate showed that at the time of his sudden death in 1923, he had still to collect over 23,000 pesos in outstanding loans.[19]

Petroch purchased his first tract of land by buying shares of his associates' two parcels in Villa de Soto in the department of Cruz del Eje. Petroch made his first series of major land purchases in 1909, most of them concentrated in the old Pueblito to the west of Córdoba's metropolitan area. Once an Indian settlement, the area had remained one of the poorest, least desirable parts of the municipality and contained a considerable amount of run-down housing, which sheltered only the marginally employed and the petty hawkers. Petroch bought three parcels on a block just south of the San Jerónimo cemetery on

Santa Rosa Street.[20] Paying less than three pesos per square meter, Petroch
bought 2,500 square meters or approximately one-seventh of the block; he
also acquired another two lots of the same size some five blocks to the south,
at the low price of less than eighty cents per square meter. In addition, Petroch
reached out beyond urban properties by buying 116 hectares of land in the
area where he first started acquiring land, Villa de Soto. The department of
Cruz del Eje, lying to the northwest of Córdoba, like the Pueblito was a traditionally poor zone containing few inhabitants and attracting fewer. Nevertheless, every year through 1914 Petroch kept adding to his properties in the Pueblito and in and around Villa de Soto. In 1910 he bought some more shares
of land in Villa de Soto, culminating in 1913 with the purchase of half of the
Estancia Melonar, measuring 780 hectares.

In the meantime, Petroch bought one parcel after another in the Pueblito,
including thirteen separate lots in Barrio Marechal in the extreme north of the
Pueblito, close to the river. He also purchased nearly 650 hectares in the richer
department of San Justo, part of a region of more recent colonization, where
agriculture was diversified to include cereals, cotton, and fine breeds of cattle.[21]
By the end of his life, Victor Petroch owned nearly 1,600 hectares from which
he collected rents and agricultural commodities for commercialization. Like
anyone else involved in lending and speculation, Petroch borrowed heavily
from both banks and friends to finance his ventures; nevertheless, when all
debts were paid, Petroch left behind a net total of approximately 31,000 pesos
in personal and real property.

More important for us than the amounts of money owed or credited is the
fact of ownership of agriculturally exploited lands by immigrants residing in
Argentine cities. Moreover, the relative number of real-property owners was
not much different from that of natives. Clearly, the Spanish landowners remained a minority within their own ethnic groups, but other data suggest that
it was not a significantly smaller proportion than the average for the general
population.[22] Our group of successful Spaniards shows conformity to the economic tenets of leading traditional Argentines, whose view that land ownership
was the basis of success arose out of political as well as economic philosophies.
Since the birth of the Argentine Republic, laws governing the awards of public
lands had been passed with a view toward establishing democratic political life
in a nation that promised a rich and great destiny. As explained by Miguel A.
Cárcano,

> The Argentine laws governing lands always attempt to deliver the ownership
> of the public soil to the individual person, and to stimulate the foreigner's
> labor, from whom lucrative work is expected.
> The very land suggests these broad and wise principles . . . The first

Argentine Congress sanctioned property mobility and abolished entailed estates and privileged exemptions, endowments and [special] privileges, and
declared the [State's] separation from public lands, which meant, at least,
that the State would no longer possess extensive, unproductive, and wild
fields.
    All men of superior mentality entertained those ideas. . . .[23]

    The intelligentsia considered that one of the foundations of "democracy is
to make property owners of the greatest number of citizens."[24] It would appear, given the availability of homestead land to new citizens, that aliens would
hasten to become naturalized citizens. However, the law allowed resident
aliens to remain unnaturalized indefinitely. Since so many immigrants were
emotionally tied more to city life than to the land, the Argentine citizenship
laws themselves were seen as having failed to provide a large enough number of
naturalizations; these laws were also blamed for the consequent lack of political
reenforcements or guarantees to facilitate the immigrants' commitments to
work the land.
    The prevalent explanation for the early urbanization of foreigners assumes
that the static pattern of land ownership was already fixed by the existence of
a small number of native latifundistas. It also assumes that the unavailability
of reasonably priced small units of land guaranteed tenancy as practically the
only way for immigrants to have worked the soil.[25] But the Spaniards with
lands in their probates usually had purchased a large proportion of them in Córdoba's suburban zones, especially around Alta Córdoba (Section 6), Nueva Córdoba, and Pueblito (both Section 9).
    Many of these areas acted as the city's green-belt, from which produce and
dairy products were brought to be consumed in the city. The lands often contained quintas on which either tenants or the owners' employees were responsible for the labor; quintas were especially prominent sources of income in the
western areas of the city. Across the Río Primero lay Alta Córdoba, with its
infamous *barrios populares.* The building of the train station for the Córdoba-
Santa Fe line in the late 1880s was a good sign for speculators hoping that the
area would become an industrial and residential section. By 1906, the municipal census showed that 32 of the 1,900 buildings in Alta Córdoba were devoted
to workshops and industrial sites. Although more than half of the residential
buildings remained straw-thatched ranchos, an almost equal number belonged
to households of industrial laborers who earned better salaries and who could
afford to pay higher rents to the speculators who had developed the area.[26]
    Most of the lands purchased by our group of Spaniards were *baldíos* or vacant
lots in marginal zones where some form of agricultural exploitation took place
in addition to tenancy. Francisco Sanjuan, for example, owned a parcel of

1,120 square meters with a house built on it, lying on the outskirts along one of the roads leading north out of the city; just south of that parcel, he also purchased over 18,000 square meters of land, including water rights and two ranchos, all of it under cultivation with fruit-bearing trees. Sanjuan rented out this land, worth a total of 2,800 pesos.[27] Pedro Sánchez Hermidas, a merchant who operated a downtown general goods store in 1869, also owned two blocks totaling 22,000 square meters of land in San Vicente, where he grew fruits and alfalfa. In addition, he owned several other plots, some with residential buildings on them from which he collected rents.[28]

Evidently, living in an urban center did not prevent immigrants from purchasing agricultural units (if they could afford the prices) any more than it prevented natives from doing so. Outright ownership of estancias was unusual, though not unknown, as shown by Ruperto Seara's 136 hectares in Río Segundo. More prevalent were purchases of shares in estancias among a few men. Moreover, immigrants appear to have taken up the Creole traditions of reliance on multiple occupations and variegated sources of income. Immigrant merchants used their money not only to purchase outright their own businesses and homes, but also to acquire land for speculative purposes, thus becoming absentee landlords themselves. The immigrants' avoidance of rural zones for residential purposes, their overwhelming preference for settling in the cities, and the prevalence of latifundist elements carry the implication that no rural middle class developed in Argentina; instead, "a process of proletarization was favored that would unfortunately result in an early urbanization . . . ."[29] Thus, while the liberals' plan for settling the rural zones with immigrants failed because of a recalcitrant latifundio system, the urban orientation of immigrants did not preclude their forming an absentee rural middle class that owned modrately sized tracts of land under agricultural exploitation.

Approximately 8.6 percent of the Spanish population of Córdoba owned real property in 1895; this figure was only 1 percent below that of the native-born. By 1906, 10.5 percent of Córdoba's Spaniards, as compared to 10.1 percent of the natives, were real-property owners. At the same time, 4.2 percent of Córdoba's Spaniards and 1.1 percent of the natives owned real property devoted to agricultural products; 5.6 percent of all foreigners and only 1.8 percent of the Argentines owned land for raising livestock.[30] Thus Spanish immigrants mirrored within their own population the economic stratification of their hosts, at least in reference to property ownership. While the absolute numbers differed, the similarities in the economic lifestyles of Creoles and Spaniards show a speedy progress in the cultural integration of the latter within the middle levels. The phenomenon of massive out-migration and its implication of lack of success indicate the unequal distribution of wealth inherent in the contemporary Argentine system. Nevertheless, the typical member of the Asociación Española did not see himself as the victim of an unequal distribution of power and privilege; despite the inconsistency between his status and his wealth, the *socio* maintained an attitude of superiority with respect to nonmembers—natives or Spaniards—excepting the elites. Members of ethnic voluntary associations in Córdoba, therefore, behaved as would others in similar situations; that is, as G. E. Lenski wrote, they strove "to maximize their satisfactions, even if necessary, at the expense of others. This means that an individual with inconsistent statuses or ranks has a natural tendency to think of himself in terms of that status or rank which is highest . . . ."[31] The existence of landowners among the members reenforced whatever positive, even if incongruent, notions they had of themselves.

Summary

The sociocultural belief-system of Argentine liberals was accepted by hundreds of thousands of immigrants who landed in the Platine area. At the base of its constructs lay the traditional and often mythical values attached to life in the New World, especially in the United States, Canada, and Argentina: an abundance of resources, an enlightened and educated leadership, almost endless opportunities in uncharted economic frontiers, and what Lipset calls a deistic optimism, interpreted as the belief in the perfectability of man.[32] Argentine nineteenth-century liberals, through seemingly endless rhetoric, catalyzed the immigrants' popular views into an acceptance of Argentina as a nonreligious theocratic political order that had, as its objective, the maintenance of the belief-systems the oligarchy had helped to create.[33]

Voluntary associations arose, in part, because of the lack of government-supported welfare bureaus to aid with medical and funeral expenses. In Córdoba the municipality held little or no responsibility for the clinical welfare of its citizens at the time that the Spaniards, Frenchmen, and Italians formed their ethnic voluntary associations. Yet, these reasons for their existence omit the philosophical implications of the theocratic system in which the associations were designed and operated. One aspect of the theocratic system is a utopian quality which permits voluntaristic structures to operate with a minimum of hierarchy, and with the intent of abolishing inequality and "allowing men to concentrate on shared values and common enterprises."[34] Hierarchy is unnecessary because the voluntaristic mechanisms will become responsible for equity and allocation. The assumptions that the system makes concerning the selflessness of human nature should now become apparent. The Argentine leadership and the heads of the "establishment" sectors of immigrant communities, however, employed such utopic norms to perpetuate the myths of a system which did, in fact, contain hierarchies, a system which had as its *modi operandi* not only their continued leaderships but also the unalterability of their own social composition. As a result, an oligarchic Creole caste coexisted with a middle class of immigrants, while both groups displayed self-enclosing mentalities toward their own ethnic cohorts.

In an era when wealth was tightly concentrated among the few, immigrants did not feel it necessary to be rich in actuality in order to consider themselves and their jobs as representing the middle class. Financial solvency to them may have been a sufficient but not a necessary condition to behave in the fashion of the bourgeoisie. What they needed, they had: *conciencia de sí*—as Ortega y Gassett used to say—but in the most parochial terms. Thus while nominally representing the interests and the patriotism of Spaniards, the members of the Asociación acted as a social class. It guarded its privileges, including the status accorded it by the local press and public figures.

The social structure of the Asociación Española underwent changes between 1872 and 1902. Some members of the semiskilled work force did join as time went by, but neither the association's leadership nor the structural hegemony of the mercantile element came under question. Furthermore, although participatory fervor was painfully lacking among members, the merchants had enough strength at the meetings to vote for the measures that would favor them and would serve to insulate them from the city's less-than-dignified Spaniards. Dignity and self-respect also demanded that members of the Asociación not become identified with the Creole masses. Such behavior, instead of sparking anti-Spanish sentiment, reenforced the institutional bonds between the Creole and Spanish leaderships. Cultural differentiation, at least in nineteenth-century Córdoba, was reconciled along lines of status, not of ethnicity. This norm served to safeguard cultural pluralism in the area for as long as the immigrant flow continued. Accordingly, the anti-immigrant sentiments that surfaced during the early 1900s in Argentina resulted from xenophobic feelings which did not originate from ethnic dissonance but rather from the threat of economic actions by radical immigrants who endangered the status of both communities. The feelings surrounding the strike against the factory of the Spaniard Farga, for example, became exacerbated only after Italian socialist organizers arrived from Buenos Aires.

Embarrassed leaders of immigrant voluntary associations could do little to counteract the sentiments of the native press against foreign radicals who were aroused by their leftist conationals. Even when members of the ethnic associations were harmed by local police, protests were addressed only to the specific incidents. Never did words or actions injurious to Spaniards strengthen their ethnic cohesion to the point of causing them to cross the boundaries of their own social classes. Among members of ethnic voluntary associations like the Spaniards', class consciousness and social insulation from lower-class immigrants may have aided in maintaining the pluralist society that liberals had so hoped to avoid. To ease their members' integration into local communities, voluntary associations simultaneously provided a needed facilitator, as evidenced by the speed with which Spaniards joined the Asociación after their arrival in Córdoba.

Although opportunities in Córdoba fell short of most Spaniards' expectations of economic mobility, a few did manage to accumulate some wealth. Through their records we see their degree of acculturation to the Argentine traditional patterns of material acquisitions. Whenever possible, they sought to acquire productive land; even if the total area was not as large as the estancias of the oligarchs, most of the Spaniards based their financial confidence on real property. Business was relegated to the role of collecting sufficient funds to facilitate agricultural property ownership.

The overwhelming majority, however, failed to accumulate any property or to move upward through the occupational scale. Why such a large proportion, therefore, of each year's group of members no longer figured in the registries for subsequent years becomes evident. Such low persistence rates within the Asociación reflected the general pattern of very high out-migration from the city. The impermanence of immigrants in Córdoba may have worked in conjunction with class disparity within the immigrant community to prevent emotions from coalescing into ethnic separatism while still maintaining a congenially pluralist culture.

7. The Limits of the Melting Pot: Marriage and Integration

When unmarried men first arrived in the city of Córdoba, they were not totally ignorant of the ways of the Argentine cities or of their new environment. The majority of Argentine natives had come there from the interior of Córdoba Province; most of the Europeans had already spent some time in Buenos Aires or Montevideo.[1] Many immigrants had passed a number of years in Argentina moving from town to town in search of an area in which to settle permanently or in which to find employment lucrative enough to enable them to return to their countries, having been "successes" in America. Upon arriving in any Argentine city, the migrants were primarily concerned with seeking their livelihoods. If they contemplated staying in the same area for some time, however, they also made efforts to cement their social ties to their new environment by, among other acts, marrying and having children.

This chapter and the next examine a random sample of the marriages which non-cordobés males contracted in the city of Córdoba between 1869 and 1909. The chapters focus on the types of brides they selected and on the degrees of social integration and mobility they achieved through marriage.[2] The Archdiocese of the city of Córdoba required affidavits from couples who planned to marry but were not natives of the city. These *expedientes matrimoniales* contain the names of all parties, including the parents, and the vital data of the couples. In addition, at least two residents of the city gave sworn testimony verifying the good character of the migrant and his or her unmarried status, and briefly describing the applicant's activities prior to and after arriving in Córdoba. From these data we are able to piece together some facets of the lives of the couples we sampled.

Without losing sight of the romantic aspect, one can view marriages—particularly during the period under study—as economic arrangements providing a measure of security for women and legal inheritances for children.[3] Economic and legal accommodations were not the only concerns that affected men, women and children, however. In addition, couples often reckoned with the social effects that marriages would have on their own communal situations—principally, on the degree of social integration facilitated by their unions. In other words, although the right to happiness in marriage may be spoken of as a norm, many societies, including that of Córdoba in the late nineteenth and early twentieth centuries, do not create the conditions necessary to guarantee that goal.[4] Concerns of economic standing, limitations of distance, ethnic animosities, human ecology and social stratification are some of the factors that condition the selection of marriage partners. No free market situation exists, even when the currency is love. As a result, we may view marital unions as representing, in part, the community's social boundaries, and thereby indicating their fluidity or rigidity. In fact, many researchers of social differentiation have accepted a subpopulation's endogamy rate as an indicator of the rigidity of the boundaries around it.[5] The selection of a mate tells us a number of things about a local society, including its norms of ethnic integration and residential patterns as well as the way in which its recent members accommodate their interests and limits to the new realities.

Residence and Romance

Organized according to broadest geographic terms, the men who arrived in the city of Córdoba migrated from the interior of the province, from elsewhere in Argentina, or from across the Atlantic Ocean. Birthplace had a distinct effect on the choices these men made in selecting their brides. When the grooms were divided between Argentines and Europeans, we discovered that on the average only one out of one hundred Argentines married a European woman during the forty years between 1869 and 1909. A family of Europeans clearly could not rely on its daughters to help enter local Argentine social circles. Moreover, no parents could expect much fulltime economic aid from their unmarried daughters: only 0.4 percent of the 516 brides who declared their occupations held fulltime jobs, and all of these labored in semiskilled and service chores. The rest were *amas de casa* (housewives) or intermittently did marginal work such as sewing or selling milk whenever the family needed additional income.

A high incidence of brides no longer had fathers and thus did not have the benefit of their financial support. Calista Sánchez, for example, was in this position when she married Felipe Pilón in 1871. Recently widowed and with no one at home to aid her, Calista Sánchez married a French coppersmith who had had an itinerant past and faced an uncertain future.[6] Arriving in the city of Córdoba barely two years before, Pilón had been employed at a French cooper's workshop. His status as a skilled worker was no guarantee of his permanence, however. He had grown up and attended school in Montevideo, where he had become a Uruguayan citizen. He then moved to Buenos Aires, where for eight years he worked as a blacksmith; after moving once more, this time to the city of Rosario, he labored in its railway yards for seven years more.[7] Nevertheless, Calista Sánchez found her husband at a period when his life indicated some stability. First, the decision to marry tells, perhaps, not only of his search for love and companionship but also of his desire finally to settle down. Second, he had devoted his efforts to cementing close personal relations with local residents, including his employer, in whose house he lived and to whose child he was godfather.

Often women without mothers or fathers at home also married at a younger age than the average. The mean age of the brides in our sample was 22.66 years; the mode, or the greatest number of cases, occurred among women who were 22 years old.[8] In conjunction with a lower age factor and deceased parents, these younger women came from poor areas of the city and often lived on small agricultural plots. Their chances of marrying European men may have been the same as those of marrying Argentines, but still they had little opportunity for real improvement of their economic levels. Poor women seldom married men in significantly higher socioeconomic positions: daughters of agricultural laborers usually married laborers, or at best, renters of small agricultural units; illiterate women usually found illiterate husbands.

Manuela Rodríguez, an illegitimate seventeen-year-old cordobesa, lived with her mother on Sarmiento Street, next to the suburb of General Paz. This section of the city, slow to develop since its first few inhabitants had settled there early in the nineteenth century, suddenly received new impetus from the building of the railroad yards servicing the Ferrocarril Central Argentino, which after 1870, linked the cities of Córdoba and Rosario.[9] In 1889, Manuela married Vicente Ravignano, an agricultural worker who lived in the suburb of San Vicente and labored on one of the many quintas in that initially agricultural area. He had arrived in the city after leaving his native Italy in 1887 and, with the aid of friends from the same Italian town, finally found work on a truck garden two years later.[10]

Manuela Rodríguez clearly found greater security in her marriage than she had had before, but it was more a function of having an employed man providing most of the family's income than of any significant improvements in actual economic and social terms. As a couple they continued to live in a fashion similar to that which they followed when they had been single; that is, in districts where "one could still find shacks of . . . [the] countryside, with [their] primitive construction of straw and sod, not too different from the Indian hut." The city of Córdoba, especially its surrounding area, was still "very far from even provisionally resolving the great problem of clean living quarters. . . ."[11] Moreover, the 1890 financial collapse followed the year of their marriage, placing them and thousands of other agricultural families under heavy economic strain. Any hopes of improving their situations were at least temporarily dashed, for the chances of obtaining land after the crisis were fewer in areas which had previously been under profitable cultivation.[12]

The decade of the 1870s had witnessed the beginning of Córdoba's speculative land pricing; the process continued through the eve of the 1890 "Baring Crisis." The 1886 issue of the *Anales* of the Sociedad Rural, for example, noted that land which had sold for 1.40 pesos per hectare now sold for 2.60 pesos. In addition, most of the land-owners were willing to sell land after 1890 only if the payments were made in gold, in order to avoid being saddled with cheap paper currency.[13] These practices ravaged the economic situations of people like Vicente Ravignano, often forcing them off their land in search of other means of livelihood.

The example of the marriage between Vicente Ravignano and Manuela Rodríguez contains one exception to the patterns of marriages in Córdoba from 1869 through 1909; the homes of the bride and groom were distant from each other. Although their surroundings were similarly low in status, they were separated by a distance of several miles and a river and hampered by poor means of direct communication.

In Tables 7.1 and 7.2, places of residence of grooms and brides show some of the relationships caused by their spatial distribution per census section. The cases of missing data largely refer to some couples marrying between 1869 and 1888, the period when reporting of addresses and occupations was scanty. As shown by the tables on the sectional distribution of grooms and brides, the proportions of men and women who came from the same sections often agreed; the rankings of the sizes of the populations of grooms and brides are the same for Sections 3, 4, 6, and 7. Section 3 held a concentrated population mass in the city's center and we should expect it to rank high for both sexes. Section 5 contained, as did Section 3, a great proportion of the city's houses of commerce, but in addition Section 5 contained two other male-dominated centers of activity: law offices and the university. This fact helps explain the higher rankings in that section among males than among females. Section 1, too, contained a significantly higher concentration of males, who primarily tilled the quintas in the western sectors of the metropolitan area. The demographic concentrations within the mixed residential and commercial Section 2 are similar.

The most striking disparity occurred in Section 8, the suburb containing most of the city's railroad yards. The differences here are significant, especially when, because of the dependence on skilled labor required by the establishments in the area, we would expect the concentrations of males to be much higher than that of females. Instead, we find that 10.5 percent of all brides, as against only 7.6 percent of the grooms, came from this area. The nearly 3 percent

Table 7.1
Areal Distribution of Couples by Section, 1869-1909
(N=648)

Section	Grooms			Brides		
	N	%	Rank	N	%	Rank
1	44	9.2	6th	33	7.4	7th
2	46	9.7	5th	43	9.6	6th
3	122	25.6	1st	109	24.4	1st
4	18	3.8	8th	22	4.9	8th
5	76	16.0	2nd	52	11.7	3rd
6	59	12.4	4th	51	11.4	4th
7	9	1.9	9th	16	3.6	9th
8	36	7.6	7th	47	10.5	5th
9	66	13.9	3rd	73	16.4	2nd
Total	476	100.0		446	100.0	
Unknown	172 (26.5% of N)			202 (31.2% of N)		

Source: Sample data.

range is supported by a difference of 4 percent between the section's total
male and female population figures in the 1906 census.[14] The smaller number
of grooms from this area also reflects the high incidence of single males who
lived in the many rooms for rent found near railroad works and terminals, and
who moved from town to town without permanent roots. In Section 9, which
spanned a wide area, we encounter a similar situation to the one in General Paz:
Section 9 contained one railroad station and a cement factory in an otherwise
rural area.

By rearranging the one-way frequency distributions of residential patterns
into a two-way frequency table, and by cross-tabulating their census sections
of residence for the years 1889-1909 (Table 7.2), we see a meaningful association which affected grooms and brides. Thus we find that the distances between the homes of men and women greatly affected the marital decisions
within each social class. The modal frequencies—the cells where the largest
number of cases took place—appear at the census sections where both grooms
and brides resided. There were no exceptions to this situation, regardless of
age, socioeconomic status or occupation. Fifty percent or more of the men in
Sections 1, 2, 3, 5, 6, 7, 8, and 9 married women from the same section. Nearly
44 percent of the grooms of Section 4, married women from the same area—

Table 7.2
Sectional Endogamy, 1889-1909
(Percentage)

Groom's Section	Bride's Section									Total
	1	2	3	4	5	6	7	8	9	
1	52.5	7.5	15.0	2.5	5.0	2.5	0.0	7.5	7.5	9.2 (40)
2	7.3	51.2	19.5	4.9	0.0	2.4	2.4	7.3	4.9	9.4 (41)
3	1.9	8.7	62.5	2.9	7.7	2.9	5.8	4.8	2.9	23.8 (104)
4	6.3	12.5	18.7	43.8	6.3	0.0	0.0	6.3	6.3	3.7 (16)
5	1.4	1.4	12.9	10.0	50.0	4.3	0.0	5.7	14.3	16.0 (70)
6	3.4	6.9	8.6	0.0	1.7	69.0	1.7	5.2	3.4	13.3 (58)
7	12.5	0.0	12.5	0.0	10.0	12.5	62.5	0.0	0.0	1.8 (8)
8	0.0	2.8	11.1	0.0	2.8	2.8	5.6	72.2	2.8	8.2 (36)
9	3.1	1.6	7.8	3.1	1.6	1.6	1.6	1.6	78.1	14.6 (64)
Total	7.6 (33)	9.6 (42)	24.3 (106)	5.0 (22)	11.2 (49)	11.7 (51)	3.7 (16)	10.5 (46)	16.5 (72)	100.0 (437)

Source: Sample data.
Note: N shown in parentheses.

a figure that falls short of the halfway point, but still remains significantly higher than the proportions of unions from disparate zones. For example, 6.3 percent of the men of Section 4 married women from Sections 1, 5, 8, or 9. What is more, Section 4 represented the smallest censal jurisdiction, thereby placing surrounding boundaries with contiguous censal divisions within easy reach and adding significance to the 44 percent figure of men marrying within it.

The least frequent cases of marriages in which the parties crossed censal sections took place between metropolitan zones farthest away from each other. No marriages occurred, for example, between men living in Section 1, lying to the west, and women from San Vicente, the seventh and easternmost metropolitan section; nor between males residing in Section 4 in the southwest corner and women living across the river in the northern suburbs, which included Alta Córdoba, San Martín and Villa Cabrera.

The district represented the censal geographic unit within the section. The city's metropolitan area contained several districts per section, and virtually none exceeded the area of a six-block rectangle. This structure meant that the farthest anyone could live from anybody else within the same central district could be easily covered by a walk of approximately five hundred meters. In fact, it was often easier to step into a neighboring district merely by crossing the dividing street one lived on or by walking just a block than to walk to the end of one's own district. We would expect, therefore, that inter- and intradistrict marriages occurred with regularity, and that it was as easy—if not easier—to wed a resident of one's own district as of another.

Table 7.3 shows the rate of intradistrict marriages in the central and peripheral areas which took place in the city between 1889 and 1909. For the twenty-one districts comprising the center the rate of geographic endogamy averaged nearly 40 percent. Put another way, four out of ten men directed their attention into the district, rather than crossing the street into an adjacent district that often was in front of their doors. The number of marriages taking place within each district, together with those between two immediately adjacent areas, accounted for the overwhelming majority of the central city's marital unions. Furthermore, in all but two central districts the values of the percentages in the table represent the modal frequencies; that is, the single occurrence per district taking place most often was that of unions within it. The rest of the 54.5 percent of the unions of men living in District 7, for example, were widely dispersed over several other districts at rates much lower than its 45.5 percent endogamy figure. The two exceptions to this norm took place among the residents of Districts 5 and 17. Another 20 percent of the men in District 5 married women of the adjacent District 4, while a surprising 42.9 percent of District 17's men also wed women from District 4.

The average geographic endogamy rate of peripheral—marginal and

Table 7.3
District Endogamy, 1889-1909
(Percentage)

Central Districts				Peripheral Districts			
District	Endogamy	District	Endogamy	District	Endogamy	District	Endogamy
1	33.3	15	36.4	22	27.3	43	43.8
2	45.5	16	45.5	23	33.3	45	33.3
3	40.0	17	28.6	24	50.0	47	100.0
4	38.9	18	30.0	25	42.9	54	0.0
5	20.0	19	33.3	26	25.0	57	70.0
6	62.5	20	25.0	27	50.0	58	100.0
7	45.5	21	42.9	29	100.0	59	0.0
8	61.1			32	60.0	60	0.0
9	16.7			33	100.0	76	100.0
10	25.0			34	87.1	80	44.4
11	30.0			35	66.7	81	0.0
12	53.8			36	75.0	82	83.3
13	40.0			37	0.0		
14	72.7			39	100.0		
		Mean Average: 39.4				Mean Average: 53.5	

Source: Sample data.

agricultural—districts was much higher than of the center area, standing at 53.5 percent. Gauging these percentages is more difficult, however, since the areas covered by these districts were considerably larger and held a much lower concentration of residents than did zones within the city's core. The absence of intradistrict unions in some of the cases may well have been a function of the nearly total lack of marriageable women in those tracts of virtually deserted lands. By the same token, the occurrences of total endogamy could have been the result of the small number of women living in those zones and of men not wishing to or not being able to travel great distances in search of potential marital relationships. Typical, too, were the marriages of distantly related members of extended families who worked together on the same or contiguous farms. In addition, it was not unusual for hired, but trusted, farm hands to be accepted into the owners' families through marriages with their daughters.

The reasons for the geographic endogamy of Córdoba's non-native male residents are based on social, cultural, and economic norms. We should remember that the grooms under study were not from the city of Córdoba originally, and they tended to settle and remain close to their initial places of residence. For the poor who had migrated mostly from the interior of the province and the north of the country, the affordability of housing was a primary concern. The cheapest living quarters for these Creoles were the numerous ranchos in the suburban and agricultural zones. These shacks were built from rough wood planks, mud and straw; sometimes they were covered by galvanized tin roofs, weighted down by bricks to prevent winds of dust storms from blowing them away. The primitive construction of ranchos permitted their residents to build them on virtually any location; if forced to move, those who could not afford to purchase new materials could easily tear them down and build elsewhere. Sometimes these dwellings were set up by squatters, but usually the residents paid a monthly rent on the land only, ranging from two to ten pesos.[15] These shacks housed from three to ten people, usually in an area of twelve square meters comprising, on the average, two rooms.

Not only were considerations of economy in housing important to these Creole migrants, but also their cultural background affected their choices of residence. The migrating Creole families consisted of displaced agricultural laborers, virtually without any abilities or experience for skilled employment in a metropolitan area. The unskilled and the service sectors were the only avenues of work for those wishing to live in the central part of the city. The lives of the migrant Creoles had been spent tilling the soil, and most of them continued their agricultural labor in and around the city of Córdoba as well. Their lifestyles, as well as the form of their homes, remained virtually unchanged after migration. "The Creole loves the rancho as an atavism, as if it brought back reminiscences of his grandparents," wrote an observer.[16]

Communication within and among marginal sections was difficult, especially after dark, which was the only available courting period for most of the men who labored from ten to fourteen hours daily, often including Sundays. Pedestrians found roadways either dusty or muddy, and tramway service between these sections was either limited or nonexistent. Although in the city of Buenos Aires a number of streetcar systems were already in operation by the early 1870s, the city of Córdoba had only three as late as the 1890s.[17] The streetcar lines of the Tramway San Vicente linked the center of the city directly to the suburb of San Vicente, at the same time that the Tramway de Córdoba and the Tramway Argentino joined General Paz to the commercial core.[18] However, no public transit lines joined the center with other suburbs until after 1900, and no streetcar systems linked any two suburban areas.

Not only did the means of contact among suburbanite cordobeses remain hampered during this period, but also the city's demographic expansion into the suburbs was blocked. In the face of economic instability residents of San Vicente and of Alta Córdoba, a suburb north of the Primero River, deserted their homes because, in the opinion of the liberal newspaper *La Carcajada,* "nobody will live at points in which a round trip to the center will cost them twenty cents."[19] The decline in the population of several suburbs continued for some time after the 1890 financial crisis.[20] Local barrio, or neighborhood, sentiments were maintained, however, in the city's suburban and rural regions throughout this period by the lack of institutionalized avenues facilitating social relations between sections. A case in point is streetcars, which the influential circles saw less as a basic social function of the municipality than as a speculative commercial venture aimed at increasing the number of potential shoppers brought to the downtown area. The route of the Tramway San Vicente, for instance, benefited merchants by following some of the important commercial streets where they owned shops. These businessmen had invested in the streetcar line in order to insure that the route laid down would serve to increase their own sales volume.[21] Localist barrio sentiments were thus reenforced by the indifference shown by centrally located business elites. Local neighborhood spokesmen even urged residents of General Paz and San Vicente to form their own musical bands to play in their areas, rather than having to travel downtown on holidays to watch the only municipal band playing at one of the central *paseos* or plazas.[22]

On the north shore of the Primero River east of the train station in Alta Córdoba (part of Section 6), lay one of the rancheríos, a slum composed of shacks. Its dark, narrow, dirty alleys delineated the boundaries of barrios that received their tragicomic names from the popular wit: "Barrio of the Frayed Clothes," "Barrio of the Moth," "Barrio of the Scraps." As described by a cordobés:

All these by-roads, which formed something like the social underground of the old Córdoba, had a reputation that was not commendable and which justifiably inspired suspicions and fears. In each of their intricate, rough and unpaved roads, in each of their uneven and irregular bends, lurked the . . . threat of a hurled rock, . . . or stabbing.

A nightly incursion into such places meant having an adventure filled with dangers. One had to walk calmly, courageously and alertly in order to avoid unpleasant surprises, since one often met with gangs of ruffians using . . . foul language, wearing provoking expressions and who were bent on aggression and assault at whatever cost. In addition, one had to be prepared by carrying a pocketful of rocks, in order to confront the furious attacks of dogs of the most diverse mixtures and sizes, which rushed out in packs from the black mouth of the area of the shacks.[23]

Street lights, even in the central zone, were neither efficient nor numerous until well into the twentieth century. By 1871, a candle served as the sole streetlight in each block of the most central area only, burning for perhaps as little as one hour and shedding light just in the immediate vicinity of its post. After 1871, when the National Exposition took place in Córdoba, the city began to use kerosene for its streetlamps, which burned somewhat brighter and considerably longer than candles. Unfortunately, the number of lamp posts remained the same, so that nightwalkers still needed to carry their own lamps for safety.[24] Municipal authorities occasionally received complaints from residents of areas without any lighting or with faulty lamps. In 1893, for example, the residents of Pueblo Nuevo protested that their kerosene lamp system was not operating. Kerosene had remained in use in poor sections during the 1890s, even after the electrification of street lights in the center.[25]

San Vicente, which had held the promise of becoming a pleasant-looking, stable quarter of middle-sized agricultural units, had become instead an unattractive location in the mid-1890s. This process resulted, inevitably, from a municipal policy which tended primarily to the needs of the center at the expense of the suburbs. Deep potholes gutted the relatively few paved streets found outside the central area, while the large ruts and holes made walking on the dirt roads precarious. Lack of street lighting made the area more dismal, and some of the city's newspapers decried the situation: "The uninhabited houses make the outlook of that town even gloomier. [It is] hidden among the brambles during the day and enveloped in darkness at night. Lighting, which is the indispensable element for population centers, and which even the most remote villages have, should be installed as soon as possible. Light is the symbol of civilization and progress."[26]

Both Creole and European migrants who settled in the metropolitan area but could not afford to pay much for lodging rented rooms in the tenements, or *conventillos,* that proliferated in Córdoba at the turn of the century in order to accommodate the hundreds of immigrants arriving weekly. The conventillos already had an infamous history in the city of Buenos Aires, beginning in the mid-nineteenth century. At first, landlords had converted deteriorating elite homes by subdividing them into multiple dwellings; by the end of the century, they began to build new tenements in the same shape as earlier converted buildings.[27] A similar situation developed in Córdoba. By 1916, the city had a total of 241 tenements in which 6,494 people lived in the 2,041 rooms. All but 35 of them were situated in the central zone, while from a total of 3,883 ranchos, only 6 percent were situated in the center.[28]

By the late 1880s, the incoming migrants who had no friends or relatives with whom to stay were banding around the inns, or *fondines,* that dotted the streets surrounding the Ferrocarril Central Argentino station. On San Gerónimo and adjacent streets these fondines offered the migrants who were willing to share the costs, "humid, damp and poorly ventilated [rooms] in which ten to twelve people slept packed like sardines." Concerned newspapers called on police and health authorities to correct the deplorable conditions.[29]

The rooms of Córdoba's tenements were perhaps the worst in the nation, not only because of their ordinarily unsafe and uncomfortable accommodations, but also because of the lack of sanitary necessities. Visitors to the city were left with unusually strong impressions after witnessing the conditions of the poor.

> As far as the lodging and health conditions of the working class are concerned, they are truly disastrous. Those who live best are the ones who dwell in the numerous ranchos on the edge [of the city]; at least they have sunlight and [fresh] air; but the city's tenements are atrocious. . . . The civilized privy has not yet made its appearance in Córdoba, and one must suspect that the tenements are no exceptions; what surprises the visitor . . . is that people can live in such conditions. The floors of the rooms are impossible; the rooms are repugnantly dirty, small, and expensive.[30]

For the middle-level workers and employees who were new to the city, the rooms of the conventillos—not the whole structure—provided some immediate relief from loneliness and boredom by accommodating two or more people who shared expenses. For Europeans it was often desirable to divide the cost of a room with fellow migrants. Many times immigrants unrelated by any familial ties would leave from the same hometown and stay together for a few years.

Numerous examples among the grooms in this study show the different ways in which foreigners associated with fellow immigrants. Whenever immigrants traveled or worked together they always maintained at least one social

link. Pedro Garrea, an Italian immigrant, signed an affidavit in 1886 in which
he testified that he had left his home fourteen years earlier, and was followed
a few months thereafter by his friend Luis Rigoni. The two met shortly after
arriving in Buenos Aires, where they stayed together for a period of four years.
When one of them decided to move to the interior, so did the other. They
shared their dwelling in Córdoba until Rigoni decided to marry a cordobesa in
the winter of 1886, when we assume the roommates separated.[31]

Fellow travelers need not have been virtual childhood friends from the same
country in order to stay together and share living expenses. Immigrants, especially single men, found it convenient to depend on each other for moral and
material support upon arrival and through their first years in Argentina. A
newly arrived Spanish immigrant explained this fact when he wrote about his
first experiences in Argentina. Thinking he could do well as an itinerant pho-
tographer, he teamed up in Buenos Aires with an experienced Armenian who
had already spent several years in the trade and who was willing to have him
as an "apprentice" in the operation of the camera and of the "business." They
immediately formed a partnership arrangement whereby the Armenian would
pay for their room, while the Spaniard, after purchasing a camera from his tu-
tor, would travel, taking photographs and expanding the volume of business
for both.[32]

The following anecdote from the Spaniard's autobiography illustrates the
advantages of having someone with experience to teach the newer arrivals the
nuances and the seemingly trivial details of regional and local culture—insights
that often proved immeasurably valuable to the thousands who scratched a
living by traveling through Argentina searching for the promised wealth. Knowledge of important dates, town celebrations, and local holidays, among other
factors, aided the immigrants in realizing some socialization while improving
their competitive abilities in a number of occupations, principally within the
retail trade. As the account goes:

> My teacher was planning to go to Goya for the festivities of Saint Anthony,
> since there was a chapel one league outside of Goya in which people prayed
> to Saint Anthony, and on that day many came from the surrounding area,
> and one could work a lot if there was good weather. A few days before
> [the festival] we went to Goya and took lodging at an inn belonging to a
> Turk. There we found six or seven additional photographers who had come
> to go to that chapel.[33]

Few migrating foreigners remained alone for very long prior to forming families of their own. For example, when Pascual Indorata departed from Naples
in the 1880s, he left behind his wife and young son. He came as a *golondrina*
(swallow)—one of the hundreds of thousands of seasonal agricultural laborers

who, each year, traveled to Argentina to work during the harvest season, then returned to their European homes. His companion during these trips was Carlos Montedonico, another "swallow." As happened to so many, Pascual Indorata decided to remain in Argentina for some time and then choose between bringing his family or returning permanently to Italy. He worked for the Córdoba-Rosario Railroad in the newly founded town of Esmeralda, in the province of Santa Fe.[34] While in Esmeralda he received news of his wife's death. He returned to Naples, where he met an old friend from Genoa, Santiago Laborio. Having no familial or financial reasons for staying in Italy, Indorata, his twelve-year-old son, and Laborio journeyed together to Argentina, where they were once again joined by Carlos Montedonico. They all settled in the city of Córdoba, where Pascual Indorata found work as a machinist with the railroad, living in a poor section of Entre Ríos Street, near the railroad station. In 1891, at the age of thirty-nine, he married Dolores Pereira, a poor cordobesa who lived in the squalid south-central suburb of Pueblo Nuevo with her unemployed father.[35] However little Pascual Indorata may have realized his dreams of comfort in Argentina, at least he had been aided by the know-how and strength of friends like Montedonico and Laborio who traveled and toiled with him.

More fortunate than the men who stayed with friends were those who came with or joined their families, as in the case of José Tossi. He came alone from Italy as a youngster to be with his older brothers, who had already established their homes and businesses in Córdoba. He lived with them and worked in the family's booth inside the Mercado Sud, one of the city's public markets. Perhaps because of the guidance given by his older brothers and the maintenance of the home culture and family traditions, young Tossi married an Italian girl who had also come to Córdoba accompanied by her older brother.[36]

Argentine authorities inadvertently encouraged this type of immigrant cultural inbreeding and introverted socialization by complying, through their propaganda and advertising techniques, with the immigrants' own work preferences and conditions for accepting employment. Through advertisements like the following, for example, the Córdoba branch of the National Office of Immigration often performed such services for the immigrants whose travel it had subsidized.

> Among other immigrants who arrived the day before yesterday and who are staying at the Asylum of Immigration are seven Spanish agricultural workers. The seven form a society and wish to find fields or quintas to farm in the city's suburbs or environs. Although they would prefer to stay together, it should not prevent anyone from offering any contract separately, as long as it suits all of their interests.[37]

Summary

Among the factors that affected the ethnic composition and orientation of Argentina were the marital choices made by foreigners and natives. This decision-making process contained its own social morphology. Marriage selections were not made randomly; even if the emotional basis for them was uniform, municipal policies created their own special circumscriptions. How and where the city wished to extend and modernize its services—transportation, lighting and security—had far-flung aftereffects which characterized the nature and extent of social relations.

Córdoba encompassed an extensive territory. By the late nineteenth century it was no longer a "walking city"; even its center was reasonably well developed and expansive. Yet it chose not to emulate the transportation models of other cities—Buenos Aires, Boston, London—thereby retaining its neighborhood parochialism. In this way, the transportation network manifested the vision of the city as a spatially fragmented corporation rather than as an integral whole. The public transportation system was not designed as a socially articular device, but as an investment to insure that the downtown area continued to command the market mechanism. City-planning, such as it was, did not encompass the notion of suburban commercial and administrative self-sufficiency along with integration to the center. By ignoring the option of an urban complex with thorough communication linkages, Córdoba did not create suburbs in which one could find the continuum of the class structure. The effects of limited transport were reenforced by the serious lack of security mechanisms, including effective police presence and safe streets, so that residents of Córdoba forged their social links within restricted territories. Marriage patterns simply reflected this reality.

The perceptions held by the newly arrived migrants of the potential social and economic results of conjugal unions were put to the test quickly. The cultural norm of proximity was partly responsible for the relatively speedy fashion in which migrants married. With narrower territorial possibilities, the field of selection also was narrower and decisions were arrived at quickly. The way in which different ethnic groups still managed to find their respective conationals is the subject of the next chapter.

8. Marriage, Nationality, and Mobility

Historians in Argentina have assumed that immigrants blended best into Creole society by the avenue of marriage. Respected social scientists agree that among the dimensions used to gauge degrees of assimilation of immigrants is their level of participation in the society's structure and their consequent functional roles in that society's modernization. Economic roles, the rational and purposeful ordering of agricultural exploitation, and mixture with the native population: these are portrayed as the measures of participation most successfully realized by the immigrants to Argentina. The argument that "because of [the immigrants'] high preponderance of males, [the immigrant] mingled, by way of marriage, with the Argentines and with different nationalities" has remained a support for the acceptance of the thesis of the Argentine melting pot.[1] José Luis Romero wrote that

> a rapid intermingling began to occur between the immigrant and the Creole masses. If this was very common at the lower ranks of society, it was no less so among the members of the middle class that was then beginning to appear and was made up to a large extent precisely of the immigrants whose economic success was leading to their role in society. . . . The creole majority could not isolate itself from the rising tide of immigration; in a few generations they would be mixed with the descendants of the immigrants.[2]

The notions of Córdoba's historians and observers of the local scene parallel national perspectives. In 1910, Manuel Río pointed out that in one out of every three marriages in Córdoba Province one or *both* partners were foreigners, with nine out of twenty children in Córdoba born from such unions. These statistics prompted him to assume that "a profound modification" in the human components of Argentina was already under way. "In this melting pot," he wrote, "the material for one of the future Argentine types is being forged."

Moreover, he felt that the fusion was proceeding rapidly.[3] Efraín Bischoff, one of Córdoba's prolific writers of local history, presently continues to echo notions of the Argentine melting-pot thesis.[4] Yet, after using the data set gleaned from the marriage sample to test the veracity and completeness of significant judgments like the ones by Germani, Romero, Río, and Bischoff, we find such statements in need of serious reevaluation. According to the head of the city's Office of Statistics, only 372 weddings took place in Córdoba during 1874, while over three thousand cordobeses were still waiting their turn. He noted a lack of enthusiasm for marriages between Argentine women and immigrants. The news prompted the editors of the weekly *La Carcajada* to report that their "female [Creole] compatriots either do not like the foreign men, or the latter do not like the former; since while twenty-nine foreign women have married foreign men, only ten Argentine females have been able to mingle with foreigners."[5]

Marriages between immigrants and Creoles were essential ingredients of the liberals' plan to form the new Argentine.[6] The family, as the foundation of society, was believed to cause the quickest and most durable cultural change. The Argentine visionaries interpreted the role of the family as does the American historian John Demos: a provider of "a kind of common denominator, or baseline, for a whole culture whose various parts may differ substantially in other respects."[7]

Since immigrants were perennially described by the liberal rhetoric as exemplary figures for the Creoles, children of mixed European-Creole couples, reasoned the elite, were to be different from birth. The offspring of mixed marriages would not need to rely, as did the Creoles, on self-discipline and good fortune in order to imitate the cultural norms of the anonymous foreign masses.

Córdoba's middle and upper levels of society were numerically small enough to diffuse widespread knowledge of those mixed couples who were courting, thereby informally setting the trend for others to follow. Although these occurred with much less frequency at the uppermost crust of the elite, the press encouraged and announced with the flair typical of the Argentine alta sociedad the mixed marriages between local women and promising European men. *El Progreso,* a daily newspaper which strongly supported large-scale immigration, printed information on forthcoming weddings not under the social events but as a regular news item, such as this statement about "one of the city's prettiest and most charming girls and a gentleman, who, though an immigrant, is our brother in terms of race, language, customs and religion!"[8]

In spite of such efforts to propagate the liberals' designs, the men who migrated to the city of Córdoba maintained clearly defined predilections for their brides, as can be shown by the tables in this chapter. Table 8.1 displays a

Table 8.1
Ethnic Endogamy, 1869-1909
(Percentage)

Grooms \ Brides	Argentine	European	Total*
Argentine	98.8	1.2	39.2 (243)
European	52.3	47.7	60.8 (377)
Total	70.5 (437)	29.5 (183)	100.0 (620)

Source: Sample data.
Note: N shown in parentheses.
* Missing observations, 28.

cross-tabulation between the places of birth of grooms and brides who married in the city between 1869 and 1909. The results are clear: European men were equally well disposed toward Argentine-born as toward European women. Over 52 percent of the European grooms married Argentine women, while the remaining 47.7 percent wed from their own ethnic cohorts.[9] Creole men, however, were extremely reticent to marry non-Argentines: only one in one hundred Creoles married a European woman. The overwhelming majority—nearly 99 percent—of the Argentine grooms married Argentine brides.

This overall picture adds some clarity to the accepted view of the Argentine melting pot. It appears that, if a melting pot existed, it was not universal; that is, not all ethnic groups comprising Argentine society were equally willing to blend with other groups. The native population, the object of the elite's tactics of change, was most resistant to foreigners. If many nineteenth-century Argentine liberals held antinativist feelings, the subelite male Creoles acted in reverse fashion by bringing no part of the foreign element into their homes as family members through marriage. Between Europeans and Creoles, the melting-pot mentality appears to have worked in only one direction in that European males married Creole women, while *criollos* remained ethnically almost totally introverted.

Did any factors affect or diverge from the general patterns shown already? We would expect age to be a factor responsible for the decision-making processes of these men: we might expect older immigrants to manifest their greater conservatism by marrying their conationals in larger proportions than younger foreigners. Table 8.2 shows, however, that such an assumption is false. In fact, the opposite took place in Córdoba. As the ages of the European grooms increased, so did the proportions of their marriages to Argentine women. A fifty-year-old Spaniard, for example, had a 33 percent greater chance of marrying an Argentine than did a younger man in his twenties, who would be more prone to marry a European than a native-born. Fifty-three percent of the European men in their twenties married within their own European group; the remaining 47 percent married Argentine-born women. We have only two cases of marriages in the interval of fifty through sixty years of age; one chose to marry an Argentine and the other a European. The overall pattern stands, however; among the overwhelming majority of European grooms, the propensity to mix with Argentine women increased with age.

The preference of European men in their twenties for their female cohorts did not hold true for the entire forty-year period, as shown in Table 8.3.

Table 8.2
Nationality of Brides and Ages of European Grooms,
1869-1909
(Percentage)

Grooms' Ages	Argentine Bride	European Bride	Total
11-20	50.0	50.0	1.1 (4)
21-30	47.0	53.0	69.0 (249)
31-40	56.7	43.3	24.9 (90)
41-50	62.5	37.5	4.4 (16)
51-60	50.0	50.0	0.6 (2)
Total	50.1 (181)	49.9 (180)	100.0 (361)

Source: Sample data.
Note: N shown in parentheses.

Table 8.3
Nationality of Brides and Ages of European Grooms, by Decade, 1869-1909
(Percentage)
(N=334)

Decade	Grooms' Ages	Argentine Bride	European Bride	Total
1869-1878	21-30	92.9	7.1	60.9 (14)
	31-40	62.5	37.5	34.8 (8)
	41-50	100.0	0.0	4.3 (1)
	Total	82.6 (19)	17.4 (4)	100.0 (23)
1879-1888	21-30	57.6	42.4	55.0 (33)
	31-40	75.0	25.0	33.3 (20)
	41-50	71.4	28.6	11.7 (7)
	Total	65.0 (39)	35.0 (21)	100.0 (60)
1889-1898	21-30	45.9	54.1	71.4 (85)
	31-40	50.0	50.0	25.2 (30)
	41-50	50.0	50.0	3.4 (4)
	Total	47.1 (56)	52.9 (63)	100.0 (119)
1899-1908	21-30	39.4	60.6	78.8 (104)
	31-40	46.2	53.8	19.7 (26)
	41-50	100.0	0.0	1.5 (2)
	Total	41.7 (55)	58.3 (77)	100.0 (132)

Source: Sample data.
Note: N shown in parentheses.

During the first decade of this study—1869 through 1878—the proportion of marriages between the youngest European grooms and brides was 7 percent, markedly lower than the 37.5 percent European endogamy rate of the thirty-one through forty-year-olds.[10] The pattern reversed itself during the following decade, however. The 7 percent rate of twenty-one through thirty-year-olds marrying immigrant females increased to over 42 percent; the years between 1889 and 1898 witnessed another increase to 54 percent, and by the twentieth century 60.6 percent of young European men were marrying young European women. Men in their thirties increased their intermarriage rate throughout the 1880s, only to drop again during the following two decades. Men in their forties fluctuated in their preferences throughout the entire period, as shown in Table 8.3. Argentine grooms maintained their overwhelming preference for marrying native women regardless of age or time factors. No clear reasons appear yet to explain the influence of age on the behavior of these European men. Possibly, some older European men felt comfortable marrying Argentines because they may have spent a longer time in the country than their younger cohorts.

Using Pearson's r correlation, the strength of the relationship between the birthplaces of grooms and brides in Córdoba, without collapsing any of the many geographic areas into discrete categories, was a reasonably strong + .48.[11] Still, interpretation of this statistic is difficult because of the large variety of birthplaces encountered in the sample, including provincial departments. In order to make better sense of the data, we computed again the strength of the relationship, keeping the same geographic spheres shown in the preceding tables: Argentina and Europe. Now the strength of the relationship is increased to a very strong value of + .68, and thereby confirming statistically the evidence which the cross-tabulations displayed earlier in their cells.[12]

The integration of immigrants into local native society may have been somewhat conditioned by economic factors, such as the disparity between the quality of life of an urban-oriented immigrant merchant family and that of a Creole peon household. But mingling familially was principally a function of, and limited by, a tendency to cluster around one's own native group. That fact is particularly true of Argentine men who were not receptive to the possibility of having immigrant wives, regardless of socioeconomic status. So far, the overall picture of European men has shown a more or less even propensity to mingle with criollas as with *extranjeras,* yet their choices, too, become less balanced when controlled for specific factors, such as time. Nor should we speak about immigrants behaviorally as a cohesive group, whose perceptions and choices are acted upon in minimally divergent fashion; the effects age had on marriage illustrate this point.

The first waves of foreigners, which augured the massive immigration into

Argentina, consisted primarily of men without their families. But while immigrant women were scarce in the latter half of the nineteenth century, it is not true that all immigrant males were either unattached or searching for brides when they arrived in Argentina. The absolute differences between the numbers of immigrant men and of all women do not in themselves dictate the inevitability of a self-perpetuating Creole-immigrant mixture.[13] In fact, the overwhelming preponderance of males among the immigrants had abated sharply toward the end of the century. The stories of successful immigrants and a modernizing economy, among other factors, had caused entire families to risk the experiment of emigrating from Europe to Argentina toward the late 1890s. In 1897, for example, nearly half—46 percent—of the immigrants came with their families.[14] Gone were the days when only men packed the hallways of the customs house of Buenos Aires. Now women and young children formed an important part of the arriving multitude.

The decline in the number of unattached immigrant men toward the end of the century was reflected in the statistics of marriage in Córdoba: marriages by Europeans dropped significantly beginning in the mid-1890s.[15] An almost total absence of marriageable European women in Córdoba during the 1870s had been, in fact, a central reason for the overwhelming proportions of marriages between immigrants and Creoles; yet by the 1880s, when males still represented by far the greatest proportion of immigrants, the percentages of intra-European unions doubled, and kept increasing through the end of the period under study.[16]

It was more difficult for the non-cordobeses to find a mate than for the natives of the city. In an Argentine urban center the size of Córdoba, natives and longtime residents knew or heard about almost everyone within the same socioeconomic circle, with the possible exception of the agricultural laborers who were somewhat isolated by the long distances and poor communications of the rural zones.[17] Geography and social ecology thus facilitated the informal network of intragroup communication within the city. Merchants had their associations or formed ad hoc organizations to petition the authorities for commercial privileges; different immigrant groups had their voluntary associations; the Creole elites had their social clubs; and, toward the end of the century, many skilled workers also had their own organizations.[18]

It took time for new residents of the urbanized areas to belong to social organizations, to seek contacts for entry into them, to establish themselves as legitimate members of the mercantile sector—in short, to "belong." Marriages for these outsiders, however, on the average took place within a relatively short time after they arrived in the city, often in only a matter of months. How, then, could the parents or guardians of courted women, in many cases recently arrived themselves, feel secure about suitors? In a very real sense men, especially outsiders, who planned on marrying also had to wed the brides' families. Marriage was not the sole province of lovers: families, especially the brides', exerted an essential influence in the execution of choices. The data show that if all other factors were held constant, the groom and the father of the bride usually employed "heritage" as a point of commonality between them. The influence exerted by the place of birth of the brides' fathers was of great magnitude; as shown in Table 8.4, it radically altered the general pattern of intra-ethnic marriages from that of the brides' birthplaces alone.

Nearly half of the European men married women from within their ethnic groups, yet approximately 80 percent of all European men actually married into families where the father was also European. Likewise, the Argentine men married into Creole families at an overwhelming rate of 92.5 percent. In fact, the strength of the association between areas of birth of grooms and brides' fathers is stronger (+.71) than the relationship between the nationalities of grooms and brides (+ .50).[19] The foregoing indicates that while over time availability of native-born women of immigrant parentage subjected the ethnic cohesion among immigrants (as measured by the rate of intra-ethnic unions) to varying degrees of dilution, nevertheless the *tradition of lineage* was strictly maintained in these unions.

Enough time had passed by 1910 to allow a population of first-generation Argentines, yet women of these households maintained their cultural traditions

Table 8.4
Ethnic Endogamy as Family Lineage, 1869-1909
(Percentage)

Nationality of Groom	Argentine Father-in-Law	European Father-in-Law	Total
Argentine	92.5	7.5	43.3 (201)
European	20.9	79.1	56.7 (263)
Total	51.9 (241)	48.1 (223)	100.0 (464)

Source: Sample data.
Note: N shown in parentheses.

not by marrying Creoles, but by keeping the families ethnically homogeneous through marriage to Europeans. An unswerving recalcitrance on the part of the traditional Creoles to marry first-generation Argentine women aided the endeavors of immigrant families with Argentine-born daughters to remain with "their own kind." Only 7.5 percent of the non-cordobés Argentines married descendants of Europeans. Of all the fathers of the brides, these Europeans represented a mere 3.2 percent throughout the forty-year period for which data exist.

The partial correlation of marital unions, controlling for the effects of the fathers' origins, indicates the impact of parentage on marital choices. A partial correlation provides us with a measure of the relationship between two variables while adjusting for the effects caused by one or more additional variables on the same relationship. Thus, we can move beyond the simple literal control permitted in cross-tabulation analysis to the use of statistical controls. In other words, so far we have been able to observe the effects of geographic heritage only simultaneously, according to the values it has taken on the three variables under study: national origins of grooms, brides, and fathers-in-law. But each category of each variable in a cross-tabulation greatly drains the average cell occurrences or frequencies; partial correlation, on the other hand, permits controls to be exerted statistically rather than literally. We may therefore remove the effects of the control variable, if any, from the relationship between the other two variables without physically withdrawing any of the data under analysis, as is necessary with cross-tabulations.[20]

Our concern with parentage as a "control variable" in interethnic marriages arises from the logical possibility that at least the father had a strong voice in deciding the type of union that took place. The result could condition the simple correlation between the geographic origins of grooms and brides by altering the correlation coefficient or, alternately, by showing its lack of effect on the results.[21] Finally, the use of partial correlation must be rationalized by one's choice of control variables. Here, the validity of using birthplace of the father as a conditioning or control variable affecting interethnic marriages becomes evident, because in order to be a true control the third variable, which we can call Z, "must be a logically or temporally prior attribute—it must somehow come before X [birthplace of groom] and Y [birthplace of bride] so that it can jointly influence those two attributes."[22]

If the birthplace of a woman mattered to her suitor, as evidenced by a correlation score of + .68, the birthplace of her father represented an even stronger factor in the dynamics of interethnic mingling in Córdoba:[23] the strength of the association between grooms and fathers of the brides on the basis of geographic background, as measured by the statistic Pearson's r, is +.71.[24] When one computes the correlation once again between grooms and brides, this time controlling for the effect of the fathers-in-law, the strength of the relationship weakened significantly to a score of + .22.[25] Interpreting these results, we find that the birthplace of the prospective father-in-law was responsible for over 41 percent of the variance, or nonhomogeneity around the average, in the choices of marriage partners; without taking into consideration the effects of the fathers, the nationalities of the brides alone accounted for only 4.8 percent of the variance.

Assumptions about the social and demographic impacts of a process of massive immigration composed mostly of men have traditionally rested upon an organic view of collective social behavior: numerical components of a society must temper and mold all group actions. Each set of actors of the evolving synthesis is, therefore, seen as "liquid" and the proportions of the inevitable mixtures of these groups must, therefore, determine the volume and quality of the resulting syncretism. Tables of aggregate censal data are used as evidence of the fusion of native-born and foreigners which massive immigration into Argentina "must have exerted."

The size of the Creole population nationwide was small throughout this period, thus it follows that Creoles were absorbed and their identity seriously altered by the immigrants. Many scholars reach this conclusion after accepting the theory that "if the absolute volume of the native population which receives the immigration (the population 'base') is very high, its capacity to assimilate or its *limit of tolerance* for the preservation of its identity—all other conditions being equal—will be high; and the opposite [will take place], if that population 'base' is small."[26] In this scheme, amalgamation is deterministic, and the resultant "types" are the perfectly acculturated offsprings of immigrants. It is this emergent mass which Romero characterizes as "hybrid."[27] Moreover, if in the nation's rural and isolated zones observers found pockets of immigrants who tenaciously held to their customs and mingled only with their own kind, the urban centers—the argument runs—provided an ambience more conducive to social and cultural integration.[28]

Nonetheless, in the case of foreign women and of immigrant family members other than the male heads of households, little evidence supports this widely shared view of social amalgamation. Gino Germani and other leading exponents of the view that Argentina evolved into a kind of ethnic monolith due to the preponderance of males among the immigrants and subsequent ethnic mixtures themselves warn of approaches to the study of migration which could reduce "it to a kind of mechanical balance of external impersonal forces. [Nevertheless, these approaches seem] to put an excessive emphasis on 'rational' or instrumental motivations, not taking into account the possible complexity of the psychological processes. . . ."[29]

The results of this study of marital unions among the different nationalities in Córdoba and our view of marriages as one of the indices of interethnic distances do not support the belief that Argentina was free from ethnic tensions or antagonisms. This belief has stemmed, in part, from the continued acceptance among Argentine and American scholars of some of the late nineteenth-century opinions on immigration—not shared by all even at that time—which considered the foreigner as a booster of the nation, since "the conscience of the history of the country of origin [would] produce among Argentines a live stimulus to work in order to be worthy of his ancestors."[30] Moreover, the selections of marriage partners in Córdoba not only display a bias between Argentines and Europeans, but also provide evidence of the strong tendencies toward endogamy within each nationality group.

In Table 8.5 we present the endogamy rates of four nationalities residing in Buenos Aires during 1893-1894, 1899-1901, and 1907-1908. Gino Germani, using figures from a work prepared by the demographer Franco Savorgnan, showed the high incidence of intermarriage in Argentina.[31] The figures attest to a decreasing rate of intra-ethnic breeding for all groups except the Spanish immigrants, who increased their rates somewhat between 1893 and 1908. Most receptive of all the ethnic groups were the Argentine nationals in Buenos Aires, whose endogamy rate revolved around 45 percent—the lowest figure of all the ethnic groups.

In Córdoba, as displayed in Table 8.6, the facts tell a different story. The rate of endogamy for these nationalities during the years between 1869 and 1909 belies the relative openness found in Buenos Aires. The Argentines maintained their first position by keeping themselves aloof—in familial terms—from all others: their endogamy rate of 98.5 percent in Córdoba stands in sharp

Table 8.5
Endogamy Rates for Buenos Aires,
1893-1894, 1899-1901, and 1907-1908
(Percentage)

Nationality	1893-1894	1899-1901	1907-1908	Average
Argentine	45.3	45.3	44.2	44.9
French	59.7	48.3	41.8	49.9
Italian	64.4	59.3	55.5	59.7
Spanish	64.9	64.3	70.8	66.6

Source: F. Savorgnan, as reported in G. Germani, *Política y sociedad,* p. 207.

Table 8.6

Ethnic Endogamy of Selected Nationalities in Córdoba, 1869-1909

(Percentage)

Grooms \ Brides	Argentine	French	Italian	Spanish	Total
Argentine	98.5	0.0	0.5	1.0	45.0 (198)
French	38.9	38.9	11.1	11.1	4.1 (18)
Italian	25.7	0.7	70.3	3.4	33.6 (148)
Spanish	32.9	2.6	10.5	53.9	17.3 (76)
Total	60.2 (265)	2.3 (10)	26.1 (115)	11.4 (50)	100.0 (440)

Source: Sample data.

Note: N shown in parentheses.

contrast to the Argentine porteño average of 45 percent (Table 8.5). Proportionately, the Frenchmen residing in Córdoba, not the Argentines, mingled the most; but Frenchmen also married as many French women as they did natives. Italian men displayed a rate of ethnic endogamy of over 70 percent. After the Frenchmen, the Spanish men had the lowest rate—not the highest as in the case of Buenos Aires—of introversion: nearly one-third of them married native-born Argentine women.

Here the data set again provides more information than earlier researchers were able to produce. Table 8.7 shows that the coincidence between grooms and fathers-in-law was once again higher than that between men and women in all groups but one, since the rate for Argentines fell by approximately 4 percent to 93.9. The proportions of marriages in which the groom and the father-in-law came from the same country, however, showed marked increases. Among Frenchmen this figure jumped to 50 percent, Italians showed a 3.3 percent increase, and Spaniards nearly 12 percent.

The proportions of unions, controlling for the effects exerted by the women's fathers, stand in sharpest contrast to the traditional assumptions about ethnic endogamy and the "melting pot" in Argentina during the period of massive immigration. When we are able to trace the lineage of each marriage, the accepted view of Argentina as having provided the ambience for an ongoing cultural and ethnic familial blend comes into serious question. Thus it seems that the data gathered by Savorgnan probably would have shown very different results if the Argentines in his study had been identified as porteño descendants of immigrants—as many of them surely were—who, in fact, were continuing their parents' heritages by marrying within their respective "communities" at a much greater rate than his results indicated.

In order to make the fairest comparisons between the accepted endogamy rates, such as Savorgnan's (Table 8.5), and the cases in Córdoba, we devised tables for the same nationalities and for the same years. Table 8.8 shows that the sharp differences between the groups remained, while in Table 8.9 controlling for the fathers-in-law once again heightened the differences.

Published results like Savorgnan's have had a long tradition of acceptance in Argentina. In fact, beginning as early as the period of germinal immigration and economic development, leading Argentines had been predicting such results. In addition to pointing to the lack of women during the first waves of immigration, they ascribed to European men a greater tendency toward being "family men" than to Creole men. Argentines who supported immigration and favored its effects on the nation gave the reasons above as evidence for the mixture of immigrant men with Creole women.[32] Moreover, they did not accept the unions of different nationalities matter of factly; they believed them to be essential and claimed that the nation's future and its rate of progress depended,

Table 8.7

Ethnic Endogamy as Family Lineage for Selected Nationalities in Córdoba, 1869-1909
(Percentage)

Grooms	Argentine	French	Italian	Spanish	Total
Argentine	93.9	0.0	4.0	2.0	45.0 (198)
French	27.8	50.0	11.1	11.1	4.1 (18)
Italian	18.9	2.0	73.6	5.4	33.6 (148)
Spanish	17.1	3.9	13.2	65.8	17.3 (76)
Total	52.7 (232)	3.4 (15)	29.3 (129)	14.5 (64)	100.0 (440)

Fathers-in-Law (column headers)

Source: Sample data.
Note: N shown in parentheses.

Table 8.8
Endogamy Rates for Córdoba,
1893-1894, 1899-1901, and 1907-1908
(Percentage)

Nationality	1893-1894	1899-1901	1907-1908	Average
Argentine	100.0	100.0	98.9	99.6
French	50.0	—	—	50.0
Italian	58.3	73.3	69.6	67.1
Spanish	25.0	80.0	40.0	48.3

Source: Sample data.

Table 8.9
Endogamy Rates for Córdoba,
1893-1894, 1899-1901, and 1907-1908,
Controlling for Birthplace of Fathers of Brides
(Percentage)

Nationality	1893-1894	1899-1901	1907-1908	Average
Argentine	100.0	100.0	100.0	100.0
French	100.0	—	—	100.0
Italian	100.0	90.9	94.1	95.0
Spanish	50.0	100.0	75.0	75.0

Source: Sample data.

in great part, on ethnic mixtures which would result in a harder working population of capitalists. Thus, according to an influential newspaper in Córdoba

> freedom, equality of conditions, the independence guaranteed by the federal form of government; everything, everything stems from the promotion of material interests, by means of increases in the population of proprietors, hands, and capital. It is necessary to buy the population, if we may use this term; and we can buy it, if not with what we can offer in exchange, then with the land we possess. Commerce, developed to its highest degree, is what gives value to our . . . [unpopulated regions], bringing the surplus of the European population to fill this empty land, [and] which, through a law of breeding reigning over the animal and plant kingdoms, will physically and intellectually improve the race . . . .[33]

Modern Argentine sociologists, such as Germani, have seen the fruition of the liberals' theories about impending miscegenation as in fact supported by censal data, other published aggregate results, and sociological inferences. Modern social scientists have virtually ignored, on the other hand, the effects on the families of the ethnically disparate young men and women of the period. Instead, the forms and the results of familial dynamics have been the subject of works in the literary field, in popular culture, and by the few Argentine historians who use those sources in the interpretations of the national culture.

The Uruguayan playwright Florencio Sánchez wrote a considerable number of plays during the late nineteenth and early twentieth centuries depicting the lives and mores of the people of the Río de la Plata area. The protagonists of one of his most famous plays, *La Gringa,* display not only stereotypical characterizations of Creoles and immigrant Italians, but also the wide social and cultural distances which they had to bridge before the two types could work and live harmoniously.[34] Sánchez ameliorated the situation during the course of the play in a fashion typical of turn-of-the-century progressives: the marriage of the Italian's daughter with the Creole's son. But this resolution through marriage took place only after considerable emotional cost. Between the Piedmontese don Nicola and the Creole don Cantalicio, distrust had always existed. Later, greed caused the relationship to turn to hatred. The gringo took over the land which the gaucho earlier had naïvely put up as collateral on a loan. In addition, don Nicola was so totally opposed to his daughter's marriage to Cantalicios' son that he threw the young man off his land, accusing him of using his daughter under false pretenses. Doña María, Nicola's wife, was even harsher in her criticism of and opposition to Creoles entering the family; she thus lent credence to the anti-Italian sentiment of the Argentines who suspected that Italian women insidiously aggravated the avarice of Italian men.[35]

José S. Alvarez, too, refers in his short stories to the obstinacy and sacrifices experienced this time by Creole parents before permitting immigrant men into their homes to marry their daughters. In a piece entitled *En Familia,* Eleuterio is the unfortunate father who is saddened by his five daughters' marriages to immigrant men. Though veiled by tragicomic rhetoric, he personifies the deeply wounded nationalist whose family and heritage are disappearing before his eyes. His friend Ramona tries to cheer him up. Her way of looking at the situation is strictly utilitarian, for she speaks with some degree of personal experience on the hidden blessings of such an arrangement:

> And I, look . . . my bliss would have been that my two daughters, poor devils, had married foreigners . . . Such fine people, so correct! . . . And afterwards, there you are! . . . even when the sons-in-law die, it is better, one suffers less . . . In any case, when Gómez, who was a Creole, died, and who, as you know, was a good-for-nothing, I cried over him so much, without even remembering all the suffering he caused my little daughter, and when Tonelli died, who had been so good to our Ernestine, and who had made her so happy, I hardly felt it . . . Perhaps, since the poor fellow was a foreigner, it hurt me less . . .

Eleuterio, though not feeling any better over his own plight, was forced to admit that Ramona had a point.[36]

The distrust between Creoles and immigrants created an animosity which prevented them from intermarrying. Marriage of a Creole to an immigrant was a social stigma for both families. A spirit conducive to ethnic endogamy existed for many years in Argentina, but it was not always successful in curbing the dilution of the different nationalities. The interethnic unions took place in the interior, to be sure, but at rates greatly divergent from those of cosmopolitan Buenos Aires.

Marriage and Social Mobility

Financial considerations often suggested Creole parents' acceptance of intermarriages. Thus some Argentine historians have argued that many of these marriages were tolerated by Creole families in the hope of benefitting financially from harder-working and more frugal immigrants, who had already, or promised to have in the near future, savings.[37] An old Creole saying went: "The little gringa is ugly, but her money makes her pretty."

Let us look at the marriage of Carlos Barruti in 1870, to illustrate such a case of economic mobility.[38] Barruti had been born in Montevideo to Italian parents, and by the time of the first national census was living with his widowed mother in downtown Córdoba. As part owners of a *confitería,* he was a general food retailer, restaurateur, and server of alcoholic beverages.[39]   At the time of his marriage to a cordobesa named Gregoria Cabanillas, daughter of middle-level Córdoba parents, he was only twenty-six years old but already well on his way to becoming a wealthy man from having joined with his brother-in-law, a Spanish Basque, in launching the confitería. It is evident from the amounts of their investments—Barruti's share was 760 gold pesos, his partner's 1,000— that neither of the two had started the business from a position of poverty: they already had considerable savings, perhaps from inherited money. More-over, they owed the business partnership additional investments of 2,000 and 3,000 gold pesos, respectively. Barruti's father-in-law, Abelino Cabanillas, bor-rowed over 800 gold pesos in goods and cash from the business, even though he had never contributed any money to the corporation. It is not surprising that such large outlays of funds were lent privately in an era lacking institu-tional banking and loan facilities, nor does it appear out of order that Barruti married Cabanillas' daughter, even though she was still a minor.

Unfortunately, the marriage lasted less than one year before the bride be-came a widow. She received, however, half of her husband's estate, the other half having been distributed among the creditors of the deceased and his part-ner. The probate proceedings and inventory read like the legacy which hun-dreds of thousands of other immigrants who came to "make America" wished for: merchandise, 2,888 gold pesos; furniture, 1,330; two houses downtown and a parcel of land outside the city, 8,759; liquid assets, 750 gold pesos.[40]

Clearly, the Cabanillas family benefited economically from young Grego-ria's wedding to Barruti. We should be cautious, however, in generalizing about this type of marriage, since the rate of occurrence of probates like Barruti's, which serve as evidence, was low in the city of Córdoba throughout the late nineteenth and early twentieth centuries.[41] It does suggest, however, that a significant number of marriages of mutual economic benefit possibly took place among the minority which comprised the exogamous unions in the city.

Data on the occupations of the parents of the wedded couples are too scanty to allow an orderly systematic analysis of economic mobility via mar-riage, but we have enough information to suggest that within the low economic levels of Córdoba's society a greater degree of intermarriage existed than that found overall. After the mid-1890s, the commonality of indicators such as illiteracy, residence in poor sectors of the city, and low occupational levels facilitated many of the marriages of poor immigrant men and Creole women.[42] Such cases occurred especially among Italian men involved in agricultural, semi-skilled, or service occupations. The incidence of intermarriage among the poor increased only after the mid-1890s.

The marriage of Juan Monti and Carmen Cuevas in 1896 provides an example.

Born in Italy, Monti emigrated to Argentina. By 1892 he had begun working with a friend, Enrique Lencina, as an agricultural laborer in Córdoba. Shortly before his marriage in October of 1896, the two friends had saved enough to purchase a *chacra,* a small parcel of land outside the city. Since Monti could neither read nor write, his socioeconomic improvement was limited to owning part of that chacra, where he maintained himself at a subsistence level at the age of forty. His new bride came from a similar social position. Carmen Cuevas, too, had been unable to attend school. Born in Córdoba to Creole parents, most of her twenty-six years of life had been spent working in the fields and at home helping to take care of her family. Her father had died some time before her wedding.[43] While her marriage to Monti did not insure that the Cuevas family would see better times, it did provide the security of having a working spouse who at least owned some real estate, however small it may have been. For Monti, too, the marriage represented an accommodation: it offered companionship in the municipality's rural zones, where he was in large part cut off from the Italian females living in the metropolitan area. As a chacarero, he would also have found it difficult to socialize with the Italians involved in commerce or skilled urban labor, for they were successfully opening avenues for integrating into the city life and would not have been amenable to their daughters' possible involvement in low-level agricultural endeavors.

A similar case occurred with Juan Roca and María Ana Ocampo. Roca, like Monti, was also an Italian agricultural worker who could not read or write. In 1903 he married the illegitimate daughter of Cecilia Ocampo, who was also very poor and who benefited from her dauther's husband at least to the extent that he provided the family with some income from his employment.[44]

The Italian José Barrera's marriage illustrates the ethnic fluidity possible among urban members of the lower class. In 1908 he worked as a milkman and lived on Tablada Street, close to the river bank in a slum area dotted with tenements, where tuberculosis cases and streetwalkers were numerous. As in the previous cases, Barrera could not sign his own name. Nearby lived Bautista Gómez, a Creole who had migrated from the town of Copacabana in the department of Ischilín, part of the poor, arid northern zone bordering the province of Catamarca. His twenty-three-year-old daughter, Gregoria, could not expect to marry much higher than the level that José Barrera represented, especially because she had an unemployed father to tend to constantly.[45]

For the men in our sample, social mobility through marriage appears to have been minimal. In fact, the occupational distribution of the men at the time of their weddings was hardly altered after their marriages. The lines of social stratification in Córdoba were too rigorously drawn to permit a man in the service sector to marry into a family of merchants, nor would the daughter of a doctor with to marry someone in petty trade—even members of the alto comercio rarely joined the families of distinguished professional cordobeses.

Immigrants who had become established merchants in the city found it somewhat easier to marry into merchant Creole families, but usually within their own social station. The marriage of Heriberto Martínez in 1890 typifies that sort of limited mobility. Martínez, a Spaniard who had arrived in Córdoba as a small child, achieved great standing in the community and became one of the largest wholesalers in Córdoba.[46] As one of the leaders within the city's commercial sector, he had numerous social and political contacts. His marriage to Manuela Carranza, daughter of a Creole merchant, cemented an economic, as well as familial relationship.[47] Still, most European merchants—who comprised almost the entirety of the nonmanual category—did not marry Argentine women, as shown in Table 8.10. Instead, the lower occupational orders were about twice as likely to marry daughters of Argentines than were members of the nonmanual group, since European manual laborers lived in the suburbs and the agricultural zones where finding daughters of Europeans was more difficult.

Integration with Creoles was easiest, though not predominant, among European professionals, whose chances for mobility were the best of all social groups. The case of Andrés de Raedemacker recapitulates for us some of the processes of social mobility via marriage in Córdoba. Raedemacker had been professor of music in the Brussels Conservatory, where he had earlier studied. After his arrival in Córdoba in the late 1880s, he became professor of piano at the newly founded National Institute of Music. The students of the Institute represented the city's fashionable, traditional, and wealthy Creole families. Although the cost of matriculation was minimal, certain basic musical requirements which could be fulfilled solely through private lessons permitted only the wealthy to attend.[48] The names of students attending this and any other musical institutions of the time read like a Córdoba "Who's Who": Yofre Díaz, Deheza, Lazcano, Luque, and Garzón, among others.[49] In this social circle Raedemacker met his bride, Luisa Novillo, the daughter of a highly successful businessman who by 1895 listed himself simply as *rentista* (landlord), indicating the ownership of a great amount of wealth in real estate.[50] One of the elder Novillo's sons also grew up to be a musician.[51]

As professor of music at the National Institute, Raedemacker could not expect to earn more than seventy pesos monthly, and his financial state could not improve significantly by tutoring students privately. Moreover, the Baring Crisis forced the Institute to close down. His marriage in 1889, however, provided Raedemacker with financial security.[52] He lived comfortably in the spacious Novillo home while devoting his time to giving private lessons until, once again, he came to teach formal classes at Córdoba's Provincial Conservatory of Music.[53] In cases of social mobility like Raedemacker's, where income was low, it was essential that the man's occupation be prestigious. Only by participating

Table 8.10
Occupational Status and Ethnic Intermarriage by European Men,
1869-1909
(Percentage)

Occupational Classification	Married Daughters of Argentines	Married Daughters of Europeans	Total
Unskilled and Menial	30.0	70.0	3.8 (10)
Semiskilled	28.6	71.4	5.4 (14)
Rural Semiskilled	33.3	66.7	5.7 (15)
Skilled	34.3	65.7	25.7 (67)
Rural Skilled	16.7	83.3	6.9 (18)
Nonmanual	15.5	84.6	34.9 (91)
Professional	33.3	66.7	1.1 (3)
Miscellaneous and Unknown	4.7	95.3	16.5 (43)
Total	19.5 (55)	80.5 (206)	100.0 (261)

Source: Sample data.
Note: N shown in parentheses.

socially in the events and festivities of the rich could anyone with little wealth expect to have some chances of breaking into the highest social class; otherwise, the odds against marrying outside one's own station were overwhelming.

Summary

Because the act of marriage was itself a fleeting event, almost insignificant in comparison to all that came before, it represented only a portion of the microcosm of interrelationships among urban residents. By examining the institution of marriage and its environment as it relates to the migrant, we have presented a study of how institutional, administrative and social factors bore upon the *decision* of marriage.

Social contacts in nineteenth-century Córdoba, as exemplified by the relations between its men and women, were conducted in parochial fashion. The geographic reach of socialization was limited. A large share of the responsibility for prolonging the residents' orientation toward whatever—or whomever—was geographically most proximate rests on the conscious neglect or the unavoidable limitations of the municipal administrations in carrying out a modern program of urban development. Poor lighting and inefficient policing made the suburbs dangerous places in which to walk after dark, and unless a man were independently wealthy his job often limited his free time to the nights, when he could spend some moments with his girl friend. Even in the central zones it was not customary to be out late at night, so that short distances between the residences of men and women were also essential to sentimental propinquity downtown.

The limited network of public transportation compounded the inhibiting effects of crime and poor lighting. It was rare to go from one suburb to another or to travel regularly from one point within the metropolitan area to a place across town. The commercially oriented transportation system was never meant to serve the needs of the public; it became, above all, a business venture meant to benefit the stockholders, some of whom had invested to see to it that their own businesses would profit from the routes. The municipal authorities did little, until the twentieth century, to expand public transportation. Only then was the parochial nature of social contacts in the neighborhoods broken, and what had previously been isolated barrios became a system of wider communication and participation in the social affairs of the city. The lack of adequate transportation, therefore, also acted to stifle any possibilities of expanding one's social frontiers: marriages took place among near neighbors.

The society of Córdoba was not egalitarian; distinct class differences maintained the system of economic inequality through much of the present century. An immigrant's professional status, as we have seen, could occasionally overcome his financial deficiencies, and by processes of emulation and socialization within the elite circle he could achieve economic mobility through marriage with one of its members. Mobility via marriage was uncommon in Córdoba, however, because an immigrant's claim to belong to a social stratum superior to the one in which he circulated was difficult to validate. As in the case with power relations, the influential clusters in a local community "may have their source of legitimacy in the folkways, some of which may be unique to the community."[54] We submit, however, that Córdoba's did not represent atypical folkways; that its social boundaries were not erected significantly more rigorously at any of the middle or upper levels than those of most contemporary Argentine cities; and that its aristocracy was not any more of a caste than the elites of Buenos Aires or Rosario, as evidenced by most subjective accounts and quantitative reports of the period.[55]

Although some opportunism by women or their families entered into the process of courtship, the degree of economic mobility through marriage was only slightly less for Creole females than for immigrant men. Not only was class distance a factor separating lowly women from men in better socioeconomic situations, but between poor Creole females and immigrant men racism also acted as an additional impediment to marital unions. Domestic service was the easiest and often the only employment that poor cordobesas could obtain: the principal employees of this type of work were "the so-called *chinas* (mestizas), undoubtedly looked upon in a deprecating fashion, perhaps not only because of class distinctions, but also because of the difference in race. It [was] common to use the word *chinita* contemptuously when someone wishe[d] to brand the behavior of a woman as lewd. *Chinitero* [was] the [label given to] the man who ha[d] sexual relations with chinas."[56]

While racism acted as an inhibitor of interethnic marriages among the poor, nationalism remained the biggest contributor to the great incidence of intra-ethnic unions, regardless of social rank, age or time period. When we analyze marriages along the broad European-Argentine dichotomy, we discover that any melting pot that may have existed in Argentina was not contributed to by the native men. The eventual appearance of the "new Argentine" was a function almost solely of the energy which immigrants—not Creoles—exerted.

Europeans were, indeed, melting into the native population by exercising their marital choices. Yet the majority of foreign men married their own co-nationals or their descendants. Ethnic endogamy, then, was not the province solely of Creoles; Argentine females born to immigrant parents married mostly foreign men, thereby prolonging the period of cultural pluralism in Argentina. It is difficult to state with certainty that mainly ethnic antagonism lay behind the ethnic endogamy in Argentina, but neither was it accidental that members of each national group kept mostly to their own in the selection of mates.[57]

The assumption behind much of the scholarship on the subject has rested on the idea of Argentina, because of its sparse native population during the nineteenth century, as a vacuum in which the varieties of immigrant elements floated freely until they all mixed. But a nation in its formative stages is not a vacuum; it merely represents a geopolitical expression capable of housing self-restricting nuclei of people, every nucleus living in harmony with every other. There was, then, no single free market but a number of them, mostly self-sufficient, and each with its own currency of ethnicity. The members of each group need not have felt any requirement or desire to radically alter its composition.

Most nineteenth-century liberal Argentine statesmen and newspaper owners wished for and envisioned the economic benefits of invigorating their country

through the formation of a "new Argentine man." Most liberal Argentine
scholars of modern times uphold the notion of the Argentine melting pot as an
accomplished fact.[58] Most present-day cosmopolitan Argentines deny the existence of ethnic separation in large urban centers, as if the recognition of cultural pluralism were a self-denigrating admission. Only those men and women
of the period we studied, it appears, in seeking to marry their own, really under-
stood their circumstances. It was not for the sake of economic benefit, nor to
substantiate subsequent sociological theories, nor to quiet the self-imposed
fears of later generations that they married whom they did; all they sought was
their own happiness. In doing so they displayed the great flexibility required
to find each other in a strange environment and adapt the cultural norms of
their native areas to their new situations.

9. Mobility and Integration in Córdoba: The Sociopolitical Legacy of Liberalism

That Argentina during the years of liberalism promised a secure future to people who would apply themselves has not been seriously questioned in Argentine historiography. The principles of laissez-faire that guided the nation's course have been condemned over the last three or four decades as acts of surrender to foreign dominant interests, but Argentina's capability to receive and to realize the dreams of millions who sought new and comfortable lives has remained unquestioned and untested. This work has tried to define both quantitatively and descriptively different modes of mobility and integration for various social and ethnic groups during the experience of massive immigration that germinated and culminated under liberal aegis.

Leaders of a land wondrous in natural resources and great in size, but populated by what they considered an atrophied and inadequately small population, the liberals of Argentina were intent on creating a new socioeconomic order. They joined different positivistic theories to liberal laissez-faire policies in order to achieve two goals: to present Argentina as a land of opportunity, and to invite European immigrants to improve the native population base. As in the case of most grand designs, however, the planners did not account for all repercussions and failed to achieve some of their basic goals. These failures resulted, to a great extent, from the options which the sociopolitical system extended to certain groups and to the individual. One part of the plan, however, held fast throughout the period: the social order and the traditional framework of the political system were maintained. Positivistic liberalism, therefore, succeeded in justifying the position of the ruling groups while they sought accommodations in the social ambience within the traditional society's modus operandi.

Though the land was wealthy in resources, the limited accessibility to that land on a proprietary basis drove native and foreigner alike into existing cities. The liberal plan to dot the country with new urban centers that would result from and service an expanding rural population augmented by European immigrants therefore failed to develop. Before and throughout the period of massive immigration the concerns of the authorities and the intelligentsia centered on achieving for Argentina the Wagnerian concept of *Volk*—that is, the communal unity of the Argentine nation.[1] Moreover, these leaders also held the formation of a new, potent Argentine race together with a unified culture as the sine qua non of recognition by and participation in the international community. Yet the genesis of this *raza cósmica* was hampered by the unwillingness of the government to force amalgamation on new and old residents of Argentina. On the contrary, national, provincial, and municipal authorities encouraged cultural pluralism both by lack of action and by design.

The practical denied the mythical dimensions of communal assimilation, when measured by the degree of immigrant integration into formal associations and informal primary groups within the Creole-established strata. The inability or unwillingness of the municipality of Córdoba to provide basic services and transportation equally throughout the city reenforced the traditional pattern of clustering around the immediate vicinity of one's residence and prevented the development of wider community social relationships.

In addition to the walking city within the center, Córdoba contained numerous walking enclaves, even downtown. Personal predilections for marriage partners worked in conjunction with administrative obstacles to prevent any amalgamation between the predominantly Creole suburbs and the significant immigrant contingent in the center. At the same time, Creole primary social groups and political figures accommodated the existence of foreigners through their institutions and legitimated their European identity (in spite of official rhetoric to the contrary) by participating in their social and patriotic affairs and by subsidizing some of their educational and commercial activities.[2]

Foreigners themselves usually paid only lip service to the promotion of ethnic cohesion; instead, they established in their associations guidelines on sponsorship and residence which generated social primacy for a few. The great majority of their conationals operated outside the framework and benefit of institutional facilitators of integration. Even though the immigrant institutions represented only a small proportion of the Europeans, the government and much of the press favored this minority with much greater attention and social import than their numbers merited. Through lending such informal assistance the liberal establishment promoted the distinction that, by their exclusionary practices, the established immigrants sought for themselves. The have-nots among the immigrants, as among the natives, were left to stake their claims in society on an individual basis as they experienced the vicissitudes of the Argentine labor market.

The concentration of different nationalities in the cities compounded the problems of ethnic differentiation inherent in the period of massive immigration. The dynamics and infrastructure (police, transportation, municipal services) of Córdoba's urban development reenforced a system of social contacts which, in addition to being limited by socioeconomic boundaries, was a function of an abbreviated geographic outreach. The *activity* of socialization may have been high, but not its *distance*. The failure of both public and private agencies to provide basic services throughout the municipality proved a hindrance to social contacts, and ethnic amalgamation.[3] In addition, all ethnic groups and associations showed varying, though high, degrees of self-imposed social restrictions, while marital contacts that excluded members of nationalities other than one's own undermined the genesis and strength of the mythical race. Thus the cultural pluralism that survived the period of massive immigration contributed toward the preservation of cultural semi-autonomy still extant in urban Argentina today, including not only Buenos Aires but also Córdoba, Rosario, Mendoza, and other major cities.

A conflict looms over the issue of ethnicity in Argentina, since immigrants held two opposing views with regard to the maintaining of ethnic cohesion. On the one hand, although belonging to the appropriate ethnic group was necessary for joining a voluntary association, very little of that ethnicity was discussed at the meetings or manifested in the association's activities. On the other, families guarded their ethnicity zealously, as evidenced in the choices of marriage partners. Moreover, because ethnic voluntary associations had two exclusionary edges—ethnic and social—conationals of different classes were prevented from sharing in any common enterprise. This fragmentation must have resulted in some dilution of ethnic unity which, in turn, was stemmed by the manner in which Europeans manifested their familial aspirations. This paradox suggests a hypothesis of ethnicity which may help us understand the meaning and perception of lineage. Class altered the parameters of ethnic awareness whenever the two concepts were or threatened to be in conflict. At the same time, ethnicity was used as a strategic device to maintain the foreign bourgeoisie linked to the ruling authorities; in turn, political elites selectively rewarded ethnic actors. Ethnicity was also employed across class lines to maintain lineage —but mostly through individual, not corporate, efforts. Thus ethnicity served both the emotional needs of Europeans conscious of their heritage and the material needs of the merchants and professionals among them.

A Successful Failure

It becomes clear that the interior, at least, was neither prepared for nor conducive to significant degrees of vertical social mobility. The rate of out-migration for the city of Córdoba was high for both cordobeses and non-cordobeses, including European immigrants. The low persistence figures may elicit

views, on the reader's part, of thousands of migrating cohorts and of chaotic
dysfunctions in the Argentine social system. Yet no radical dislocation took
place within the socioeconomic order during this period. Did the discontented
population remain a voiceless majority? Or should we conclude that the Argentine system, in fact, managed somehow to satisfy enough claims to stifle potential disruptions? Or were the 1890 uprisings, for example, representative of
pent-up emotions arising from social inequalities?

The explosive situation of the early 1890s did not represent a basic alteration of the national political structure. The participants of several revolts
which in 1890 took place throughout the country were moral activists committed to a "modernization" of the Argentina political system. This modernizing
spirit dictated an end to the personalistic, insular political organizations of
constituents whose loyalties were limited to their own leaders and whose concerns focused on their own perquisites. The function of the political system
was not questioned; only its operational mode was repudiated. With President
Juárez Celman's resignation, his rivals—Roca, Alem, and Pellegrini—succeeded
in removing "a sick organ, [something] that it was necessary to extirpate in
order to prevent the putrefaction of the whole system, which would subsist for
many years longer."[4]   On the issue of revamping the economic system the
Unión Cívica remained silent; in fact, some argue that the UC acted in traditionalist, rightist fashion by dwelling merely on the moral indignation caused
by the exaggerated attention of the Generation of '80 to pecuniary matters.[5]

Thus, most reformers were not concerned with economic directions, the
industrial infrastructure, or the dependence on neocolonialist European powers.
Nor did the participants of uprisings during this period represent the aspirations of those victimized by the social stratification system we have described
in previous chapters. Not surprisingly, neither Roca nor Alem saw the solutions
to the nation's predicaments as resting on the separation of political power
from the social and economic power centers. Leftists, too, demanded constitutional guarantees, the Australian ballot, and universal suffrage but contended
in addition that democratic political mechanisms did not address the heart of
the matter. Thus socialists and anarchists viewed those actors with suspicion
and remained divorced, on the whole, from the events of 1890.[6]   These principles summarized primarily the political aspirations of the bourgeoisie comprised of the people involved in small-scale commercial and artesanal forms of
production and of some elite members who were threatened by serious cyclic
economic crises.[7]   In view of the limited political goals posited by middle-class
revolutionists, and considering the lack of subsequent fulfillment for so many
people, Roca's and Alem's actions would prove inadequate outlets for social
dissension. The Córdoba of the nineteenth century and the first few years of
the twentieth remained, nevertheless, relatively free of labor unrest and

completely free of revolts. The oligarchs in the Argentine interior, at least, maintained both their political patrimony and their social predominance because of the very same chaotic migrations to which we have referred. The impermanence of expansive marginal sectors of the society insured the continued unquestionability of the social order. The fluidity of Córdoba's population, as it streamed in and out of the city, maintained a labor pool of constant size and changing constituents. Simultaneously, the high rate of population turnover helped to prevent the formation and solidifying of class consciousness.

The same laborers did not persist in Córdoba long enough to protest against prevalent inequalities. No grass-roots opposition could last, and local labor leadership did not provide sufficient organization to catalyze any important movements. In the case of shoe workers or bakers, most strikes in late nineteenth- and early twentieth-century Córdoba died out quickly—sometimes within forty-eight hours. If they promised to last any great length of time, the activists were helped by socialist labor organizers imported from Buenos Aires. The local and regional oligarchy did not subscribe to restructuring socioeconomic norms, any more than it even began to question the nature of the existing state of affairs. In fact, most of Córdoba's leadership was strongly committed to the societal status quo, although some cleavages developed over issues such as the acceptable size and correct type of immigration. Through their organs, several deliberative and political bodies such as the Asociación Juventud Católica, the Club Unión Cívico de la Juventud, and the Unión Cívica, propagated issue- but not system-oriented dialectics. Thus the relative lack of social improvement in Córdoba did not carry with it the expected social tensions during this period: such a movement lacked not only leadership, but also followers. Marriage patterns and the exclusive character of the principal immigrant institutions, such as the mutual-aid associations, worked to isolate socially marginal groups of cordobeses and non-cordobeses and, eventually, to drive them out of the city in search of more receptive surroundings.

If life in Córdoba was a disappointment for so many, did all of Argentina also fail to satisfy the socioeconomic expectations of its people? How can we explain the growth of the Argentine middle class? Any specific discussion of similar experiences in other Argentine urban centers must remain limited for now.[8] Some evidence already indicates that the persistence rates for some Buenos Aires residents stood much higher than Córdoba's.[9] We can only speculate on the reasons for the differences, but they coexist on two levels: the economic and the practicable. While Buenos Aires did not achieve the same degree of industrialization as did other western metropolises, its potential for growth and industrial output were so much greater than the interior's that chances for finding the *adequate accommodation* of one's expectations were much improved in the port city. Moreover, Buenos Aires' larger population afforded improved marketability even for home- or workshop-tooled products.

Residents of Córdoba experienced lower persistence rates because they enjoyed a greater number of options than those available to porteños. Cordobeses had three alternatives in guiding their lives: 1) they could stay in the city; 2) they could move to another, presumably larger, Argentine city; or 3) they could move out of the country (especially true for immigrants). For most of Buenos Aires' population the second alternative was neither reasonable nor viable, while the economic and emotional costs involved in moving out of the country, on the other hand, were certainly much greater. Still, even the total European out-migration rate from Argentina between 1871 and 1906 averaged approximately 50 percent.[10] Most of the immigrants who stayed remained in Buenos Aires, and we can assume that most out-migrants, too, had formerly resided in that city.

The Argentine middle class that is said to have begun developing toward the end of the nineteenth century was, to a large degree, a fiction. Distinctions must be made between the economic parameters that we normally associate with membership in the middle class, and the labels and cultural values of bourgeoisie that were ascribed to certain occupational groups in Argentina. The high number of comerciantes among the immigrants did not generally signify vertical mobility from lower occupational and manual levels. Between a retail merchant renting and living in a small shop and getting by with the free labor of his family, and a brick-maker with his own kiln and living in the impoverished outskirts of the city, the basic distinctions were not economic. Yet the distinctions that have been made presumed that the first case represented a socioeconomic improvement over his previous level. If the merchant was an immigrant, so much the better, since his existence legitimated both the government's program of immigration and, by extension, the beneficent governance by an exceptional native group. The growth of the mercantile element in Córdoba (and, we suspect, in the rest of Argentina as well) did not result from upward socioeconomic movement as much as from the lateral mobility of people who had never been involved in unskilled and semiskilled tasks. The gap between the self-employed skilled operations and the mercantile trades was narrow, and often the two levels meshed.

Also, the high incidence of business bankruptcies nationally, and in Córdoba specifically, raises questions about the financial stability under which these comerciantes operated. Approximately 2,300 bankruptcies were declared by businessmen of the city of Córdoba between 1895 and 1935; in addition, nearly 500 suits were filed to reach agreements on debt liquidations between creditors and merchants.[11] Nearly all these businessmen were foreigners, with Jews and "Arabs" (as the Argentines called all Middle Easterners), who formed a significant contingent of hawkers, figuring disproportionately high. Many comerciantes worked from small inventories that could be easily wiped out by disruptions in either the transportation network of the manufacturing processes. In spite of the small scale on which even stationary merchants operated, the majority culture ascribed to them a role higher than that to which they belonged financially. Immigrants, especially those in nonmanual categories, were quite receptive to the ascriptions given to them by the majority culture.

The experiences of the members of the French and Spanish voluntary associations underline two premises in the processes of socialization and integration among immigrants in Argentina: 1) commonality of birthplace was a necessary but not a sufficient condition to coalesce each nationality; 2) while the proportions of different occupational groups varied within each immigrant institution, a minority of Europeans in Córdoba succeeded in their socialization by conforming to the official mores, and thereby positively oriented themselves to the norms of a nonmembership group which they took as their frame of reference.[12] It mattered little if the economic basis existed to legitimate such social mobility by orientation to a higher reference group; as we saw in the French case, the cooperation among the press, liberal leadership, and certain types of immigrants permitted the continuance of the scheme. Spaniards showed similar tendencies by accepting their ascribed importance in the local society and, in addition, generated their own separation from lower social classes, especially when those class constituents were Creoles.

Our investigation of the Spanish group also points out some shortcomings in the prevalent reasoning used to explain the immigrants' preponderantly urban settlement. Obstacles to land ownership were indeed difficult to surmount and undoubtedly played a crucial role in the Europeans' predilection for cities. But urban residence did not at all preclude land ownership by immigrants. The principal inhibiting factor was the lack of funds with which to purchase real property, and this obstacle straddled nationality. Moreover, migrants and natives had similar patterns of land ownership. Both groups favored urban real estate and were similarly oriented toward rural landholdings in that they were not multiprovincial but were restricted to Córdoba. The great majority of immigrants were not latifundists, but such, too, was the situation among Creoles. Neither cohort contained many estancia owners; instead, propertied individuals normally owned only small and medium parcels of land. In sum, absentee landlordism, usually associated with oligarchs, was not a trait monopolized by Creoles. For strong mercantile groups, commerce did not serve as a means unto itself but as the facilitator of collateral for acquiring the real basis of status and wealth: the means to speculate in land. In this mode, too, Europeans mirrored one of the norms of the majority culture. Nevertheless, the occurrences of propertied cases remained rare for the whole society because even commercial enterprise proved an unreliable source of funding.

The nature of materialistic culture persisted beyond liberal Argentina. As the nation's exports increased, they provided fabulous sums to the few who owned the sources of wealth. Economic behavior altered cultural norms, and conspicuous consumption became the obsession of the rich. The disparity between the poor and the wealthy would in time become more visible until the resulting tension generated today's apparently unbridgeable schism.

Notes

Introduction

1. *Hacer la América* became the expression commonly used to denote the goals of most European immigrants: to accumulate wealth in the western hemisphere, then to return home where they could live on their earnings, set up businesses, or purchase their own lands (see Ezequiel Martínez Estrada, *X-Ray of the Pampa,* p. 3). The immigrant represented to Martínez Estrada, as to many other Argentines, "a dreamer of personal dreams," but always a dangerous person in the end: ". . . the immigrant who came with the idea of returning and then stayed is an unattached, impervious and refractory being. He carries hidden intentions in his native soul, landscape, climate, and language and he is determined to return to his medium before dying" (*X-Ray,* pp. 370-371).

2. *El Progreso,* January 25, 1876, published a review of what some European observers were writing about opportunities for immigrants in Argentina. Some of the more scathing criticisms were being written by an Italian named Giovanni Florenzano, who argued that Italian emigration was socially, economically, and culturally detrimental to Italy and to the emigrants themselves. In his view, European and Argentine promoters, especially in France and Italy, were employing deception and get-rich-quick rhetoric to lure people to Argentina. Some opportunities did exist, he pointed out, in the area of the Gran Chaco; he quoted a returned Italian's memoirs of his days in Argentina that in

five years, after an initial investment of two thousand to three thousand pesos, a group of men could cut and sell enough timber for all to become rich.

3. *El Progreso*, February 23, 1876.

4. Miguel Angel Cárcano, *El estilo de vida argentino*, p. 100.

5. Gino Germani, "La movilidad social en la Argentina," in *Movilidad social en la sociedad industrial*, ed. Seymour M. Lipset and Reinhard Bendix, pp. 354-355.

6. Jorge Balán, Harley L. Browning, and Elizabeth Jelin, *Men in a Developing Society: Geographic and Social Mobility in Monterrey, Mexico;* Thomas Lynn Smith, *Colombia: Social Structure and the Process of Development;* and Ruben E. Reina, *Paraná: Social Boundaries in an Argentine City.*

7. Stephan Thernstrom, *Poverty and Progress: Social Mobility in a Nineteenth Century City.*

8. Tulio Halperín Donghi, *El revisionismo histórico argentino*, p. 71.

9. For examples of North American works in this vein, see Stephan Thernstrom, *Poverty and Progress: Social Mobility in a Nineteenth Century City;* Stephan Thernstrom, "Urbanization, Migration, and Social Mobility in Late Nineteenth Century America," in *Towards a New Past*, ed. Barton J. Bernstein; Stephan Thernstrom and Peter R. Knights, "Men in Motion: Some Data and Speculations about Urban Population Mobility in Nineteenth Century America," *Journal of Interdisciplinary History* 1 (Autumn 1970): 7-35; Peter R. Knights, *The Plain People of Boston, 1830-1860: A Study in City Growth;* Clyde Griffen, "Workers Divided: The Effect of Craft and Ethnic Differences in Poughkeepsie, New York, 1850-1880," in *Nineteenth Century Cities: Essays in the New Urban History*, ed. Stephan Thernstrom and Richard Sennett; Clyde Griffen, "Occupational Mobility in Nineteenth Century America: Problems and Possibilities," *Journal of Social History* 5 (Spring 1972): 310-330; Howard P. Chudacoff, *Mobile Americans: Residential and Social Mobility in Omaha, 1880-1920;* and Herbert G. Gutman, "The Reality of the Rags-to-Riches 'Myth': The Case of Paterson, New Jersey, Locomotive, Iron, and Machinery Manufactures, 1830-1880," in *Nineteenth Century Cities.*

10. Córdoba (Province), *Compilación de leyes, decretos, acuerdos de la Excelentísima Cámara de Justicia y demás disposiciones de carácter público dictadas en la provincia de Córdoba.* II (1810-1870): 271-272; III (1870-1873): 89, 92-93; IV (1874-1876): 94; XXIII (1896): 324-327.

11. Córdoba (Province), *Leyes* IX (1882): 93; XIII (1886): 156; XV (1888): 315; XX (1893): 292-293; XXII (1895): 249; XXVI (1899): 112-114.

12. Eugene F. Sofer and Mark D. Szuchman, "Educating Immigrants: Voluntary Associations in the Acculturation Process," in *Educational Alternatives in Latin America: Social Change and Social Stratification*, ed. Thomas J. La Belle, pp. 342-345.

13. Gino Germani, *Estructura social de la Argentina*, p. 74.

14. The data not significant to the .05 level are to be found in Tables 3.2 and 3.3. These statistical data refer to the individuals within the sample who persisted in Córdoba from one census to the next (1869-1895). Since most

people moved out of the city during the intercensal period, the number of persisters remained low, the tables reflect this phenomenon. Tests of significance applied to the group of persisters are not valid since they do not form a true random sample. It was impossible to determine how large the rate of out-migration was going to be found prior to the end of the research. Had it been possible, the solution might have been to increase the size of each sample N, thereby assuring that we would be left with an appropriately large subgroup of persisters n. But this solution would have entailed such great efforts that it would be several more years before any results would appear, all the time being spent on the tracing of a large multiple of the N cases presented here. To illustrate this point, consider that the accuracy of the estimate made from the sample comes from $\sigma/\sqrt{N}$, where σ is the population standard deviation, and N the absolute size of the sample. Thus the sample's accuracy, if we double the sample size, would increase only by $\sqrt{2}=1.41$ times. Doubling the precision of the sample estimates requires the quadrupling of sample size ($\sqrt{4}=2$). (See Roderick Floud, *An Introduction to Quantitative Methods for Historians*, p. 175.) Reliance on statistical tests of significance in order to add weight to historical evidence has obvious limitations. But we can also find support for our contentions through the patterns which hold up all the way from the sample size N to subgroups n, especially when we can add illustrative and representative cases to trace the human reliability behind the data (see Charles M. Dollar and Richard J. Jensen, *Historian's Guide to Statistics: Quantitative Analysis and Historical Research*, pp. 13-15). This is also relevant in our own case, in which several computer runs testing the 1,583 individuals drawn from sample cases and members of their households showed patterns identical to the runs employing only the 696 cases of the sample group.

15. James Lockhart, *Spanish Peru, 1532-1560: A Colonial Society*, p. 269.

16. Natalie Rogoff, "Social Stratification in France and in the United States," *American Journal of Sociology* 58 (January 1953): 348.

17. S. M. Miller, "Comparative Social Mobility," *Current Sociology* 9, no. 1 (1960): 1-89; Peter M. Blau and Otis Dudley Duncan, Occupational Mobility in the United States," in *Structured Social Inequality: A Reader in Comparative Social Stratification*, ed. Celia S. Heller, pp. 340-352; Seymour M. Lipset and Reinhard Bendix, *Social Mobility in Industrial Society*; Gerhard Lenski, *Power and Privilege;* C. Wright Mills, "The Middle Classes in Middle-Sized Cities," *American Sociological Review* 11 (December 1946): 520-529; Robert W. Hodge, Donald J. Treiman, and Peter H. Rossi, "A Comparative Study of Occupational Prestige," in *Class, Status, and Power: Social Stratification in Comparative Perspective*, ed. Reinhard Bendix and Seymour M. Lipset, 2nd ed., pp. 309-321; and Robert W. Hodge, Paul M. Siegel, and Peter H. Rossi, "Occupational Prestige in the United States: 1925-1963," *American Journal of Sociology* 70 (November 1964): 286-302. For a discussion of comparative survey studies, see Sidney Verba, "Cross-National Survey Research: The Problems of Credibility," in *Comparative Methods in Sociology: Essays on Trends and Applications*, ed. Ivan Vallier, pp. 309-356.

18. Joseph A. Kahl and James Davis, "A Comparison of Indexes of Socioeconomic Status," *American Sociological Review* 20 (June 1955): 317-325; Alex Inkeles and Peter H. Rossi, "National Comparisons of Occupational Prestige," *American Journal of Sociology* 61 (January 1956): 329-339.

19. Thernstrom, *Poverty and Progress,* pp. 224-239.

20. Fernando H. Cardoso and José L. Reyna, "Industrialization, Occupational Structure, and Social Stratification in Latin America," in *Constructive Change in Latin America,* ed. Cole Blasier, pp. 22-55; Roberto Cortés Conde, "Problemas del crecimiento industrial (1870-1914)," in *Argentina, sociedad de masas,* ed. Torcuato S. Di Tella, Gino Germani, and Jorge Graciarena, pp. 59-84.

21. Phillip Wagner and Marvin Mikesell, eds., *Readings in Cultural Geography,* pp. 1-2.

22. David Sopher, "Place and Location: Notes on the Spatial Patterning of Culture," in *The Idea of Culture in the Social Sciences,* ed. Louis Schneider and Charles Bonjean, p. 113.

23. On pp. 19-20 of *The Varieties of History: From Voltaire to the Present* (ed. Fritz Stern) is a discussion of some of the implications. Negative repercussions of "official histories" also took place in Argentina; for example, *mitristas* preparing a history of San Martín injudiciously edited the correspondence between the general and the Buenos Aires authorities in order to hide the rough language that he sometimes used in his demands for speedier responses to his requests from the field.

24. Enrique Martínez Paz, *La formación histórica de la provincia de Córdoba.*

25. Efraín U. Bischoff, *Historia de la provincia de Córdoba.*

Chapter 1: Prospects of the City

1. Rodolfo de Ferrari Rueda, *Historia de Córdoba,* p. 89.

2. For an adequate historical overview of the University of Córdoba and a good presentation of how it was regarded by Argentina's intelligentsia, see Francisco Jurado Padilla, *La Universidad de Córdoba, tribuna del pensamiento nacional.*

3. Emilio E. Sánchez, *Del pasado cordobés en la vida argentina,* p. 21.

4. Padilla, *La Universidad,* pp. 19-22.

5. *El Eco de Córdoba,* January 14, 1863.

6. Córdoba (Province), *Leyes* I (1810-1870): 147.

7. Córdoba (Province), *Leyes* I (1810-1870): 165.

8. Córdoba (Province), *Leyes* II (1810-1870): 142.

9. Juan Bautista Alberdi, *Bases y puntos de partida para la organización política de la República Argentina,* p. 73.

10. Raúl Scalabrini Ortíz, *Historia de los ferrocarriles argentinos,* 5th ed., pp. 94-95.

11. *El Eco de Córdoba,* February 24, 1863.

12. *El Eco de Córdoba,* April 16, 1863.

13. *El Eco de Córdoba,* September 17, 1863.

14. H. C. Ross Johnson, *Vacaciones de un inglés en la Argentina,* p. 74. This account comes from the author's travels in the country in 1867.

15. Manuel E. Río and Luis Achával, *Geografía de la provincia de Córdoba,* II, 452-453.

16. Argentine Republic, A.G.N. (see list of abbreviations), *Primer censo de la República Argentina* (1869) (hereafter cited as *Censo 1869*), pp. 672-673.

17. The relationship between living quarters and industrial patterns is reviewed in J. E. Havel, *Habitat y vivienda,* 3rd ed., pp. 5-21.

18. Azucena Perla Della Casa de Tauro, "Censo de la ciudad de Córdoba del año 1832. Estudio demográfico," p. 12.

19. *La Patria,* July 4, 1895.

20. Sample data.

21. A.G.N., *Censo 1869,* pp. 642-669.

Chapter 2: On Being Poor and Moving On

1. Aníbal Arcondo, "Notas para el estudio del trabajo compulsivo en la región de Córdoba," in *Homenaje al Doctor Ceferino Garzón Maceda,* p. 133.

2. A.G.N., *Censo 1869,* pp. 236-237.

3. Córdoba (Province), *Reglamento para la administración de justicia y policía en la campaña de Córdoba,* n.p.

4. *La Carcajada,* May 31, 1873.

5. Arcondo, "Notas para el . . . trabajo compulsivo," p. 140. Argentine literature on the relationship between economic distention and family disruption is exiguous. Some similarities become apparent, though not yet provable, by the experiences of other areas; see Harold Perkin, *The Origins of Modern English Society,* pp. 149-160, for some examples.

6. Julio S. Maldonado, *La Córdoba de mi infancia,* 2nd ed., pp. 32-34, 102.

7. Emiliano Endrek, *El mestizaje en Córdoba, siglo XVIII y principios del XIX,* p. 98.

8. Endrek, *El mestizaje,* p. 25.

9. Maldonado, *La Córdoba,* p. 108.

10. Maldonado, *La Córdoba,* p. 73.

11. Córdoba (City), R.C. (see list of abbreviations), *Protocolos de Defunciones,* 1884, p. 269.

12. R. C., *Protocolos de Defunciones,* 1891, VI, 69; A.G.N., *Segundo censo de la República Argentina (1895)* (hereafter cited as *Censo 1895*), Leg. 885.

13. R.C., *Protocolos de Defunciones,* 1877, No. 233.

14. A.G.N., *Censo 1895,* Leg. 885; R.C., *Protocolos de Matrimonios, 1895;* A.H.P.A.T. (see list of abbreviations), 2a Nominación, 1922, Leg. 58, Exp. 13, Declaratoria de Herederos.

15. *La Carcajada,* December 1, 1872.

16. Javier Marrazzo, *Ciudades, pueblos y colonias de la República Argentina,* 2nd ed., p. 156.

17. James R. Scobie, *Buenos Aires: Plaza to Suburb, 1870-1910,* pp. 182, 186.

18. Joseph Tulchin, "Agricultural Credit and Politics in Argentina, 1910-1922," p. 304.

19. Tulchin, "Agricultural Credit," p. 10.

20. *La Carcajada,* January 22, 1882.

21. Córdoba (Province), *Guía general de Córdoba* (1901, 1904, 1918, 1921), *passim.*

22. A.C. (see list of abbreviations), *Defunciones,* 1870, No. 235.

23. A.G.N., *Censo 1869,* Legs. 156-163; A.G.N., *Censo 1895,* Legs. 883-894; A.C., *Defunciones,* 1869-1880; R.C., *Defunciones,* 1881-1895.

24. *El Eco de Córdoba,* March 13, 1878.

25. *El Porvenir,* August 30, 1892.

26. *El Porvenir,* October 8, 1886.

27. The amount represented 5.3 percent of the annual budget. Córdoba (Province), *Leyes* II, (1810-1870): 440-443.

28. Córdoba (Province), *Leyes* II (1810-1870): 552; III (1870-1873): 83.

29. Córdoba (Province), *Leyes* II (1810-1870): 576.

30. Córdoba (Province), *Leyes XVI* (1889): 212-249; A.H.P. (see list of abbreviations), *Gobierno,* "Diversos Asuntos," 1891, Tomo 11, f. 38.

31. For example, in 1890 private donations amounted to 1,977 pesos, while subventions from the province totaled 4,200 pesos (A.H.P., *Gobierno,* "Diversos Asuntos," 1891, Tomo 11, f. 38.

32. A.H.P., *Gobierno,* "Diversos Asuntos," 1894, Tomo 18, ff. 108-111.

33. *El Porvenir,* May 2, 1891.

34. Córdoba (Province), *Leyes* XII (1885): 92-93; XVI (1889): 55.

35. Córdoba (Province), *Leyes* XIV (1887): 26-28.

36. Córdoba (Province), *Leyes* XII (1885): 70-71; Arcondo, "Notas para el . . . trabajo compulsivo," p. 142.

37. *El Porvenir,* September 30, 1887.

38. The sample cases were extracted, by means of a table of random numbers, from the 1869 census and traced into the 1895 census schedules for the city of Córdoba, which are kept in the Archivo General de la Nación. Stratified into cordobés (N=369) and non-cordobés (N=327) samples, the statistical results are significant to the .05 level. We accept a confidence level of 95 percent, and a confidence interval of plus or minus 5 percent. This means that if we were to draw an infinite number of samples of sizes 369 and 327, respectively, the results from 95 percent of these samples would be within 5 percent of the "true" values of the universe from which the samples were drawn, that is, the values found in the populations of cordobeses and non-cordobeses in the city.

39. *La Carcajada,* July 13, 1873.

40. *La Carcajada,* June 14, 1874.

41. *El Progreso,* January 15, 1876.

42. *La Carcajada,* June 9, 1878.

43. *El Porvenir,* June 18, 1887.

44. *La Carcajada,* November 6, 1887, and December 8, 1888.

45. *La Carcajada,* August 14, 1877.

46. Córdoba (City), *Memorias del Intendente Municipal, 1885-1888,* in Hilda Iparraguirre, "Notas para el estudio de la demografía de la ciudad de Córdoba en el período, 1869-1914," in *Homenaje al Doctor Ceferino Garzón Maceda,* p. 277.

47. Juan B. González, *El encarecimiento de la vida en la República Argentina,* p. 40.

48. González, *El encarecimiento,* p. 41.

49. Córdoba (City), *Censo general de la población . . . de 1906,* p. xvi.

50. Iparraguirre, "Notas para . . . la demografía," pp. 275-276.

51. Córdoba (City), *Memoria municipal correspondiente al ejercicio 1888,* p. 49.

52. José M. Alvarez, *La lucha por la salud: Su estado actual en la ciudad de Córdoba,* p. 205; *La Patria,* November 17, 1894.

53. *El Porvenir,* July 8, 1888.

54. *La Carcajada,* April 23, 1882.

55. *La Carcajada,* November 18, 1880.

56. Stephan Thernstrom, "Reflections on the New Urban History," *Daedalus* 100 (Spring 1971): 367.

57. Howard P. Chudacoff, *The Evolution of American Urban Society,* pp. 83-84; and *Mobile Americans: Residential and Social Mobility in Omaha, 1880-1920.*

Chapter 3: On Being Rich and on Getting By

1. During two fifty-six-year periods (1869-1925 and 1895-1951) through which we traced both sets of sample members and attached households drawn from two random samples out of the 1869 and 1895 census schedules, the yearly incidence of probated estates of all magnitudes increased by approximately 9 percent.

2. For comparisons of urban dwellings at this time in Buenos Aires, see James Scobie, *Buenos Aires: Plaza to Suburb, 1870-1910,* pp. 43-45, and "Buenos Aires as a Commercial-Bureaucratic City, 1880-1910: Characteristics of a City's Orientation," in *The American Historical Review* 77 (October 1972): 1035-1073; Diana Hernando, "*Casa y familia:* Spatial Biographies in 19th Century Buenos Aires."

3. Azucena Perla Della Casa de Tauro, "Censo de la ciudad de Córdoba del año 1832: Estudio demográfico," p. 17.

4. Emiliano Endrek, *El mestizaje en Córdoba, siglo XVIII y principios del XIX,* p. 47; Della Casa, "Censo de 1832," pp. 19, 25 ff.

5. Dora Estela Celson, "Censo de la ciudad de Córdoba del año 1840: Estudio demográfico," Cuadro VII d. The existence of slavery well into the nineteenth century was not unique to Córdoba; the 1824 census schedules for the city of Paraná, for example, also show that most white families had either servants (probably indentured) or slaves. (see Ruben E. Reina, *Paraná: Social Boundaries in an Argentine City,* pp. 16-17).

6. Della Casa, "Censo de 1832," p. 56; Celson, "Censo de 1840," pp. 10-11, Cuadro V d.

7. *La Carcajada,* March 8, 1874.

8. *La Carcajada,* May 31, 1874.

9. Scobie, *Buenos Aires,* p. 250.

10. Aníbal Arcondo, "Tierra y política de tierras en Córdoba," *Revista de Economía y Estadística* 13, nos. 3-4 (1969): 36.

11. Sample data.

12. A.H.P.A.T., 2a Nominación, 1887, Leg. 7, Exp. 5, Sucesorio.

13. *El Eco de Córdoba,* August 26, 1869.

14. Manuel E. Río and Luis Achával, *Geografía de la provincia de Córdoba,* II, 319-321.

15. A.H.P.A.T., 2a Nominación, 1887, Leg. 7, Exp. 5, Sucesorio.

16. Sample data.

17. A.G.N., *Censo 1869,* Legs. 161-162.

18. A.H.P.A.T., 1a Nominación, 1898, Leg. 18, Exp. 1, Sucesorio.

19. A.G.N., *Censo 1869,* Leg. 159.

20. A.U.N.C. (see list of abbreviations), *Libro 2° de Grados,* 1806-1893.

21. A.U.N.C., *Libro 3° de Grados,* 1894-1913.

22. A.H.P.A.T., 3a. Nominación, 1909, Leg. 4, Exp. 3, Declaratoria de Herederos.

23. Sample data.

24. A.H.P.A.T., 2a Nominación, 1908, Leg. 10, Exp. 4, Sucesorio; 2a Nominación, 1903, Leg. 7, Exp. 13, Sucesorio.

25. Tulio Halperín Donghi, *Revolución y guerra: Formación de una élite dirigente en la Argentina criolla,* p. 22.

26. H. S. Ferns, *Britain and Argentina in the Nineteenth Century,* p. 144.

27. *La Patria,* August 4, 1898.

28. Roberto Cortés Conde, *Corrientes inmigratorias y surgimiento de industrias en Argentina (1870-1914),* pp. 10-11.

29. Cortés Conde, *Corrientes inmigratorias,* p. 18.

30. Santiago Juan Albarrancín, *Bosquejo histórico, político y económico de la provincia de Córdoba,* pp. 258-263.

31. Río and Achával, *Geografía,* II, p. 277.

32. Sample data.

33. A.G.N., *Censo 1869,* Leg. 159.

34. A.H.P.A.T., 1a Nominación, 1888, Leg. 14, Exp. 7.

35. A.G.H., *Censo 1869,* Leg. 163.

36. A.C., *Defunciones,* 1878, No. 24.

37. R.C., *Defunciones,* 1891, I, p. 265 v.

38. A.H.P.A.T., 2a Nominación, 1919, Leg. 21, Exp. 7.

39. R.C., *Defunciones,* 1883, p. 403.

40. A.G.N., *Censo 1895,* Leg. 888.

41. Córdoba (City), *Censo general de 1906,* p. xv.

42. Córdoba (City), *Censo de 1906,* pp. 116, 122.

43. A.G.N., *Censo 1895,* Leg. 888.

44. A.G.N., *Censo 1895,* Leg. 890.

45. A.H.P.A.T., 4a Nominación, 1912, Leg. 16, Exp. 11, Declaratoria de Herederos.

46. A.G.N., *Censo 1869,* Leg. 160.

47. R.C., *Defunciones,* 1887, p. 530; A.H.P.A.T., 1a Nominación, 1890, Leg. 6, Exp. 1, Sucesorio.

Chapter 4: Urbanism, Racism, and Social Differentiation

1. Roberto Cortés Conde, *Corrientes inmigratorias y surgimiento de industrias en Argentina (1870-1914),* p. 5.

2. Gino Germani, in *Assimilation of Immigrants in Urban Areas: Methodological Notes,* 2nd ed., proposes a number of psychosocial approaches which may prove useful for those researching the reactions of recently arrived migrants to urban centers. The applicability of some of his formulations to historical research of nineteenth-century Argentine cities is, however, somewhat limited. Of the histories of immigrant assimilation in the United States, perhaps the best known is Oscar Handlin's *The Uprooted.*

3. Gino Germani, "Mass Immigration and Modernization in Argentina," in *Masses in Latin America,* ed. Irving L. Horowitz, p. 322.

4. David Crew, "Definitions of Modernity: Social Mobility in a German Town, 1880-1901," *Journal of Social History* 7 (Fall 1973): 53-60. Crew's sample of workers in the German town of Bochur in the Ruhr showed that between 1880 and 1890, 87.1 percent of the unskilled and semiskilled remained in their occupational levels.

5. Crew, p. 68.

6. Eric J. Hobsbawm, "Labor History and Ideology," *Journal of Social History* 7 (Summer 1974): 375.

7. Clyde Griffen, "Public Opinion in Urban History," *The Journal of Interdisciplinary History* 4 (Winter 1974): 471-472.

8. Virginia Yans-McLaughlin convincingly uses a functionalist approach to the study of immigrant assimilation. Drawing upon the premise of cultural anthropologists that traditional values can be adapted to integrate with modern practices and result in economic development, Ms. Yans-McLaughlin uses Clifford Geertz' framework to show the similarities in the socioeconomic behavior of south Italians in their native Mezzogiorno and in Buffalo, New York, at the turn of the century ("A Flexible Tradition: South Italian Immigrants Confront a New York Experience," *Journal of Social History* 7 [Summer 1974]: 492).

9. Max Weber, "Class, Status, Party," in *From Max Weber: Essays in Sociology,* eds. Hans H. Gerth and C. Wright Mills, pp. 183-185.

10. Domingo F. Sarmiento, *Life in the Argentine Republic in the Days of the Tyrants or Civilization and Barbarism,* p. 33.

11. Sarmiento, *Life in the Argentine Republic,* p. 34.

12. Eric J. Hobsbawm, *The Age of Revolution, 1789-1848,* pp. 359-362.

13. The liberals' philosophy resembled some thoughts of twentieth-century United States sociologists, such as Robert Park ("Human Migration and the Marginal Man," *American Journal of Sociology* 33 [May 1928]: 881-893).

14. A.G.N., Ministerio del Interior, VII (1869), *Informe del agente en Suiza y Alemania,* Carlos Beck, 23 de noviembre, 1868.

15. Domingo F. Sarmiento, *Conflicto y armonías de las razas en América.*

16. Héctor Félix Bravo, *Sarmiento, pedagogo social,* pp. 17-18.

17. Hobart A. Spalding, Jr., *Argentine Sociology from the End of the Nineteenth Century to World War I,* p. 7. One of the better known works expounding on the interior quality of the racial mixtures that developed in Argentina (and other Latin American countries) is Carlos O. Bunge's *Nuestra América;* José Ingenieros lamented the exiguous Argentine cultural traditions in *Las direcciones filosóficas de la cultura argentina,* 3rd ed., pp. 8-10.

18. José Ramos Mejía, *Las multitudes argentinas: Estudios de psicología colectiva . . .*

19. Manuel E. Río, "Córdoba, 1810-1910," *Revista de la Junta Provincial de Historia de Córdoba* 1 (1960): 11-76; and "Consideraciones históricas y sociológicas sobre la provincia de Córdoba, deberes de la juventud en la época presente," in *Córdoba: Su fisonomía, su misión. Escritos y discursos,* p. 95.

20. Stanislav Andreski, *The Uses of Comparative Sociology,* p. 223.

21. David Rock, *Politics in Argentina, 1890-1930: The Rise and Fall of Radicalism,* p. 12.

22. Córdoba (Province), *Leyes* XXIII (1896): 418.

23. Don H. Doyle, "The Social Functions of Voluntary Associations in a Nineteenth-Century American Town," *Social Science History* 1 (Spring 1977): 336.

24. Gino Germani writes that manifestations of patriotism often came about for the Italians after emigration—not before, when identification with their country of origin was quite low. Expressions of national identity, according to Germani, came from the elites of each nationality, yet the position of the elites varied among classes; with the exception of a few journalists, the professionals among the elite often became spokesmen for the majority culture and operated within the existing political framework (see "Mass Immigration," p. 312).

25. Amilcar Razori, *Historia de la ciudad argentina,* III, 104.

26. When we excluded priests, who were barred from membership, the percentage of professionals outside the Société (4.8 percent) fell below that of the professionals who joined (6.2 percent). The data for this research came from the manuscript census returns for the city of Córdoba from 1869 and 1895, kept in the Archivo General de la Nación, and from the *Livres des societaires* of the Société Française de Secours Mutuels du Córdoba (hereafter cited as S.F.S.M.), kept in the association's archive.

27. S.F.S.M., *Procès-Verbaux,* I, 1.

28. S.F.S.M., *Réglement de 1877 modifié en 1881,* p. 1.

29. S.F.S.M., *Procès-Verbaux,* I, 1.

30. S.F.S.M., *Procès-Verbaux,* II, 63.

31. S.F.S.M., *Procès-Verbaux,* I, 18-19.

32. S.F.S.M., *Procès-Verbaux,* II, 28.

33. Unlike what occurred in the United States, little evidence seems to exist of joint political activities in Córdoba by different nationalities much before 1900. For a view of the long tradition of political activities of immigrants in the United States, see Oscar Handlin, *Boston's Immigrants, 1790-1880,* rev. ed., pp. 153-155. By the end of the nineteenth century, Córdoba began to feel a few of the waves of social unrest which were taking place in the littoral area. For an overview of these movements, see José Panettieri, *Los trabajadores.*

34. There are indications, moreover, that some of those listing themselves as skilled workers were in fact the owners of small workshops or *talleres.* In such an event, we must suspect that the figures for the nonmanual category are somewhat depressed by excluding those petty proprietors who fell within the skilled group.

35. Eugene F. Sofer, "Voluntary Associations and the Achievement of Bourgeois Norms: The Case of the Jews of Buenos Aires, 1890-1930."

36. S.F.S.M., *Procès-Verbaux,* II, 55. Year after year, however, the new recruits fit into the social patterns of the successful, older members.

37. *El Porvenir,* September 30, 1887.

38. *El Progreso,* September 4, 1878.

39. In 1895, 72.3 percent of the city's immigrants were literate, compared to only 45.5 percent of the Creoles (Argentine Republic, *Segundo Censo* (1895), II 281; Córdoba (City), *Censo de 1906,* p. lxi). For a general discussion of the oligarchy's educational policies, see Hobart A. Spalding, Jr., "Education in Argentina, 1890-1914: The Limits of Oligarchical Reform," *Journal of Interdisciplinary History* 3 (Summer 1972): 31-61.

40. Córdoba (Province), *Leyes* XXI (1894): 221. For a broader view of the role of voluntary associations in nonformal education in Argentina, see Eugene Sofer and Mark Szuchman, "Educating Immigrants: Voluntary Associations in the Acculturation Process," in *Educational Alternatives in Latin America: Social Change and Social Stratifications,* ed. Thomas J. LaBelle, pp. 334-359.

41. A.G.N., *Censo 1895,* Leg. 890.

42. *El Porvenir,* January 9, 1889.

43. Louis Wirth, "Urbanism as a Way of Life," *American Journal of Sociology* 44 (July 1938): 23-24.

44. *El Progreso,* January 15, 1876.

45. *La Patria,* June 25, 1895.

46. *La Patria,* June 19, 1895.

Chapter 5: Class Formation and Cultural Pluralism

1. In this study we are not concerned with statistical inferences such as levels of significance or probability, since we are not studying a sample of the available membership but its universe or totality.

2. Argentine Republic, *Primer censo (1869)*, pp. 636-637.

3. A.G.N., *Censo 1869*, Leg. 156.

4. *La Carcajada*, March 25, 1882.

5. Manuel Ugarte, *El porvenir de América Latina*, p. 36; Carl Solberg, *Immigration and Nationalism: Argentina and Chile, 1890-1914*, p. 20.

6. Juan F. Marsal, *Hacer la América: Autobiografía de un inmigrante español en la Argentina*, p. 126.

7. Group data.

8. *La Carcajada*, October 8, 1876.

9. Efraín U. Bischoff, *Historia de la provincia de Córdoba*, II, 225.

10. *Los Principios*, October 15, 1895.

11. Oscar Handlin, *Boston's Immigrants, 1790-1880*, rev. ed., pp. 155-156.

12. Asociación Española de Socorros Mútuos de Córdoba (hereafter cited as A.E.S.M.), *Centenario*, p. 18.

13. A.G.N., *Censo 1869*, Leg. 162.

14. A.E.S.M., *Libro de actas de asambleas generales, 1872-1915*, Sesión preparatoria, June 2, 1872, pp. 1-2.

15. A.E.S.M., *Libro de asambleas*, Asamblea constituyente, June 9, 1872, p. 5.

16. A.E.S.M., *Libro de asambleas*, February 6, 1881, pp. 63-65.

17. A.E.S.M., *Libro de asambleas*, January 22, 1882, p. 73.

18. Group data.

19. A.E.S.M., *Actas de la Junta Directiva, 1872-1885*, I, July 28, 1876, 92.

20. A.E.S.M., *Actas*, I, August 4, 1876, pp. 93-95.

21. A.E.S.M., *Libro de asambleas*, August 8, 1886, pp. 109-110.

22. Group data.

23. A.E.S.M., *Actas*, I, August 15, 1874, 42-43.

24. A.E.S.M., *Libro de registro de socios, 1902*, n.p.

25. Group data.

26. Group data.

27. Manuel Bejarano, "Inmigración y estructuras tradicionales en Buenos Aires (1854-1930)," in *Los fragmentos del poder*, eds. Torcuato S. DiTella and Tulio Halperín Donghi, p. 81.

28. A.E.S.M., *Libro de registro, 1902*, n.p.

29. *Guía general de Córdoba, 1901*.

30. *Guía general de Córdoba, 1904*.

31. A.E.S.M., *Libro de registro, 1902*, n.p.

32. A.H.P.A.T., 2a Nominación, 1905, Leg. 12, Exp. 27, Declaratoria de Herederos.

33. Felix Garzón Maceda, *La medicina en Córdoba*, I, 448-451.

34. One can make this observation by scanning through Córdoba's extant city directories for the years 1901, 1904, 1918, and 1921. The principal change was increased concentration of these low-status residents within those sections.

35. A.E.S.M., *Libro de asambleas*, August 8, 1886, pp. 109-110.

36. A.E.S.M., *Libro de asambleas,* August 4, 1889, p. 125.

37. A.E.S.M., *Libro de asambleas,* October 14, 1888, p. 122.

38. Victims of the turmoil of the early 1890s were the attendance records of the Asociación for the years 1890-1892.

39. Group data.

40. Gino Germani, "Mass Immigration and Modernization in Argentina," in *Masses in Latin America,* ed. Irving L. Horowitz, p. 312.

41. A.E.S.M., *Actas,* I, October 13, 1883, 213.

42. A.E.S.M., *Actas,* I, June 25, 1872, 7-8.

43. A.E.S.M., *Actas,* I, January ?, 1883, 205.

44. Iparraguirre and Pianetto write of wide participation during the period of the Spanish American War; however, that political activity was neither conducted nor sanctioned by the Asociación Española officially, but by ad hoc groups composed of members and nonmembers (Hilda Iparraguirre and Ofelia Pianetto, *La organización de la clase obrera en Córdoba, 1870-1895,* p. 28).

45. For an overview of the difficulties in Spanish foreign policy during this period, see Raymond Carr, *Spain, 1808-1939,* pp. 359 ff.

46. A.E.S.M., *Actas,* II, October 2, 1885, 2-6.

47. A.E.S.M., *Actas,* II, October 25, 1885, 6-8.

48. A.E.S.M., *Actas,* II, August 21, 1885, 2.

49. We gathered the figures from A.E.S.M., *Libro de asambleas,* and *Actas,* I and II.

50. Ramón Menéndez Pidal, *The Spaniards in Their History,* p. 44.

51. Sample data.

52. Juan José Sebreli, *Buenos Aires, vida cotidiana y alienación,* 4th ed., pp. 74-75.

53. Germani, "Mass Immigration," p. 313.

54. *La Patria,* September 15, 1896.

55. A.E.S.M., *Libro de asambleas,* August 30, 1901, p. 217.

56. A.E.S.M., *Libro de asambleas,* August 30, 1901, p. 218.

57. David E. Apter, "Radicalization and Embourgeoisement: Some Hypotheses for a Comparative Study of History," *Journal of Interdisciplinary History* 1 (Winter 1971): 277; and E. Digby Baltzell, *The Protestant Establishment,* p. 70.

58. Iparraguirre and Pianetto, *La organización,* p. 28.

Chapter 6: Mobility Patterns among Spaniards

1. Group data.

2. Evidence of this can be gleaned from an in-depth look into A.H.P.A.T., Escribanías Nos. 1-4, 1869-1882, and Nominaciones Nos. 1-5, 1883-1925.

3. Charles S. Sargent, *The Spatial Evolution of Greater Buenos Aires, Argentina, 1870-1930,* p. 29.

4. Sargent, *The Spatial Evolution,* p. 30.

5. Ofelia Pianetto, "Industria y formación de la clase obrera en la ciudad de Córdoba, 1880-1906," in *Homenaje al Doctor Ceferino Garzón Maceda,* pp. 342-343.

6. Marta Sánchez, "Movimientos de lucha y organización de la clase obrera en la ciudad de Córdoba, 1895-1905," in *Homenaje al Doctor Ceferino Garzón Maceda,* p. 393.

7. Juan Bialet-Massé, *El estado de las clases obreras argentinas a comienzos del siglo,* p. 216.

8. *Los Principios,* May 21, 1901.

9. Pianetto, "Industria y formación," p. 352.

10. Bialet-Massé, *El estado,* p. 217.

11. Bialet-Massé, *El estado,* p. 219.

12. This phase of the research involved going beyond the litigation records held in the Archivo de Tribunales of the Archivo Histórico de la Provincia, since they did not contain data beyond the year 1925. Because we had no knowledge of dates of deaths beyond 1902, we had to trace the members into the juridical records through a timespan during which we would find anyone's death involving probates or financial litigations. In order to do so, we extended the tracing process into the Archivo de Tribunales of the Palacio de Justicia through 1951. In this manner we made sure to find any extant probate cases.

13. A.E.S.M., *Libro de registro, 1883,* n.p.

14. A.G.N., *Censo 1895,* Leg. 886.

15. *Guía general de Córdoba, 1901,* p. 82.

16. A.H.P.A.T., 1a Nominación, 1907, Leg. 20, Exp. 22, Declaratoria de Herederos.

17. Horatio Alger, *Ragged Dick and Mark, the Match Boy,* p. 46.

18. Javier Marrazzo, *Ciudades, pueblos y colonias de la República Argentina,* 2nd ed., p. 293.

19. A.H.P.A.T., la Nominación, 1923, Leg. 19, Exp. 19, Sucesorio.

20. *Catastro Machado. Copia fiel del plano de la ciudad de Córdoba del año 1890.*

21. Aníbal Arcondo, "Tierra y política de tierras en Córdoba," *Revista de Economía y Estadística* 13 (1969): 38.

22. See data of probates from the sample of Córdoba's general population in 1869.

23. Miguel Angel Cárcano, *Evolución histórica del régimen de la tierra pública, 1810-1916,* 3rd ed., p. 382.

24. Cárcano, *Evolución,* p. 392.

25. For examples of writings using such theories, see Tomás Roberto Fillol, *Social Factors in Economic Development: The Argentine Case,* p. 27; Ricardo M. Ortíz, *Historia económica de la Argentina, 1850-1930,* I, 200-205; and James R. Scobie, *Revolution on the Pampas: A Social History of Argentine Wheat, 1860-1910,* pp. 121-122, et passim.

26. Córdoba (City), *Censo de 1906,* pp. 113, 114, 130.

27. A.H.P.A.T., 2a Nominación, 1895, Leg. 1, Exp. 7, Testamentaria.

28. A.H.P.A.T., 3a Escribanía, 1874, Leg. 157, Exp. 17, Sucesorio.

29. Gustavo Beyhaut, et al., "Los inmigrantes en el sistema ocupacional argentino," in *Argentina, sociedad de masas,* eds. Torcuato S. Di Tella, Gino

Germani, and Jorge Graciarena, p. 94.

30. Córdoba (City), *Censo de 1906*, pp. 177, 193. The census did not break down by nationalities the population owning land devoted to livestock.

31. Gerhard E. Lenski, *Power and Privilege*, p. 87.

32. Seymour M. Lipset, *The First New Nation*.

33. David Apter, "Radicalization and Embourgeoisement: Some Hypotheses for a Comparative Study of History," *Journal of Interdisciplinary History* 1 (Winter 1971): 268.

34. Apter, "Radicalization and Embourgeoisement," p. 300.

Chapter 7: The Limits of the Melting Pot

1. A glance at the tables presented in the studies and reports by Juan A. Alsina and Guillermo Wilcken verify that a considerable number of European immigrants entered Argentina from Montevideo (Juan A. Alsina, *La inmigración europea en la República Argentina*, esp. pp. 83, 84, 110, 125, and 128; Guillermo Wilcken, *Memoria sobre inmigración al Ministro del Interior*).

2. The data presented here were gathered from the marriages recorded in the archive of the archbishopric of Córdoba and in the city's Municipal Civil Registry, and from the notarial records in the Judicial Archive and in the Archivo Histórico de la Provincia. The sample, randomly selected from a universe of approximately 3,240 relevant unions contracted between 1869 and 1909, totaled 648 cases. We based the selection of marriages on the ones in which the grooms were not natives of the city of Córdoba but were marrying in it. All statistical results are significant to the .0001 level. We accept a confidence level of 99 percent and a confidence interval of plus or minus 5 percent. This means that if we were to draw an infinitely large number of samples of size 648, the results from 99 percent of these samples would be within 5 percent of the "true" values of the universe from which the samples were drawn, that is, the values found in all the marriages contracted in Córdoba in which the groom was not born in the city.

3. Max Weber, "Religious Rejections of the World and Their Directions," in *From Max Weber: Essays in Sociology*, ed. Hans H. Gerth and C. Wright Mills, pp. 343-344.

4. William J. Goode, "Marital Satisfaction and Instability: A Cross Cultural Class Analysis of Divorce Rates," *International Social Science Journal* 14 (1962): 507-526.

5. Examples of historical and sociological uses of marriage in this vein are Frank G. Mittelbach and Joan W. Moore, "Ethnic Endogamy—The Case of Mexican Americans," *American Journal of Sociology* 74 (July 1968): 50-62; Emily R. Coleman, "Medieval Marriage Characteristics: A Neglected Factor in the History of Medieval Serfdom," *Journal of Interdisciplinary History* 2 (Autumn 1971): 205-219; Richard A. Griswold del Castillo, "La Raza Hispano Americana: The Emergence of an Urban Culture among the Spanish Speaking of Los Angeles, 1850-1880," pp. 125-186, esp. pp. 137-142; Ruby Jo Reeves Kennedy, "Single or Triple Melting Pot? Intermarriage Trends in New Haven,

1870-1940," *American Journal of Sociology* 49 (January 1944): 331-339; and Bertram Hutchinson, "Some Evidence Related to Matrimonial Selection and Immigrant Assimilation in Brazil," *Population Studies* 11 (November 1957): 149-156.

6. A.G.N., *Censo 1869,* Leg. 159.

7. A.C., *Expedientes Matrimoniales,* Leg. 149, I, Exp. 12, May 8, 1871.

8. Sample data.

9. Miguel Potel Junot, *Plano de la ciudad y suburbios de Córdoba, República Argentina delineado y grabado por Miguel Potel Junot, 1878.*

10. A.C., *Expedientes Matrimoniales,* Leg. 167, Exp. 105, July 18, 1889; R.C., *Protocolos de Matrimonios,* 1889.

11. Manuel E. Río and Luis Achával, *Geografía de la provincia de Córdoba,* II, 455.

12. Aníbal Arcondo, "Población y mano de obra agrícola: Córdoba, 1880-1914," *Revista de Economía y Estadística* 14 (1970): 19.

13. Aníbal Arcondo, "Tierra y política de tierras en Córdoba," *Revista de Economía y Estadística* 13 (1969): 35.

14. Córdoba (City), *Censo de 1906,* p. 3.

15. Juan F. Cafferata, "El saneamiento de la vivienda en la profilaxis contra la tuberculosis. Relación entre las condiciones de la vivienda y la mortalidad por tuberculosis en el municipio de Córdoba," *Revista de la Universidad Nacional de Córdoba* 4 (December 1917): 367.

16. Cafferata, "El saneamiento," p. 366. For another contemporary view of living conditions among Córdoba's poor, see José M. Alvarez, *La lucha por la salud: Su estado actual en la ciudad de Córdoba,* esp. pp. 320-325, 490-494.

17. James R. Scobie, *Buenos Aires: Plaza to Suburb, 1870-1910,* pp. 160-166.

18. Santiago J. Albarracín, *Bosquejo histórico, político y económico de la provincia de Córdoba,* p. 424.

19. *La Carcajada,* July 20, 1890.

20. *La Carcajada,* September 30, 1894.

21. *La Carcajada,* October 17, 1880.

22. *La Carcajada,* November 18, 1880.

23. Bernabé A. Serrano, *Córdoba de ayer,* pp. 144-145.

24. Julio S. Maldonado, *La Córdoba de mi infancia,* 2nd ed., pp. 39-40.

25. *La Carcajada,* April 23, 1893.

26. *La Libertad,* January 19, 1894.

27. Scobie, *Buenos Aires,* pp. 147-148.

28. Cafferata, "El saneamiento," p. 376.

29. *La Carcajada,* September 15, 1889.

30. Juan Bialet-Massé, *El estado de las clases obreras argentinas a comienzos del siglo,* p. 229.

31. A.C., *Expedientes Matrimoniales,* Leg. 164, Exp. 64, July 6, 1886.

32. Juan F. Marsal, *Hacer la América: Autobiografía de un inmigrante español en la Argentina,* pp. 163-165.

33. Marsal, *Hacer la América*, p. 166.

34. Javier Marrazzo, *Ciudades, pueblos y colonias de la República Argentina*, 2nd ed., p. 151.

35. A.C., *Expedientes Matrimoniales*, Leg. 169, Exp. 25, February 21, 1891.

36. A.C., *Expedientes Matrimoniales*, Leg. 169, Exp. 84, May 27, 1891.

37. *El Progreso*, June 7, 1876.

Chapter 8: Marriage, Nationality and Mobility

1. Gino Germani, *Política y sociedad en una época de transición: De la sociedad tradicional a la sociedad de masas*, p. 207.

2. José Luis Romero, *A History of Argentine Political Thought*, p. 176.

3. Manuel E. Río, "Córdoba, 1810-1910," *Revista de la Junta Provincial de Historia de Córdoba* 1 (1960): 15-16.

4. Efraín U. Bischoff, *Historia de la provincia de Córdoba*, II, 221-228.

5. *La Carcajada*, March 4, 1874.

6. Carl Solberg, *Immigration and Nationalism: Argentina and Chile, 1890-1914*, p. 20; Manuel Gálvez, *El solar de la raza*, pp. 61-62; José Ramos Mejía, *Las multitudes argentinas*, pp. 296-301.

7. John Demos, *A Little Commonwealth: Family Life in Plymouth Colony*, p. lx.

8. *El Progreso*, December 17, 1875.

9. Sample data.

10. Sample data.

11. Sample data.

12. Sample data.

13. The population figures for the city of Córdoba, according to sex and nationality for people fifteen years of age and older are the following:

	Argentines		Immigrants	
	M	F	M	F
1869*	7,626	11,057	511	124
1895	11,716	17,824	3,417	1,820
1906	20,567	26,196	6,771	4,499

* Estimated.

14. *La Libertad*, January 20, 1898.

15. Sample data.

16. Sample data.

17. For a brief view of isolation in rural zones and some psychological implications, see James R. Scobie, *Revolution on the Pampas: A Social History of Argentine Wheat, 1860-1910*, pp. 61-63.

18. For a comprehensive view of workers' organizations, see José Panettieri, *Los trabajadores*, pp. 113-134; the structures in Córdoba during our period are reviewed in Marta Sánchez, "Movimientos de lucha y organización de la clase

obrera en la ciudad de Córdoba, 1895-1905," in *Homenaje al Doctor Ceferino Garzón Maceda*, pp. 393-408; Ofelia Pianetto, "Industria y formación de clase obrera en la ciudad de Córdoba, 1880-1906," in *Homenaje*, pp. 335-354; and Hilda Iparraguirre and Ofelia Pianetto, *La organización de la clase obrera en Córdoba, 1870-1895*, pp. 34-42, 47-55.

19. Sample data. Here we used the statistic "phi."

20. For a clear overview of the uses and advantages of partial correlations, see Norman H. Nie, et al., *SPSS: Statistical Package for the Social Sciences*, pp. 158-161.

21. Charles M. Dollar and Richard J. Jensen, *Historian's Guide to Statistics: Quantitative Analysis and Historical Research*, p. 92.

22. Dollar and Jensen, *Historian's Guide*, p. 94. For a discussion of causal analysis and the importance of temporal priority of variables, see Hubert M. Blalock, *Causal Inferences in Non-experimental Research*, pp. 9-14.

23. Sample data.

24. Sample data.

25. Sample data.

26. Germani, *Política y sociedad*, p. 199.

27. José Luis Romero, in *Argentina: Imágenes y perspectivas*, threads this synthetic quality throughout his writing.

28. The argument of immigrant insularity in rural regions has been prompted by works of Gastón Gori, especially *La pampa sin gaucho;* it has been echoed more recently in Germani, *Política y sociedad*, pp. 202-203.

29. Gino Germani, *Assimilation of Immigrants in Urban Areas: Methodological Notes*, 2nd ed., p. 1.

30. *El Eco de Córdoba*, February 28, 1889, quoted in *El Porvenir*, March 1, 1889.

31. The figures come from an untitled study by Savorgnan and used by Germani in *Política y sociedad*, p. 207.

32. *El Eco de Córdoba*, April 13, 1878, described the immigrants' desires to settle down with their families; allusions to the rootlessness of Creoles in Córdoba can be found in Manuel E. Río, "Consideraciones históricas y sociológicas sobre la Provincia de Córdoba," in *Córdoba: Su fisonomía, su misión. Escritos y discursos*, p. 95. Even José Bianco, who did not advocate massive immigration programs, admitted that contrary to Creole behavior immigrants tended to form and remain with their families (Bianco, *Educación pública; ensayo sociológico*, p. 40).

33. *El Eco de Córdoba*, September 17, 1863.

34. Florencio Sánchez, *El caudillaje criminal en Sud América*, p. 10; and *La Gringa.*

35. Antonio J. Pérez Amuchástegui, *Mentalidades argentinas, 1860-1930*, 3rd ed., p. 440.

36. José S. Alvarez (Fray Mocho), *Cuadros de la ciudad*, pp. 16-20.

37. Pérez Amuchástegui, *Mentalidades*, p. 443.

38. A.C., *Expedientes Matrimoniales*, Leg. 148, Exp. 78, November?, 1870.

39. A.G.N., *Censo 1869*, Leg. 159.

40. A.H.P.A.T., 1a Escribanía, 1871, Leg. 150, Exp. 1, Sucesorio.

41. Sample data.

42. Sample data.

43. A.C., *Expedientes Matrimoniales*, Leg. 174, Exp. 107, October 13, 1896; R.C., *Protocolos de Matrimonios, 1896*.

44. A.C., *Expedientes Matrimoniales*, Leg. 181, Exp. 29, March 20, 1903; R.C., *Protocolos de Matrimonios, 1903*.

45. A.C., *Expedientes Matrimoniales*, Leg. 186, II, Exp. 325, July 10, 1908; R.C., *Protocolos de Matrimonios, 1908*.

46. *Guía general de Córdoba, 1901* provides, as do city directories for other years, listings and addresses of commercial enterprises in Córdoba.

47. A.C., *Expedientes Matrimoniales*, Leg. 168, Exp. 68, April 22, 1890.

48. Rafael Moyano López, *La cultura musical cordobesa*, p. 56.

49. Moyano López, *La cultura*, pp. 76-79.

50. A.G.N., *Censo 1895*, Leg. 890.

51. A.G.N., *Censo 1869*, Leg. 162; A.G.N., *Censo 1895*, Leg. 890.

52. A.C., *Expedientes Matrimoniales*, Leg. 167, Exp. 98, July 8, 1889.

53. Moyano López, *La cultura*, p. 74.

54. Richard A. Schermerhorn, "Power in the Local Community," in *Structured Social Inequality: A Reader in Comparative Social Stratification*, ed. Celia S. Heller, p. 168.

55. The 1912 "social register" of Córdoba, for example, contains virtually the same proportions of established Creole families as the ones for Buenos Aires (*Guía social de Córdoba, 1912*).

56. Adolfo H. Muschietti, *El prejuicio de la prostitución y la lucha anti-venérea*, quoted in Miguel Bravo Tedín, *Historia del barrio Clínicas*, p. 116.

57. Sociologist William J. Goode illustrates the virtual inevitability of the usual pattern of homogamy by using the market system as an analogy:

Although the patterns of homogamy—"like marries like"—is found in all societies, it is more than an expression of preference for a mate similar to oneself or one's family. It is the resultant of a market process in which either elders or courting young people attempt to locate the most desirable mate, just as a seller attempts to obtain the very best price for his commodities. However, since others in marriageable ages are doing precisely the same thing, the net result is that in general those who marry will be able to choose a spouse who has roughly the same market value.

Homogamy, then, is not merely ethnocentricism [sic]. It is also the blind result of many individuals who, in seeking the very best possible spouse for their children or themselves, and by virtue of the types of offers made or rejections received, come to find a spouse at their own social or economic level.

William J. Goode, "Family and Mobility," in *Class, Status, and Power: Social Stratification in Comparative Perspective*, 2nd ed., eds. Reinhard Bendix and

Seymour M. Lipset, p. 593.

58. Notable exceptions to this general feeling, Argentines would agree, take place principally among Jews and Orientals.

Chapter 9: Mobility and Integration in Córdoba: The Sociopolitical Legacy of Liberalism

1. William J. McGrath, "*Volksseelenpolitik* and Psychological Rebirth: Mahler and Hofmannstahl," *Journal of Interdisciplinary History* 4 (Summer 1973): 56.

2. Eugene F. Sofer and Mark D. Szuchman, "Educating Immigrants: Voluntary Associations in the Acculturation Process," in *Educational Alternatives in Latin America: Social Change and Social Stratification,* ed. Thomas J. La Belle, pp. 343-344, 354.

3. For alternative attitudes on the part of the public and administrators, which increased urban growth and transportation without sacrificing human traffic, see Sam B. Warner, Jr., *Streetcar Suburbs: The Process of Growth in Boston, 1870-1900,* pp. 21-34.

4. Roberto Etchepareborda, *La revolución argentina del 90,* p. 78.

5. Ezequiel Gallo (H.) and Silvia Sigal, "La formación de los partidos políticos contemporáneos: La U.C.R. (1890-1916)," in *Argentina, sociedad de masas,* eds. Torcuato S. Di Tella, Gino Germani, and Jorge Graciarena, pp. 128-129.

6. José Ratzer, *Los marxistas argentinos del 90,* pp. 74-77.

7. Gallo and Sigal, "La formación," p. 129. See also David Rock, "Radicalism and Urban Working Class in Buenos Aires, 1916-1922," for a detailed discussion of the political aspirations of the bourgeoisie and of the working class.

8. Currently, young scholars are involved in urban social histories of Rosario (Lance Query), of early Buenos Aires (1810-1850) (Karl Graeber), and of Buenos Aires since 1890 (Eugene Sofer).

9. Data from Eugene Sofer's study of Jewish porteños show persistence rates of thirty years and more. See "From Pale to Pampa: Eastern European Jewish Social Mobility in Gran Buenos Aires, 1890-1945."

10. Ernesto Tornquist & Co., *The Economic Development of the Argentine Republic in the Last Fifty Years,* p. 15.

11. Archivo Histórico de la Provincia. *Archivo de Tribunales,* 1a and 2a Nominación Civil, Capital, 1883-1925; 3a Nominación Civil y Comercial, Capital, 1881-1925; 4a Nominación Civil y Comercial, Capital, 1898-1925; 5a Nominación Civil y Comercial, Capital, 1912-1925; 1a Nominación Comercial, Capital, 1880-1925; 2a Nominación Comercial, Capital, 1895-1925; Archivo de Tribunales, 1a through 7a Nominación Civil y Comercial, Capital, 1926-1935. The litigation cases that provide information on Córdoba's commercial operations include *Cesión de Bienes, Inventarios, Quiebra, Convocatoria de Acreedores, Desolución de Sociedad,* and *División.* The great majority of businesses in Córdoba were small and thus subject to brief lives. The per

capita cost of business mortality rates nationwide in Argentina between 1910 and 1914 amounted to US $7.40 per person per year; during the same period, the figure in the United States, on the other hand, was US $2.55 per person per year. See Roger W. Babson, *The Future of South America*, p. 243; Theodore Hershberg et al., "Occupation and Ethnicity in Five Nineteenth Century Cities," *Historical Methods Newsletter* 7 (June 1974): 214.

12. Robert K. Merton and Alice Kitt Rossi, "Contributions to the Theory of Reference Group Behavior," in *Continuities in Social Research,* eds. Robert K. Merton and Paul F. Lazarsfeld, pp. 40-105.

Bibliographic Note

The basis of most quantitative studies of urban dwellers, at least in the United States, is formed by the manuscript census returns. Samples from the general population of Argentina, too, can be gathered from the manuscript census returns from the first (1869) and second (1895) censuses.[1] The originals, housed in the Archivo General de la Nación in Buenos Aires, contain the name, age, sex, marital status, province or country of birth, occupation, physical defects, ownership of real property, and type of housing of each resident. The last two variables were recorded in 1895 only. Census officials divided each city into numbered sections and districts; no map of the divisions has survived, however. The census returns are ordered without regard to geographic sequence and had to be arranged to make sense of where each numbered area lay before the geographic mobility patterns within the city could be studied. This lengthy process required thorough familiarity with the city's landmarks and street layout as well as a good amount of detective work in order to match each numbered district with its proper geographic boundaries.

The occupations provided by the different manuscript sources had to be clustered and ranked in a systematic manner so that the occupational mobility patterns of the sampled cases could be measured. Shifts within the occupational structure are one of the bases of social mobility most often studied because, as Michael B. Katz states, "to trace the movements of a man from occupation to occupation is, to a considerable extent, to trace his vertical movement within social space; the sum of these movements determines the patterns and rate of social mobility, the degree of openness, within a society."[2]

Eleven occupational categories were devised, including Miscellaneous and Unknown, and ranging from Unskilled and Menial to High Professional. All occupations reflected twelve characteristics which, therefore, all categories possessed to varying degrees: 1) age required; 2) education required; 3) training required; 4) training period required; 5) mode of operation; 6) level of complexity; 7) dependence on local and national economic situations; 8) financial security; 9) job schedule; 10) audience to which classification is primarily directed; 11) financial remuneration; and 12) duties on a daily basis. The

occupations were classified according to how they conform to each characteristic of the categories: an occupation which fulfilled a minimum of seven of a
category's characteristics fit within that category. An occupation could have a
multiple classification, depending on information about the person holding
that occupation. Unspecified occupations (e.g., *peón*) were occasionally classified differently from more precisely listed occupations (e.g., *peón de albañil*).[3]

Each individual was sampled together with his or her family in order to
verify the identity of the sampled person throughout the tracing process. For
example, we encountered many common last names in Córdoba—Moyano,
Ludueña, Toledo, to give a few—but having references to a wife, husband, or
children made it possible to confirm or discard those found in the documents
having the same first and last names. Because people sampled in the first census may have been absent from the city in 1895, either due to out-migration or
to death, it was necessary to trace them through the parish and civil registry
death records in order to identify cases in which death was the cause of absence.

The city of Córdoba was the first in Argentina to operate a civil registry,
preceding the rest of the province and the nation by ten years when it opened
its doors in 1880. From the beginning it kept the city's complete death records;
the births and marriages were not kept perfectly until the end of the decade.
The municipal civil registry's archive is not open to the public, and permission
to enter it was nearly impossible to secure; to the best of our knowledge, we
were the only ones ever permitted to use it. Although the provincial *Dirección
General del Registro Civil* does not contain volumes prior to 1890, its archive
is open to the public. The death acts contain data concerning occupation,
address, literacy, the relationship of the next of kin, and whether or not the
deceased had made a last will and testament. Each volume has an index alpha-
betized only by the first letter of the last name of the deceased, which, together
with a surprisingly high degree of commonality of first *and* last names, made
this phase of the tracing extremely tedious.

The Archdiocese of Córdoba has the city's best-ordered archive, in which
records are kept under excellent conditions. The archive served a number of
functions in the course of the research. Its records of deaths, which antedate
those of the civil registry, were used to complete the search of names through
the intercensal period. The marriage records helped to answer major questions
on the issues of immigrant integration and social mobility through marriage.
The archive of the Archdiocese of Córdoba contains all the *expedientes matrimoniales,* or special requests for marriage, through the year 1914. All persons
who wished to be married by the church but who were not natives of the city
were required to present applications for marriage; the information on these
forms provides the researcher with valuable data on the brides and grooms.

The expedientes matrimoniales are contained in nearly two hundred volumes
encompassing two and a half centuries, from 1664 through 1914. Our research
covered forty-two volumes spanning the years 1869-1909, during which approximately 3,250 forms were filed. The format of these expedientes hardly
changed over time. It included the names of the bride and grooms, and their

parents'; places of birth and residence; ages; and the sworn statements of at least two members of the community who knew the non-native bride or groom and who testified that no impediments precluded the marriage. The witnesses' affidavits often rounded out information on the early Argentine experiences of European immigrants, including their years of travel through the country, their activities, and their families.

The expedientes matrimoniales did not provide data on occupations or addresses; that information was gathered in the archive of the municipal civil registry. Data for the same individuals was thus gleaned from different sources in order to fill any gaps within their life histories. The Archdiocesan archive was helpful in the question of intermarriage between cordobeses and noncordobeses, but only the civil registry could provide data on geographic and occupational mobility. The civil registry's marriage records become reliably complete toward the end of the 1880s; between 1889 and 1909 all but very few of the couples sampled from the church records also appeared as having been married by the state.

Of the official provincial archives, Córdoba's present the most complete and perhaps the best organized. The extent to which their volumes provide information depends on the questions asked. Sometimes it became necessary to make adjustments in the questions in order to get the available data; such is the case with the study of economic status. The province did not keep yearly assessments of the residents' personal and real property during the nineteenth and early twentieth centuries. The national civil code, however, provided that any divisible goods left behind by a deceased must go to probate court for subdivision. Economic questions can thus be studied through the notarial and judicial records, which provide a complete accounting of the items left at the time of death: number, type, and worth of animals; land measurements, assessments, and locations, and often dates and methods of acquisition; jewelry; cash; tools of the trade; clothes. Finally, the subdivision of goods states each survivor's share.

The notarial and judicial archives contain other important economic data as well. The researcher may look into issues involving embargoes; debt payment (*cobro de pesos*); legalization, proof, or measurement of land possession (*treintanario* or *mensura*). Often, an inheritance case may be listed as other than "probate" (*juicio sucesorio*), yet its contents yield the same information (e.g., *declaraciones de herederos, testamentaria, inventarios, posesión de herencia, por herencia,* and *división*).

For answers to the commercial aspects of the city or of sampled groups, the commercial court records begin to be reliably maintained at the turn of the century. The indices contain both civil and commercial cases. Printed matter relating to merchants of the late nineteenth and early twentieth centuries usually refers to them generically as comerciantes, or *miembros del comercio,* and sometimes misguidedly as industriales. The commercial court records offer data on activities indicating the intricacies of a given business—its volume and solvency—and the peculiarities of a financial system in which borrowing from lending institutions was exceptional. The types of commercial cases include: *cobro de pesos, disolución de sociedad, cesión de bienes, convocatoria de acreedores,* and *quiebra.*

An inherent bias is in effect when using the civil and commerical judicial records, since only those who had some stake (usually money) in presenting themselves before the court appear in the records. The destitute are usually not found, although cases of legitimization of squatters' settlements and declarations of poverty occur with regularity. On the other hand, these records by no means reflect only the economic data of the elite; instead, the middle levels of the urban society form the bulk of the court cases.

The indices are kept excellently from 1883 through 1925, the last year of judicial cases housed in the Archivo Histórico de la Provincia; thereafter, one must work in the provincial Archivo de Tribunales, where the indexing is done yearly by first letter of each person's last name. The cases preceding 1883 are kept in the Archivo Histórico, filed within the four *Registros de Escribanías* and totaling 1,163 volumes, of which nearly 200 cover the period from 1869 through 1882. The total number of volumes from 1883 to the present is unknown. We can point to our experience, however, to state that tracing sample members for a period of nearly a century (from 1869 through 1951) involved perusing thousands of cases.

The educational mobility of children present in the sampled households can be traced only at the university level, since no lists exist of primary or secondary school enrollments. The archive of the Universidad Nacional de Córdoba contains the *Libros de Grados,* in which all the graduates appear with their degrees and disciplines.

The voluntary associations provided some of the best source for viewing Córdoba's European communities at closer range. A number of European voluntary associations sprang up in the city during the second half of the nineteenth century. Of the three largest immigrant groups, only the Spanish and French voluntary associations retain nineteenth-century materials for examination. One of the Italian associations destroyed its records, while the other was formed too late to be of use in this study. The Spanish and French associations' membership registries yielded the names which were traced into subsequent years of membership, into the census, into the city's death records, and into the probate archives. Both voluntary associations kept records of the members' names, ages, places of birth, occupations, addresses, marital statuses, dates of leaving the association, and reasons for leaving. In addition to the registries of members, the books containing the minutes of the meetings gave a picture of the associations' activities as well as their members' needs and preoccupations.

Once having started any one phase of tracing, we found it imperative to carry the phase to its (chronological) conclusion; otherwise, the effort would have been wasted. Nothing would have been gained by tracing through only half of the intercensal period, for example, or by tracing only a portion of the names in the random sample.

Looking into documentation authored by the individuals who together form social histories is essential for observing the differences between the ideal and the real, between symbolic expressions and executions of choices. Good histories involve the ideational and the actual; unfortunately, too much of Argentine history has been drawn from the use of documentation not subjected to tests of veracity. Perhaps we are fortunate at this stage in not having the literary support that Barthold Niebuhr saw as essential to historical truth. For him, no further detailed evidence would be required to make an inference in history when it has already been generally accepted bo other scholars. Such common persuasion "furnishes the same reinforced verification as would new sources of evidence."[4] We have the opportunity to go beyond inferences, however, thanks to new techniques and to a healthy initial skepticism toward what some see as evidence. In this manner, those of us interested in the process of Argentine history can share in actuating James Harvey Robinson's philosophy that "history should not be regarded as a stationary subject which can only progress by refining its methods and accumulating, criticizing, and assimilating new material, but it is bound to alter its ideas and aims with the general progress of society and of the social sciences and that it should ultimately play an infinitely more important role in our intellecutal life than it has hitherto done."[5]

Notes

1. An expanded version of this section appears in Eugene Sofer and Mark D. Szuchman, "City and Society: Their Connection in Latin American Historical Research," *Latin American Research Review* 14 (1979): 113-129.

2. Michael B. Katz, "Occupational Classification in History," *Journal of Interdisciplinary History* 3 (Summer 1972): 62-68.

3. For a fuller discussion of these matters, see Mark D. Szuchman and Eugene F. Sofer, "The State of Occupational Stratification Studies in Argentina: A Classificatory Scheme," *Latin American Research Review* 11 (1976): 159-171.

4. Barthold Georg Niebuhr, "Vorrede zu der ersten Ausgabe," in *The Varieties of History*, ed. and trans. Fritz Stern, p. 48.

5. James Harvey Robinson and Charles A. Beard, "Preface," from *The Development of Modern Europe*, in *The Varieties of History*, ed. and trans. Fritz Stern, p. 266.

Bibliography

I. PRIMARY SOURCES

A. *Manuscript Materials.*
Archivo de la Universidad Nacional de Córdoba, *Libro 2° de Grados.* Año
1806-1893. Córdoba.
————. *Libro 3° de Grados.* Año 1894-1913. Córdoba.
————. *Libro 4° de Grados.* Año 1913-1930. Córdoba.
Archivo General de la Nación. Ministerio del Interior. *Informe de Carlos Beck
a la Comisión de Inmigración.* Buenos Aires, 1869.
————. *Sección Gobierno; Ministerio del Interior.* 7 vols. Buenos Aires,
1869.
Archivo General de los Tribunales (Córdoba). *Expedientes de Pleitos.* Juzgado
1a Nominación Civil y Comercial. Capital. 1926-1951.
————. *Expedientes de Pleitos.* Juzgado 2a Nominación Civil y Comercial.
Capital. 1926-1951.
————. *Expedientes de Pleitos.* Juzgado 3a Nominación Civil y Comercial.
Capital. 1926-1951.
————. *Expedientes de Pleitos.* Juzgado 4a Nominación Civil y Comercial.
Capital. 1926-1951.
————. *Expedientes de Pleitos.* Juzgado 5a Nominación Civil y Comercial.
Capital. 1926-1951.
————. *Expedientes de Pleitos.* Juzgado 6a Nominación Civil y Comercial.
Capital. 1926-1951.
————. *Expedientes de Pleitos.* Juzgado 7a Nominación Civil y Comercial.
Capital. 1926-1951.
Archivo Histórico de la Provincia de Córdoba. Archivo General de los Tribu-
nales. *Escribanía No. 1.* Legajos 530-580. (1869-1882)
————. *Escribanía No. 2.* Legajos 171-234. (1869-1882)
————. *Escribanía No. 3.* Legajos 142-181. (1869-1882)
————. *Escribanía No. 4.* Legajos 124-168. (1869-1882)
Archivo Histórico de la Provincia de Córdoba. *Gobierno.* 1891, Tomo 11.

"Diversos asuntos" (Asilo de Mendigos), f. 38.

_____. *Gobierno.* 1892, Tomo 13. "Diversos asuntos" (Sociedad Francesa de Socorros Mútuos de Córdoba), f. 95.

_____. *Gobierno.* 1894, Tomo 18. "Diversos asuntos" (Memoria de Asilo de Mendigos), f. 107.

_____. *Gobierno.* 1895, Tomo 16. "Diversos asuntos" (Club de Residentes Estranjeros), f. 251.

_____. *Gobierno.* 1895, Tomo 16. "Diversos asuntos" (Sociedad Francesa de Socorros Mútuos), f. 238.

_____. *Gobierno.* 1895, Tomo 16. "Diversos asuntos" (Pueblo de la Toma e Indígenas de Soto), f. 175.

_____. *Gobierno.* 1895, Tomo 1. "Ministerios y autoridades nacionales" (Segundo Censo Nacional), f. 229.

_____. *Gobierno.* 1894, Tomo 1. "Ministerios nacionales" (Departamento Nacional de Inmigración), f. 123.

_____. *Gobierno.* 1892, Tomo 6. "Municipalidades" (Córdoba), f. 1-86.

Archivo Histórico de la Provincia de Córdoba. Archivo General de los Tribunales. *Indice de la Escribanía No. 1.* "Escribanía de Hipotecas." Vol. 2. 1764-1882.

_____. *Indice de la Escribanía No. 2.* "Escribanía de Hacienda." Vol. 2. 1809-1882.

_____. *Indice de la Escribanía No. 3.* "Escribanía Guerrero." 1679-1882.

_____. *Indice de la Escribanía No. 4.* "Escribanía Olmos y Aguilera," 1690-1882.

_____. *Expedientes de Pleitos.* Juzgado 1a Nominación Civil. Capital. 1883-1925. 1,003 legajos.

_____. *Expedientes de Pleitos.* Juzgado 2a Nominación Civil. Capital. 1883-1925. 1,107 legajos.

_____. *Expedientes de Pleitos.* Juzgado 3a Nominación Civil y Comercial. Capital. 1881-1925. 831 legajos.

_____. *Expedientes de Pleitos.* Juzgado 4a Nominación Civil y Comercial. Capital. 1898-1925. 571 legajos.

_____. *Expedientes de Pleitos.* Juzgado 5a Nominación Civil y Comercial. Capital. 1912-1929. 203 legajos.

_____. *Expedientes de Pleitos.* Juzgado 1a Nominación Comercial. Capital. 1880-1926.

_____. *Expedientes de Pleitos.* Juzgado 2a Nominación Comercial. Capital. 1895-1925.

_____. *Expedientes de Pleitos.* Juzgado 1a a 4a Nominación Civil y Comercial. Capital. 1926-1930.

Archivo Histórico de la Provincia de Córdoba. *Indice Gobierno.* 1880-1889. 1890-1895.

Argentine Republic. *Primer censo de la República Argentina (1869)* (Población). Legajos 156-163 (Córdoba. Capital).

_____. *Segundo censo de la República Argentina (1895)* (Población).

Legajos 883-894 (Córdoba. Capital).

Arzobispado de Córdoba. *Indice de Defunciones* (Catedral). Vols. 7-12. 1865-1886.

————. *Libros de Actas de Defunciones* (Catedral). Vols. 7-12. 1865-1886.

————. *Indices de expedientes matrimoniales de la Catedral de Córdoba.*

————. *Expedientes matrimoniales.* Legajos 147-192. 1869-1914.

Asociación Española de Socorros Mútuos de Córdoba. *Actas de la Junta Directiva.* 2 vols. 1872-1888.

————. *Libro de actas de asambleas generales, 1872-1915.*

————. *Libro de registro de socios.* 1872.

————. *Libro de registro de socios.* 1883.

————. *Libro de registro de socios.* 1889.

————. *Libro de registro de socios.* 1902.

————. *Libro de registro de socios.* 1916.

————. *Libro de registro de socios.* 1927.

Córdoba (Municipalidad). Archivo Histórico. *Concejo Deliberante. Actas.* 1868-1906.

Córdoba (Municipalidad). *Presupuesto de la Municipalidad de la Ciudad de Córdoba para 1869.* Departamento de Gobierno, 9 de noviembre de 1868.

————. Oficina del Registro Civil. *Protocolos de Defunciones.* 1881-1895. 68 vols.

————. *Protocolos de Matrimonios.* 1881-1909. 103 vols.

————. *Protocolos de Nacimientos.* 1881-1895. 26 vols.

Société Française de Secours Mutuels du Córdoba. *Livres des Societaires.* 1875-1973. 4 vols.

————. *Procès-Verbaux.* 1875-1902. 3 vols.

————. *Reglamente de 1877 modifié en 1881.*

B. Printed Materials.

Archivo General de la Nación. *Mapas y planos. Colección Biedma-Pillado. Carpeta II.* "Plano de la ciudad de Córdoba. Levantado y dibujado por el Ingeniero Albano M. de Laberge—1860." Buenos Aires.

————. *Mapas y planos. Colección Biedma-Pillado. Carpeta II.* "Segundo censo de la República Argentina. Administración del Dr. Uriburu, 10 de mayo de 1895." Buenos Aires.

Archivo Histórico de la Provincia de Córdoba. Archivo General de los Tribunales. *Indice de los expedientes tramitados por ante las escribanías Nros. 1, 2, 3 y 4.* Córdoba, 1930.

————. *Indice de expedientes. Juzgado de 1a Nominación Civil. Capital. 1883-1926.* Córdoba, 1931.

————. *Indice de expedientes. Juzgado de 2a Nominación Civil. Capital. 1883-1926.* Córdoba, 1932.

————. *Indice de expedientes de 3a Nominación Civil. Capital. 1888-1925.* Córdoba, 1933.

————. *Indice de expedientes. Juzgado 1a a 4a Civil y Comercial. 1926-*

1930. Córdoba, 1934.

Argentine Republic. *Memoria del Ministro del Interior ante el Congreso Nacional. 1895.* 3 vols. Buenos Aires, 1896.

_____. *Memoria presentada por el Ministro de Estado en el Departamento del Interior al Honorable Congreso Nacional en las sesiones de 1869.* Buenos Aires, 1870.

_____. *Primer censo de la República Argentina (1869).* Buenos Aires, 1872.

_____. *Segundo censo de la República Argentina, mayo 10 de 1895.* 3 vols. Buenos Aires, 1898.

_____. *Tercer censo nacional, levantado el 1° de junio de 1914.* 10 vols. Buenos Aires, 1916-1919.

_____. *Cuarto censo nacional.* 3 vols. Buenos Aires, 1947.

_____. *Ley de inmigración y colonización de la República Argentina, sancionada por el Congreso Nacional de 1876.* Buenos Aires, 1882.

_____. *Argentine Republic; agricultural and pastoral census of the nation. Stockbreeding and agriculture in 1908.* 3 vols. Buenos Aires, 1909.

_____. *Censo nacional agropecuario. Año 1937.* 2 vols. Buenos Aires, 1940.

_____. *Censo industrial de 1935.* Buenos Aires, 1938.

_____. *Censo de comercio, 1954.* 2 vols. Buenos Aires, 1959.

_____. *Censo de los empleados administrativos, funcionarios judiciales y personal docente de la República Argentina correspondiente al 31 de diciembre de 1892.* Buenos Aires, 1893.

_____. *Censo escolar correspondiente a fines de 1883 y principios de 1884.* 3 vols. Buenos Aires, 1885.

Catastro Machado. Copia fiel del plano de la ciudad de Córdoba del año 1890. Córdoba, 1949.

Córdoba (Municipalidad). *Censo general de la población, edificación, comercio, industria, ganadería y agricultura de la ciudad de Córdoba, capital de la provincia del mismo nombre (República Argentina) levantado en los días 31 de agosto y 1° de septiembre de 1906.* Córdoba, 1910.

Córdoba (Province). *Censo industrial, 1954.* Córdoba, 1959.

_____. *Las colonias de la provincia de Córdoba en el año 1887.* Buenos Aires, 1888.

Córdoba (Municipalidad). *Comisión administradora de la municipalidad. Memoria. Año 1872.* Córdoba, 1872.

Córdoba (Province). *Compilación de leyes, decretos, acuerdos de la Excelentísima Cámara de Justicia y demás disposiciones de carácter público dictadas en la Provincia de Córdoba.* 33 vols. Córdoba, 1810-1906.

Córdoba (Municipalidad). *Compilación de ordenanzas y acuerdos de la municipalidad de Córdoba desde el día su instalación hasta el presente.* Córdoba, 1874.

Córdoba (Municipalidad). *Digesto de ordenanzas y acuerdos de la municipalidad de Córdoba, 1856 a 1879.* Córdoba, 1889.

Córdoba (Municipalidad). *Leyes de municipalidades número 1,819-1,994-2,389 y decretos reglamentarios.* Córdoba, 1916.

Córdoba (Province). *Mapa oficial de la provincia de Córdoba.* Departamento Topográfico. Buenos Aires, 1924.

Córdoba (Municipalidad). *Memoria. Año 1872.* Córdoba, 1872.

Córdoba (Province). *Población, 1869-1960.* Córdoba, 1961.

_____. *Reglamento para la administración de justicia y policía en la campaña de Córdoba.* Córdoba, 1856.

France. *Ministère de l'Intérieur. Dénombrement de la population. 1891.* Paris, 1892.

France. Ministère du Commerce. Service de la Statistique Générale. *Resultats statistiques du dénombrement de 1881. France et Algérie.* Paris, 1883.

Guía almanaque de la ciudad y provincia de Córdoba. Córdoba, 1888.

Guía general de Córdoba, 1901. Córdoba, 1901.

Guía general de Córdoba, 1904. Córdoba, 1904.

Guía Córdoba. Guía descriptiva y comercial de la provincia, 1918. Córdoba, 1918.

Guía Córdoba. Guía descriptiva y comercial de la provincia de Córdoba, 1921. 3rd ed. Córdoba, 1921.

Guía de la ciudad de Córdoba. Córdoba, 1896.

Guía social de Córdoba, 1912. Córdoba, 1912.

Potel Junot, Miguel. *Plano de la ciudad y suburbios de Córdoba, República Argentina, delineado y grabado por Miguel Potel Junot, 1878.* Córdoba, 1878.

Wilcken, Guillermo. *Las colonias; informe sobre el estado actual de las colonias agrícolas de la República Argentina, 1872.* Buenos Aires, 1873.

_____. *Memoria sobre inmigración al Ministro del Interior.* Buenos Aires, 1874.

II. SECONDARY SOURCES

A. Books.

Academia Nacional de la Historia. *Historia argentina contemporánea, 1862-1930.* Buenos Aires: 1965.

Agulla, Juan Carlos. *Eclipse de una aristocracia: Una investigación sobre las élites dirigentes de la ciudad de Córdoba.* Córdoba: 1968.

Albarracín, Santiago Juan. *Bosquejo histórico político y económico de la provincia de Córdoba.* Buenos Aires: 1889.

Alberdi, Juan Bautista. *Bases y puntos de partida para la organización política de la República Argentina.* Buenos Aires: 1966.

Alger, Horatio. *Ragged Dick and Mark, the Match Boy.* New York: 1962.

Alsina, Juan A. *La inmigración en el primer siglo de la independencia.* Buenos Aires: 1910.

_____. *La inmigración europea en la República Argentina.* Buenos Aires: 1898.

Alvarez, José M. *La lucha por la salud: Su estado actual en la ciudad de Córdoba.* Córdoba: 1898.

Alvarez, José S. (Fray Mocho). *Cuadros de la ciudad*. Buenos Aires: 1961.

Anderson Imbert, Enrique. *Genio y figura de Sarmiento*. Buenos Aires: 1967.

Andreski, Stanislav. *The Uses of Comparative Sociology*. Berkeley: 1965.

Andrews, Joseph. *Journey from Buenos Ayres, through the provinces of Córdova, Tucumán, and Salta*. . . . 2 vols. London: 1827.

Aragón, Roque Raúl and Jorge Calvetti. *Genio y figura de José Hernández*. Buenos Aires: 1973.

Arcondo, Aníbal B. *La agricultura en Córdoba, 1870-1880*. Córdoba: 1965.

Armaignac, Henry. *Viaje por las pampas de la República Argentina*. Ed. and trans. Alfredo Amaral Insiarte. Buenos Aires: 1961.

Arzobispado de Córdoba. *Boletín oficial del Arzobispado de Córdoba, enero a marzo 1971*. Córdoba: 1971.

Asociación Española de Socorros Mútuos de Córdoba. *Centenario*. Córdoba: 1972.

Ayarragaray, Lucas. *La inmigración y el nacionalismo*. Buenos Aires: 1920.

Babson, Roger W. *The Future of South America*. Boston: 1915.

Bagú, Sergio et al. *Bibliografía crítica sobre la historia de la estratificación social en la Argentina durante el período 1880-1959*. Buenos Aires: 1960.

Bagú, Sergio. *Evolución histórica de la estratificación social en la Argentina*. Buenos Aires: 1961.

_____. *La sociedad de masas en su historia*. Córdoba, 1961.

Balán, Jorge, Harley L. Browning, and Elizabeth Jelin. *Men in a Developing Society: Geographic and Social Mobility in Monterrey, Mexico*. Austin: 1973.

Baltzell, E. Digby. *The Protestant Establishment*. New York: 1964.

Banco de la Provincia de Córdoba. *Noventa años sirviendo a la producción. Breve historia de una institución de crédito*. Córdoba, 1963.

Barbieri, C. A. *Epopeya romántica (Córdoba en 1840-1843)*. Buenos Aires: n.d.

Bardet, G. *El urbanismo*. Buenos Aires: 1959.

Bendix, Reinhard and Seymour M. Lipset, eds. *Class, Status, and Power: Social Stratification in Comparative Perspective*. 2nd ed. New York: 1966.

Berkhofer, Robert F., Jr. *A Behavioral Approach to Historical Analysis*. New York: 1969.

Beyer, Glenn H., ed. *The Urban Explosion in Latin America: A Continent in Process of Modernization*. Ithaca: 1967.

Beyhaut, Gustavo et al. *Inmigración y desarrollo económico*. Buenos Aires: 1961.

Bialet-Massé, Juan. *El estado de las clases obreras argentinas a comienzos del siglo*. Córdoba: 1968.

Bianco, José. *Educación pública; ensayo sociológico*. Córdoba: 1898.

Bischoff, Efraín U. *La Córdoba de antaño*. Córdoba: 1949.

_____. *Historia de la provincia de Córdoba*. 3 vols. Buenos Aires: 1968-70.

Blalock, Hubert M. *Causal Inferences in Nonexperimental Research*. Chapel Hill: 1964.

Blau, Peter Michael and Otis Dudley Duncan. *The American Occupational*

Structure. New York: 1967.

Bórea, Domingo. *La mutualidad y el cooperativismo en la República Argentina. (Tercer Censo Nacional).* Buenos Aires: 1917.

Bosch, Beatriz. *Urquiza y su tiempo.* Buenos Aires: 1971.

Bravo, Hector Félix. *Sarmiento, pedagogo social.* Buenos Aires: 1965.

Bravo Tedín, Miguel. *Historia del barrio Clínicas.* Córdoba: 1970.

Bunge, Alejandro E. *Los problemas económicos del presente.* Vol. 1. Buenos Aires: 1920.

Bunge, Carlos O. *Nuestra América.* Barcelona: 1903.

Byars, Robert S. and Joseph L. Love, eds. *Quantitative Social Science Research on Latin America.* Urbana: 1973.

Cabrera, Pablo. *Universitarios de Córdoba.* Córdoba: 1916.

Cacopardo, María Cristina. *República Argentina, cambios en los límites nacionales, provinciales y departamentales a través de los censos nacionales de población.* Buenos Aires: 1967.

Cafferata, Juan Félix. *De la Córdoba de ayer.* Córdoba: 1949.

Canal Feijoo, Bernardo. *Teoría de la ciudad argentina.* Buenos Aires: 1951.

Cantón, Dario and José Luis Moreno. *Pequeño censo de 1927.* Buenos Aires: 1971.

Cárcano, Miguel Angel. *El estilo de vida argentino.* Buenos Aires: 1969.

————. *Evolución histórica del régimen de la tierra pública, 1810-1916.* 3rd ed. Buenos Aires: 1972.

Cárcano, Ramón J. *Mis primeros ochenta años.* Buenos Aires: 1965.

Carr, Raymond. *Spain, 1808-1939.* London: 1966.

Centro Latino-Americano de Investigaciones en Ciencias Sociales. Publicación no. 6. *Estratificación y movilidad social en Argentina; fuentes bibliográficas (1880-1958).* Río de Janeiro: 1959.

Chudacoff, Howard P. *Mobile Americans: Residential and Social Mobility in Omaha, 1880-1920.* New York: 1972.

————. *The Evolution of American Urban Society.* Englewood Cliffs, New Jersey: 1975.

Chueco, Manuel. *Los pioneros de la industria Argentina.* Buenos Aires: 1886.

————. *La República Argentina en su Primer Centenario.* Vol. 1. Buenos Aires: 1910.

Comisión Nacional de Homenaje a Lisandro de la Torre. *Lisandro de la Torre y el régimen municipal.* Buenos Aires: 1956.

Conil, P. A. *La provincia de Córdoba. Su presente y su porvenir.* 2nd ed. Córdoba: 1873.

Cortés Conde, Roberto. *Corrientes inmigratorias y surgimiento de industrias en Argentina, 1870-1914.* Buenos Aires: 1964.

Couchón, Emilio. *Inmigración y colonización.* Buenos Aires: 1889.

Demos, John. *A Little Commonwealth: Family Life in Plymouth Colony.* New York: 1970.

Di Tella, Torcuato S., Gino Germani, and Jorge Graciarena, eds. *Argentina, sociedad de masas.* Buenos Aires: 1971.

Dollar, Charles M. and Richard J. Jensen. *Historian's Guide to Statistics: Quantitative Analysis and Historical Research.* New York: 1971.

Eizaguirre, José Manuel. *Córdoba, primera serie de cartas sobre la vida y las costumbres del interior.* Córdoba: 1898.

Endrek, Emiliano. *El mestizaje en Córdoba, siglo XVIII y principios del XIX.* Córdoba: 1966.

Etchepareborda, Roberto. *La revolución argentina del 90.* Buenos Aires: 1966.

Farber, Bernard. *Guardians of Virtue: Salem Families in 1800.* New York: 1972.

Fernández, Raúl. *Historia de la educación primaria en Córdoba.* Córdoba: 1960.

Ferns, H. S. *Britain and Argentina in the Nineteenth Century.* Oxford: 1960.

Ferrari Rueda, Rodolfo de. *Historia de Córdoba.* Córdoba: 1964.

Fillol, Tomás Roberto. *Social Factors in Economic Development: The Argentine Case.* Cambridge, Massachusetts: 1961.

Floud, Roderick. *An Introduction to Quantitative Methods for Historians.* Princeton: 1975.

Furlong, Guillermo, S. J. *Cartografía histórica argentina.* Buenos Aires: 1964.

Galletti, Alfredo. *Vida e imagen de Roca.* Buenos Aires: 1965.

Gallo, Ezequiel. *Agrarian Expansion and Industrial Development in Argentina (1880-1930).* Buenos Aires: 1970.

Gálvez, Manuel. *El solar de la raza.* Buenos Aires: 1913.

Garzón, Félix T. *Historia de Banco Provincial y Banco de Córdoba.* Buenos Aires: 1923.

Garzón Funes, José. *Discurso pronunciado en la colación de grados del 8 de diciembre de 1907 por José Garzón Funes.* Córdoba: 1907.

Garzón Maceda, Félix. *Discurso del Doctor Félix Garzón Maceda en la colación de grados del año 1910, Universidad Nacional de Córdoba.* Córdoba: 1906.

_____. *La medicina en Córdoba.* 3 vols. Buenos Aires: 1916-1917.

Germani, Gino. *Assimilation of Immigrants in Urban Areas: Methodological Notes.* 2nd ed. Buenos Aires: 1966.

_____. *Estructura social de la Argentina.* Buenos Aires: 1955.

_____. *La movilidad social en la Argentina.* Buenos Aires: 1956.

_____. *Política y sociedad en una época de transición: De la sociedad tradicional a la sociedad de masas.* Buenos Aires: 1962.

_____. *El proceso de urbanización en la Argentina.* Buenos Aires: 1959.

Germani, Gino, Jorge Graciarena, and Miguel Murmis. *La asimilación de los inmigrantes en la Argentina y el fenómeno del regreso en la inmigración reciente.* Buenos Aires: 1964.

Gil de Oto, Manuel. *La Argentina que yo he visto.* Buenos Aires: n.d.

González, Juan B. *El encarecimiento de la vida en la República Argentina.* Buenos Aires: 1908.

Gordon, Michael, ed. *The American Family in Social-Historical Perspective.* New York: 1973.

Gordon, Milton M. *Assimilation in American Life: The Role of Race, Religion, and National Origins.* New York: 1964.

Gori, Gastón. *Inmigración y colonización en la Argentina.* Buenos Aires: 1964.

_____. *La pampa sin gaucho.* Buenos Aires: 1952.

Gouchón, Emilio. *Apuntes sobre inmigración y colonización.* Buenos Aires: 1889.

Gutiérrez, Leandro H. *El movimiento inmigratorio y las crisis económicas en la República Argentina.* Buenos Aires: 1965.

Halperín Donghi, Tulio. *Historia de la Universidad de Buenos Aires.* Buenos Aires: 1962.

_____. *El revisionismo histórico argentino.* Buenos Aires: 1971.

_____. *Revolución y guerra: Formación de una élite dirigente en la Argentina criolla.* Buenos Aires: 1972.

Handlin, Oscar. *Boston's Immigrants, 1790-1880.* Rev. ed. New York: 1970.

_____. *The Uprooted.* Boston: 1952.

Hardoy, Jorge Enrique and Richard P. Schaedel, eds. *El proceso de urbanización en América desde sus orígenes hasta nuestros días.* Buenos Aires: 1969.

Havel, J. E. *Habitat y vivienda.* 3rd ed. Trans. Ricardo I. Zelarayán. Buenos Aires: 1970.

Heath, Dwight B. and Richard N. Adams, eds. *Contemporary Cultures and Societies of Latin America.* New York: 1965.

Heller, Celia S., ed. *Structured Social Inequality: A Reader in Comparative Social Stratification.* New York: 1970.

Hernández, José. *Martín Fierro.* 7th ed. Buenos Aires: 1956.

Hobsbawm, E. J. *The Age of Revolution, 1789-1848.* New York: 1964.

Huerta Palau, Pedro. *Los transportes en la provincia de Córdoba, Año 1876.* Córdoba: 1951.

Ibarguren, Carlos. *La historia que he vivido.* Buenos Aires: 1969.

Imaz, José Luis de. *Los que mandan.* 9th ed. Buenos Aires: 1972.

Ingenieros, José. *Las direcciones filosóficas de la cultura argentina.* 3rd. ed. Buenos Aires: 1971.

Instituto de Investigaciones Históricas. Instituto de Desarrollo Económico y Social. *Jornadas de historia y economía argentina en los siglos XVIII y XIX.* Buenos Aires: 1964.

Instituto Torcuato Di Tella. *Censos nacionales de países de América Latina. Generales y de población.* 2nd ed. Buenos Aires: 1966.

International Labor Office. *International Standard Classification of Occupations.* Geneva: 1969.

Iparraguirre, Hilda and Ofelia Pianetto. *La organización de la clase obrera en Córdoba, 1870-1895.* Córdoba: 1968.

Johnson, H. C. Ross. *Vacaciones de un inglés en la Argentina.* Buenos Aires: 1943.

Knights, Peter R. *The Plain People of Boston, 1830-1860: A Study in City Growth.* New York: 1971.

Lanuza, José Luis. *Genio y figura de Lucio V. Mansilla.* Buenos Aires: 1965.

Lattes, Alfredo E. *La migración como factor de cambio de la población en la Argentina.* Buenos Aires: 1972.

Lenski, Gerhard E. *Power and Privilege.* New York: 1966.

Lipset, Seymour M. and Reinhard Bendix. *Movilidad social en la sociedad industrial.* 2nd ed. Trans. Ricardo Malfé. Buenos Aires: 1969.

————. *Social Mobility in Industrial Society.* Berkeley: 1959.

Lipset, Seymour M. and Richard Hofstadter, eds. *Sociology and History: Methods.* New York: 1968.

Lipset, Seymour M. *The First New Nation.* New York: 1963.

Lloyd, Reginald. *Impresiones de la República Argentina en el siglo veinte.* Buenos Aires: 1911.

Lockhart, James. *Spanish Peru, 1532-1560: A Colonial Society.* Madison: 1974.

López, Lucio V. *La gran aldea.* 4th ed. Buenos Aires: 1970.

López Cepeda, Manuel. *La confitería Oriental. Cien años después.* Córdoba: 1963.

————. *Gentes, casas y calles de Córdoba.* Córdoba: 1966.

López de Gómara, Justo S. *Un gran problema español en América; vida política del emigrado, su acción y trascendencia.* Buenos Aires: 1915.

Maldonado, Julio S. *La Córdoba de mi infancia.* 2nd ed. Buenos Aires: 1939.

Mansilla, Lucio V. *Mis memorias.* Buenos Aires: 1966.

Marrazzo, Javier. *Ciudades, pueblos y colonias de la República Argentina.* 2nd ed. Buenos Aires: 1910.

Marsal, Juan F. *Hacer la América: Autobiografía de un inmigrante español en la Argentina.* Buenos Aires: 1969.

Martínez, Alberto R. and Maurice Lewandowski. *The Argentine in the Twentieth Century.* London: 1911.

Martínez, Isidoro. *La Universidad Nacional de Córdoba. Síntesis histórica.* Córdoba: 1968.

Martínez Estrada, Ezequiel. *X-Ray of the Pampa.* Trans. Alain Swietlicki. Austin: 1971.

Martínez Paz, Enrique. *La formación histórica de la provincia de Córdoba.* Córdoba: 1941.

Martínez Villada, Luis G. *Religión y sociología.* Córdoba: 1909.

Máximo, Virgolini. *Córdoba de ayer, de hoy, y de mañana.* Córdoba: 1953.

McGann, Thomas F. *Argentina, the United States and the Inter-American System, 1880-1914.* Cambridge: 1957.

Melo, Carlos R. *Constituciones de la Provincia de Córdoba.* Córdoba: 1950.

Menéndez Pidal, Ramón. *The Spaniards in Their History.* Trans. Walter Starkie. New York: 1966.

Miatello, Roberto A. *Población de la Provincia de Córdoba. Estudios de las poblaciones departamentales.* Córdoba: 1959.

Miller, Delbert C., Eva Chamorro Greca, and Juan Carlos Agulla. *De la industria al poder.* Buenos Aires: 1966.

Miller, Delbert C. *International Community Power Structures.* Bloomington: 1970.

Moyano López, Rafael. *La cultura musical cordobesa.* Córdoba: 1941.

Muschietti, Adolfo H. *El prejuicio de la prostitución y la lucha antivenérea.* Buenos Aires: 1914.

Navarro Viola, Jorge. *El club de residentes extranjeros.* Buenos Aires: 1941.

Novara, Juan J. and Horacio J. L. Palmieri. *Contribución a la historia de los precios en Córdoba, 1887-1907.* Córdoba: 1968.

Oddone, Juan Antonio. *La emigración europea al Río de la Plata.* Montevideo: 1966.

Oliver, Isidro. *El socialismo en el interior argentino.* Rosario: 1951.

Ortiz, Ricardo M. *Historia económica de la Argentina, 1850-1930.* 2 vols. Buenos Aires: 1955.

Padilla, Francisco Jurado. *La Universidad de Córdoba, tribuna del pensamiento nacional.* Córdoba: 1969.

Panettieri, José. *Los trabajadores.* Buenos Aires: 1968.

Patroni, Adriani. *Los trabajadores en la Argentina: Datos acerca de salarios, horarios, habitaciones obreras, costo de vida, etc.* Buenos Aires: 1898.

Pennock, J. Roland and John W. Chapman, eds. *Voluntary Associations.* New York: 1969.

Pérez Amuchástegui, Antonio J. *Mentalidades argentinas, 1860-1930.* 3rd ed. Buenos Aires: 1972.

Pérez Rosales, Vicente. *Recuerdos del pasado.* Buenos Aires: 1964.

Perkin, Harold. *The Origin of Modern English Society.* London: 1969.

Peyret, Alejo. *Una visita a las colonias de la República Argentina.* Buenos Aires: 1889.

Pirenne, Henri. *Medieval Cities: Their Origins and the Revival of Trade.* Trans. Frank D. Halsey. Garden City: 1956.

Rabinovitz, Francine F. and Felicity M. Trueblood. *Latin American Urban Research.* Vol. 1. Beverly Hills: 1971.

Ramos Mejía, José María. *Historia de la instrucción primaria en la República Argentina, 1810-1910.* 2 vols. Buenos Aires: 1910.

_____. *Las multitudes argentinas: Estudios de psicología colectiva.* Buenos Aires: 1899.

Ratzer, José. *Los marxistas argentinos del 90.* Córdoba: 1969.

Razori, Amilcar. *Historia de la ciudad argentina.* 3 vols. Buenos Aires: 1945.

Recchini de Lattes, Zulma and Alfredo Lattes. *Migraciones en la Argentina: Estudio de las migraciones internas e internacionales basado en datos censales, 1869-1960.* Buenos Aires: 1969.

Reina, Ruben E. *Paraná: Social Boundaries in an Argentine City.* Austin: 1973.

Reiss, Albert J. et al. *Occupations and Social Status.* New York: 1961.

Río, Manuel E. *Córdoba: Su fisonomía, su misión. Escritos y discursos.* Córdoba: 1967.

_____. *Las finanzas de Córdoba en los últimos veinte años.* Córdoba: 1900.

Río, Manuel E. and Luis Achával. *Geografía de la provincia de Córdoba.* 2 vols. Buenos Aires: 1904-1905.

_____. *Síntesis histórica de la deuda pública en Córdoba.* Córdoba: 1899.

Rock, David. *Politics in Argentina, 1890-1930: The Rise and Fall of Radicalism.* London: 1975.

Rodríguez de la Torre, Miguel. *Significado histórico de las calles de Córdoba.*

Buenos Aires: 1945.

Rofman, Alejandro and Luis Alberto Romero. *El proceso de formación urbano-regional en la Argentina.* Buenos Aires: 1970.

Rojas, Ricardo. *Las provincias.* Buenos Aires: 1927.

Romero, José Luis. *A History of Argentine Political Thought.* Trans. Thomas F. McGann. Stanford: 1963.

—————. *Argentina: Imágenes y perspectivas.* Buenos Aires: 1956.

—————. *Breve historia de la Argentina.* 3rd ed. Buenos Aires: 1971.

—————. *El desarrollo de las ideas en la sociedad argentina del siglo XX.* México, D. F.: 1965.

Roque, Emilio H. *La provincia de Córdoba.* Buenos Aires: 1903.

Russell-Wood, A. J. R. *Fidalgos and Philanthropists: The Santa Casa de Misericordia of Bahia, 1550-1755.* Berkeley: 1968.

Sánchez, Emilio E. *Del pasado cordobés en la vida.* Córdoba: 1968.

Sánchez, Florencio. *El caudillaje criminal en Sud América.* Buenos Aires: 1966.

—————. *La gringa.* Buenos Aires: 1961.

Sánchez, Nazario F. *Hombres y episodios de Córdoba.* Córdoba: 1928.

Sargent, Charles S. *The Spatial Evolution of Greater Buenos Aires, Argentina, 1870-1930.* Tempe: 1974.

Sarmiento, Domingo F. *Conflicto y armonías de las razas en América.* Buenos Aires: 1915.

—————. *Life in the Argentine Republic in the Days of the Tyrants or Civilization and Barbarism.* New York: 1961.

Scalabrini Ortiz, Raúl. *Historia de los ferrocarriles argentinos.* 5th ed. Buenos Aires: 1971.

Scandin, Francesco. *La Argentina y el trabajo; impresiones y notas.* Buenos Aires: 1906.

Schneider, Louis and Charles Bonjean, eds. *The Idea of Culture in the Social Sciences.* London: 1973.

Scobie, James R. *Argentina: A City and a Nation.* New York: 1964.

—————. *Buenos Aires: Plaza to Suburb, 1870-1910.* New York: 1974.

—————. *Revolution on the Pampas: A Social History of Argentine Wheat, 1860-1910.* Austin: 1964.

Sebreli, Juan José. *Buenos Aires, vida cotidiana y alienación.* 4th ed. Buenos Aires: 1965.

Segreti, Carlos. *La gobernación de José Javier Díaz en 1820.* Córdoba: 1960.

Sennett, Richard, ed. *Classic Essays on the Culture of Cities.* New York: 1969.

Serrano, Bernabé A. *Córdoba de ayer.* Córdoba: 1969.

Shorter, Edward. *The Historian and the Computer: A Practical Guide.* Englewood Cliffs, New Jersey: 1971.

Smith, T. Lynn. *Colombia: Social Structure and the Process of Development.* Gainesville: 1967.

Solberg, Carl. *Immigration and Nationalism: Argentina and Chile, 1890-1914.* Austin: 1970.

Somoza, Jorge L. *La mortalidad en la Argentina entre 1869 y 1960.* Buenos

Aires: 1971.
Somoza, Jorge L. and Alfredo E. Lattes. *Muestras de los dos primeros censos nacionales de población, 1869-1895.* Buenos Aires: 1967.
Spalding, Hobart A. *Argentine Sociology from the End of the Nineteenth Century to World War I.* Buenos Aires: 1968.
Stern, Fritz, ed. *The Varieties of History: From Voltaire to the Present.* Cleveland: 1965.
Swierenga, Robert P. *Quantification in American History: Theory and Research.* New York: 1970.
Teubal, Nissim. *El inmigrante: De Alepo a Buenos Aires.* Buenos Aires: 1953.
Thernstrom, Stephan and Richard Sennett, eds. *Nineteenth Century Cities: Essays in the New Urban History.* New Haven: 1969.
Thernstrom, Stephan. *Poverty and Progress: Social Mobility in a Nineteenth Century City.* New York: 1969.
Thiriot, Luis F. *Situación económica y financiera de la provincia de Córdoba.* Córdoba: 1892.
Tornquist y Compañía, Ernesto. *The Economic Development of the Argentine Republic in the Last Fifty Years.* Buenos Aires: 1919.
Ugarte, Manuel. *El porvenir de América Latina.* Buenos Aires: 1953.
Universidad Nacional de Córdoba. *Homenaje al Doctor Ceferino Garzón Maceda.* Córdoba: 1973.
Vallier, Ivan, ed. *Comparative Methods in Sociology: Essays on Trends and Applications.* Berkeley: 1971.
Vázquez, Juan Adolfo. *Antología filosófica argentina del siglo XX.* Buenos Aires: 1965.
Vázquez Presedo, Vicente. *El caso argentino: Migración de factores, comercio exterior y desarrollo, 1875-1914.* Buenos Aires: 1971.
Wagner, Phillip and Marvin Mikesell, eds. *Readings in Cultural Geography.* Chicago: 1962.
Ward, David. *Cities and Immigrants: A Geography of Change in Nineteenth Century America.* New York: 1971.
Warner, Sam B., Jr. *Streetcar Suburbs: The Process of Growth in Boston, 1870-1900.* New York: 1974.
Warner, W. Lloyd and Leo Srole. *The Social Systems of American Ethnic Groups.* New Haven: 1945.
Weinberg, Félix. *Vida e imagen de Sarmiento.* Buenos Aires: 1963.
Whiteford, Andrew. *Two Cities of Latin America: A Comparative Description of Social Classes.* New York: 1964.
Wilde, José A. *Buenos Aires desde 70 años atrás (1810-1880).* 3rd ed. Buenos Aires: 1964.
Zinny, Antonio. *Historia de los gobernadores de las provincias argentinas.* Buenos Aires: 1920.

B. Articles.

Agulla, Juan Carlos. "La aristocracia en el poder: Estudio de un estrato tradicional en una comunidad en desarrollo," *Aportes* 7 (1968): 76-88.

_____. "Aspectos sociales del proceso de industrialización en una comunidad urbana," *Revista Mexicana de Sociología* 25 (1963): 747-772.

_____. "Poder, comunidad y desarrollo industrial, La estructura de poder en una comunidad en desarrollo: Córdoba," *Aportes* 2 (1966): 80-105.

Albarracín, Santiago J. "Córdoba hace 60 años," *Revista Geográfica Americana* 28, no. 171 (1947): 241-247.

Anderson, Bo. "Commentary on Markos J. Mamalakis' 'Theory of Sectoral Clashes'," *Latin American Research Review* 4 (Fall 1969): 47-50.

Anonymous. "The Immigrant in South America," *Blackwood's Edinburgh Magazine* 190 (November 1911): 608-618.

Ansel, Bernard D. "European Adventurer in Tierra del Fuego: Julio Popper," *Hispanic American Historical Review* 50 (February 1970): 89-110.

Apter, David E. "Radicalization and Embourgeoisement: Some Hypotheses for a Comparative Study of History," *Journal of Interdisciplinary History* 1 (Winter 1971): 265-303.

Arcondo, Aníbal. "Notas para el estudio del trabajo compulsivo en la región de Córdoba." In *Homenaje al Doctor Ceferino Garzón Maceda.* Córdoba: 1973, pp. 133-145.

_____. "Población y mano de obra agrícola: Córdoba, 1880-1914," *Revista de Economía y Estadística* 14, nos. 1-4 (1970): 3-32.

_____. "Tierra y política de tierras en Córdoba," *Revista de Economía y Estadística* 13, nos. 3-4 (1969): 13-44.

Bacigalupo, José Luis. "Proceso de urbanización en Argentina." In *La urbanización en América Latina.* Ed. Jorge Enrique Hardoy and C. Tobar. Buenos Aires: 1969, pp. 389-417.

Bagú, Sergio. "La clase media en la Argentina." In *Materiales para el estudio de la clase media en la América Latina.* Washington, D.C.: 1950.

Balán, Jorge. "Migrant-native Socioeconomic Differences in Latin American Cities: A Structural Analysis," *Latin American Research Review* 4 (Spring 1969): 3-51.

Baltzell, E. Digby. *"Who's Who in America* and *The Social Register:* Elite and Upper Class Indexes in Metropolitan America." In *Class, Status, and Power: Social Stratification in Comparative Perspective.* Ed. Reinhard Bendix and Seymour M. Lipset. 2nd ed. New York: 1966, pp. 266-275.

Bazán, Armando Raúl. "Las bases sociales de la montonera," *Revista de Historia Americana y Argentina* 4, nos. 7-8 (1962-1963): 113-132.

Bejarano, Manuel. "Inmigración y estructuras tradicionales en Buenos Aires (1854-1930)." In *Los fragmentos del poder.* Ed. Torcuato S. Di Tella and Tulio Halperín Donghi. Buenos Aires: 1969, pp. 75-149.

Bendix, Reinhard and Seymour M. Lipset. "Karl Marx's Theory of Social Classes." In *Class, Status, and Power: Social Stratification in Comparative Perspective.* 2nd ed. New York: 1966, pp. 6-11.

Beyhaut, Gustavo et al., "Los inmigrantes en el sistema ocupacional argentino." In *Argentina, sociedad de masas*. Ed. Torcuato S. Di Tella, Gino Germani, and Jorge Graciarena. Buenos Aires: 1971, pp. 85-123.

Bischoff, Efraín U. "Batalla de Oncativo o Laguna Larga," *Anuario del Departamento de Historia* 1, no. 1 (1963): 9-61.

Blau, Peter M. and Otis Dudley Duncan. "Occupational Mobility in the United States." In *Structured Social Inequality: A Reader in Comparative Social Stratification*. Ed. Celia S. Heller. New York: 1969.

Bloomberg, Susan E. et al., "A Census Probe into Nineteenth Century Family History: Southern Michigan, 1850-1880," *Journal of Social History* 5 (Fall 1971): 26-45.

Blumin, Stuart. "The Historical Study of Vertical Mobility," *Historical Methods Newsletter* 1 (September 1968): 1-3.

————. "Mobility and Change in Ante-Bellum Philadelphia." In *Nineteenth Century Cities: Essays in the New Urban History*. Ed. Stephan Thernstrom and Richard Sennett. New Haven: 1969, pp. 165-208.

Buchanan, William I. "La moneda y la vida en la República Argentina," *Revista de Derecho y Letras* 1 (December 1898): 197-221.

Bunge, Alejandro E. "Costo de la vida en la Argentina de 1910 a 1917," *Revista de Economía Argentina* 1 (July 1918): 39-63.

————. "Costo de la vida, salarios y rendimiento, República Argentina," *Revista de Economía Argentina* 21 (September-December 1928): 1-39.

Cafferata, Juan F. "El saneamiento de la vivienda en la profiláxis contra la tuberculosis. Relación entre las condiciones de la vivienda y la mortalidad por la tuberculosis en el municipio de Córdoba," *Revista de la Universidad Nacional de Córdoba* 4 (December 1917): 355-429.

Cardoso, Fernando H. and José L. Reyna. "Industrialization, Occupational Structure, and Social Stratification in Latin America." In *Constructive Change in Latin America*. Ed. Stewart Cole Blasier. Pittsburgh: 1968, pp. 22-55.

Clubb, Jerome M. and Howard Allen. "Computers and Historical Studies," *Journal of American History* 54 (December 1967): 599-607.

Coleman, Emily R. "Medieval Marriage Characteristics: A Neglected Factor in the History of Medieval Serfdom," *Journal of Interdisciplinary History* 2 (Autumn 1971): 205-219.

Cornblit, Oscar. "Inmigrantes y empresarios en la política argentina," *Desarrollo Económico* 6 (January-May 1967): 641-691.

Cornblit, Oscar, Ezequiel Callo (H.), and Alfredo A. O'Connell. "La generación del 80 y su proyecto: Antecedentes y consecuencias." In *Argentina, sociedad de masas*. Ed. Torcuato S. Di Tella, Gino Germani, and Jorge Graciarena. Buenos Aires: 1971, pp. 18-58.

Cortés Conde, Roberto. "Cambios históricos en la estructura de la producción agropecuaria en la Argentina: Utilización de los recursos," *Desarrollo Económico* 5 (January-March 1966): 493-509.

————. "Problemas del crecimiento industrial (1870-1914)." In *Argentina,*

sociedad de masas. Ed. Torcuato S. Di Tella, Gino Germani, and Jorge
Graciarena. Buenos Aires: 1971, pp. 59-84.

————, "Tendencias en el crecimiento de la población urbana en Argentina."
In *Homenaje al Doctor Ceferino Garzón Maceda.* Córdoba: 1973, pp. 191-
205.

Crew, David. "Definitions of Modernity: Social Mobility in a German Town,
1880-1901," *Journal of Social History* 7 (Fall 1973): 51-74.

Critto, Adolfo. "Análisis del campo y de la ciudad, después de la migración.
Campo-ciudad en Córdoba." In *El proceso de urbanización en América
Latina desde sus orígenes hasta nuestros días.* Ed. Jorge E. Hardoy and
Richard P. Schaedel. Buenos Aires: 1969, pp. 339-359.

Davis, Kingsley and Wilbert E. Moore. "Some Principles of Stratification,"
American Sociological Review 10 (April 1945): 242-249.

Di Tella, Torcuato S. "Desarrollo económico y estructura ocupacional. Revi-
sión de la tesis de Colin Clark." In *La urbanización en América Latina.* Ed.
Jorge E. Hardoy and Carlos Tobar. Buenos Aires: 1969, pp. 257-269.

Dickinson, Robert E. "The Scope and Status of Urban Geography: An Assess-
ment," *Land Economics* 14 (August 1948): 221-238.

Fleming, John V. "Historians and the Evidence of Literature." *Journal of
Interdisciplinary History* 4 (Summer 1973): 95-105.

Ford, A. G. "Argentina y la crisis de Baring de 1890." Trans. Lelia Bustos
Vocos de Ortíz. *Revista de Economía y Estadística* 13, nos. 3-4 (1969): 133-
167.

Forni, Floreal H. "Aspectos sociales de la urbanización." In *La urbanización
en América Latina.* Ed. Jorge E. Hardoy and Carlos Tobar. Buenos Aires:
1969, pp. 205-234.

Fox, Thomas and S. M. Miller. "Occupational Stratification and Mobility:
Intra-Country Variations," *Studies in Comparative International Development* 1, no. 1 (1965): 3-10.

Fracchia, Alberto, Haydee Goróstegui de Torres, and Roberto Cortés Conde.
"Producto bruto en el período 1869-1914. Identificación de fuentes y suge-
rencias sobre métodos de estimación posibles." In *Jornadas de historia y
economía argentina en los siglos XVIII y XIX.* Buenos Aires-Rosario: 1964,
pp. 79-120.

Frías, Luis Rodolfo. "Simón Luengo, el constante revolucionario de Córdoba,"
Anuario del Departamento de Historia, 2-3, no. 2 (1968): 263-280.

Frisch, Michael H. "The Community Elite and the Emergence of Urban Poli-
tics: Springfield, Massachusetts, 1840-1880." In *Nineteenth Century Cities:
Essays in the New Urban History.* Ed. Stephan Thernstrom and Richard
Sennett. New Haven: 1969; pp. 277-296.

Gallo, Ezequiel (H.) and Silvia Sigal. "La formación de los partidos políticos
contemporáneos: La U.C.R. (1890-1916)." In *Argentina, sociedad de masas.*
Ed. Torcuato S. Di Tella, Gino Germani, and Jorge Graciarena. Buenos
Aires: 1971, pp. 124-176.

Gandia, Enrique de. "Fuentes de la historiografía en el siglo XX," *Revista*

Interamericana de Bibliografía 17 (January-March 1967): 3-50.

Germani, Gino. "Antisemitismo ideológico y antisemitismo tradicional." In *Los fragmentos del poder.* Ed. Torcuato S. Di Tella and Tulio Halperín Donghi. Buenos Aires: 1969, pp. 461-475.

————. "The City as an Integrating Mechanism." In *The Urban Explosion in Latin America.* Ed. G. Beyer. Ithaca: 1967, pp. 175-214.

————. "La clase media en la Argentina, con especial referencia a sus sectores urbanos." *Materiales para el estudio de la clase media en la América Latina.* Washington, D.C.: 1950, pp. 1-33.

————. "Mass Immigration and Modernization in Argentina." In *Masses in Latin America.* Ed. Irving L. Horowitz. New York: 1970, pp. 289-330.

————. "Mass Society, Social Class, and the Emergence of Fascism." In *Masses in Latin America.* Ed. Irving L. Horowitz. New York: 1970, pp. 577-600.

————. "La movilidad social en la Argentina." In *Movilidad social en la sociedad industrial.* Ed. Seymour M. Lipset and Reinhard Bendix. 2nd ed. Trans. Ricardo Malfé. Buenos Aires: 1969, pp. 317-366.

————. "La sociología en la Argentina," *Revista Latinoamericana de Sociología* 4 (November 1968): 385-420.

Glasco, Laurence A. "Computerizing the Manuscript Census." *Historical Methods Newsletter* 3 (December 1969): 1-4, and 3 (March 1970): 20-25.

Glass, D. V. "Social Stratification and Social Mobility," *International Social Science Bulletin* 1, no. 1 (1954): 12-25.

Goode, William J. "Family and Mobility." In *Class, Status, and Power: Social Stratification in Comparative Perspective.* Ed. Reinhard Bendix and Seymour M. Lipset. 2nd ed. New York: 1966, pp. 582-601.

————. "Marital Satisfaction and Instability: A Cross Cultural Class Analysis of Divorce Rates," *International Social Science Journal* 14, no. 3 (1962): 507-526.

Goróstegui de Torres, Haydee. "Aspectos económicos de la organización nacional." In *Los fragmentos del poder.* Ed. Torcuato S. Di Tella and Tulio Halperín Donghi. Buenos Aires: 1969, pp. 151-170.

Grenón, Pedro, S. J. "Medio siglo de periodismo cordobés (los de la tercera imprenta)," *Anuario del Departamento de Historia* 2-3, no. 2 (1968): 281-412.

Griffen, Clyde. "Occupational Mobility in Nineteenth Century America: Problems and Possibilities," *Journal of Social History* 5 (Spring 1972): 310-330.

————. "Public Opinion in Urban History," *Journal of Interdisciplinary History* 4 (Winter 1974): 469-474.

————. "Workers Divided: The Effect of Craft and Ethnic Differences in Poughkeepsie, New York, 1850-1880." In *Nineteenth Century Cities: Essays in the New Urban History.* Ed. Stephan Thernstrom and Richard Sennett. New Haven: 1969, pp. 49-97.

Gutman, Herbert G. "The Reality of the Rags-to-Riches 'Myth': The Case of Paterson, New Jersey, Locomotive, Iron, and Machinery Manufacturers,

1830-1880." In *Nineteenth Century Cities: Essays in the New Urban History.* Ed. Stephan Thernstrom and Richard Sennett. New Haven: 1969, pp. 98-124.

Hardoy, Jorge E. et al. "El caso de Argentina [urbanización]," *Revista de la Sociedad Interamericana de Planificación* 2, nos. 5-6 (1968): 31-38.

Hardoy, Jorge E. "Dos mil años de urbanización en América Latina." In *La urbanización en América Latina.* Ed. Jorge E. Hardoy and Carlos Tobar. Buenos Aires: 1969, pp. 23-64.

Hardoy, Jorge E. and Carmen Aranovich. "Urban Scales and Functions in Spanish America Towards the Year 1600: First Conclusions," *Latin American Research Review* 5 (Fall 1970): 57-91.

Hareven, Tamara K. "The History of the Family as an Interdisciplinary Field," *Journal of Interdisciplinary History* 2 (Autumn 1971): 399-414.

Hays, Samuel P. "Historical Social Research: Concept, Method, and Technique," *Journal of Interdisciplinary History* 4 (Winter 1974): 475-482.

Hershberg, Theodore et al. "Occupation and Ethnicity in Five Nineteenth Century Cities: A Collaborative Inquiry," *Historical Methods Newsletter* 7 (June 1974): 174-216.

Hobsbawm, Eric J. "Labor History and Ideology," *Journal of Social History* 7 (Summer 1974): 371-381.

Hodge, Robert, Paul M. Siegel, and Peter H. Rossi. "Occupational Prestige in the United States: 1925-1963," *American Journal of Sociology* 70 (November 1964): 286-302.

Hodge, Robert W., Donald J. Treiman, and Peter H. Rossi. "A Comparative Study of Occupational Prestige." In *Class, Status and Power: Social Stratification in Comparative Perspective.* Ed. Reinhard Bendix and Seymour M. Lipset. 2nd ed. New York: 1966, pp. 309-321.

Hutchinson, Bertram. "Some Evidence Related to Matrimonial Selection and Immigrant Assimilation in Brazil," *Population Studies* 11 (November 1957): 149-156.

Inkeles, Alex and Peter H. Rossi. "National Comparisons of Occupational Prestige," *American Journal of Sociology* 61 (January 1956): 329-339.

Iparraguirre, Hilda. "Notas para el estudio de la demografía de la ciudad de Córdoba en el período 1869-1914." In *Homenaje al Doctor Ceferino Garzón Maceda.* Córdoba: 1973, pp. 267-288.

Kahl, Joseph and James A. Davis. "A Comparison of Indexes of Socioeconomic Status," *American Sociological Review* 20 (June 1955): 317-325.

Katz, Michael B. "Occupational Classification in History," *Journal of Interdisciplinary History* 3 (Summer 1972): 63-88.

————. "Social Structure in Hamilton, Ontario." In *Nineteenth Century Cities: Essays in the New Urban History.* Ed. Stephan Thernstrom and Richard Sennett. New Haven: 1969, pp. 209-244.

Knights, Peter R. "Population Turnover, Persistence, and Residential Mobility In Boston, 1830-1860." In *Nineteenth Century Cities: Essays in the New Urban History.* Ed. Stephan Thernstrom and Richard Sennett. New Haven:

1969, pp. 258-274.

Korn, Francis. "Algunos aspectos de la asimilación de inmigrantes en Buenos Aires." In *Los fragmentos del poder*. Ed. Torcuato S. Di Tella and Tulio Halperín Donghi. Buenos Aires: 1969, pp. 439-460.

Larsson de Reinhold, Karin. "Notas para el estudio del comercio entre Córdoba y las demás provincias en 1820," *Anuario del Departamento de Historia* 1, no. 1 (1963): 135-165.

Lees, Lynn H. "Patterns of Lower-Class Life: Irish Slum Communities in Nineteenth-Century London." In *Nineteenth Century Cities: Essays in the New Urban History*. Ed. Stephan Thernstrom and Richard Sennett. New Haven: 1969, pp. 359-385.

Lipset, Seymour M. and Hans L. Zetterberg. "A Theory of Social Mobility," *Transactions of the Third World Congress of Sociology* 2 (1956): 155-177.

Lockhart, James. "The Social History of Colonial Spanish America: Evolution and Potential," *Latin American Research Review* 7 (Spring 1972): 6-45.

MacDonald, John S. "Agricultural Organization, Migration and Labour Militancy in Rural Italy," *Economic History Review* 14 (August-April 1963-1964): 61-75.

MacDonald, John S. and Leatrice D. MacDonald. "Italian Migration to Australia: Manifest Functions of Bureaucracy Versus Latent Functions of Informal Networks," *Journal of Social History* 3 (Spring 1970): 249-275.

Mamalakis, Markos J. "The Theory of Sectoral Clashes," *Latin American Research Review* 4 (Fall 1969): 9-46.

McGrath, William J. "Volksseelenpolitik and Psychological Rebirth: Mahler and Hofmannstahl," *Journal of Interdisciplinary History* 4 (Summer 1973): 53-72.

McGreevey, William P. "Recent Material and Opportunities for Quantitative Research in Latin American History: Nineteenth and Twentieth Centuries," *Latin American Research Review* 9 (Summer 1974): 72-82.

Melo, Carlos R. "Las provincias durante la presidencia de Sarmiento, 1868-1874," *Humanidades* 37, no. 3 (1961): 149-196.

Merkx, Gilbert W. "Recessions and Rebellions in Argentina, 1870-1970," *Hispanic American Historical Review* 53 (May 1973): 285-295.

Merton, Robert K. and Alice Kitt Rossi. "Contributions to the Theory of Reference Group Behavior." In *Continuities in Social Research*. Ed. Robert K. Merton and Paul F. Lazarsfeld. New York: 1950, pp. 40-105.

Miller, S. M. "Comparative Social Mobility," *Current Sociology* 9 (1960): 1-89.

Mills, C. Wright. "The Middle Classes in Middle-Sized Cities," *American Sociological Review* 11 (December 1946): 520-529.

Mittelbach, Frank G. and Joan W. Moore. "Ethnic Endogamy—The Case of Mexican Americans," *American Journal of Sociology* 74 (July 1968): 50-62.

Modell, John. "The Peopling of a Working-Class Ward: Reading, Pennsylvania, 1850," *Journal of Social History* 5 (Fall 1971): 71-95.

Mörner, Magnus. "The History of Race Relations in Latin America: Some Comments on the State of the Research," *Latin American Research Review*

1 (Summer 1966): 17-44.

Morse, Richard M. "Cities and Society in Nineteenth Century Latin America: The Illustrative Case of Brazil." In *El proceso de urbanización en América desde sus orígenes hasta nuestros días*. Ed. Jorge E. Hardoy and Richard P. Schaedel. Buenos Aires: 1969, pp. 303-322.

_____. "A Prolegomenon to Latin American Urban History," *Hispanic American Historical Review* 52 (August 1972): 359-394.

_____. "Recent Research on Latin American Urbanization: A Selective Survey with Commentary," *Latin American Research Review* 1 (Fall 1965): 3574.

_____. "Trends and Issues in Latin American Urban Research, 1965-1970 (Part I)," *Latin American Research Review* 6 (Spring 1971): 3-52.

_____. "Trends and Issues in Latin American Urban Research, 1965-1970 (Part II)," *Latin American Research Review* 6 (Spring 1971): 19-75.

Newton, Ronald C. "On 'Functional Groups,' 'Fragmentation,' and 'Pluralism' in Spanish American Political Society," *Hispanic American Historical Review* 50 (February 1970): 1-29.

Niebuhr, Barthold Georg. "Vorrede zu der ersten Ausgabe." From *Römische Geschichte*. Ed. M. Isler. Rev. ed. 3 vols. Berlin: 1873. Trans. and ed. Fritz Stern. In *The Varieties of History: From Voltaire to the Present*. Cleveland: 1956.

Noé, Julio. "La religión, la familia, y la propiedad en la sociedad argentina a fines del siglo XVIII," *Anales de la Facultad de Derecho y Ciencias Sociales* 2 (1916): 152-181.

Padilla, Francisco Jurado. "La Universidad de Córdoba en la última década del siglo XIX," *Revista de la Universidad Nacional de Córdoba* 38 (September-December 1951): 1145-1173.

Park, Robert E. "Human Migration and the Marginal Man," *American Journal of Sociology* 33 (May 1928): 881-893.

Pianetto, Ofelia. "Industria y formación de clase obrera en la ciudad de Córdoba, 1880-1906." In *Homenaje al Doctor Ceferino Garzón Maceda*. Córdoba: 1973.

Pinto, Juan. "El inmigrante en nuestro teatro," *Universidad* 49 (January-March 1964): 41-62.

Portes, Alejandro. "Sociology and the Use of Secondary Data." In *Quantitative Social Science Research on Latin America*. Ed. Robert S. Byars and Joseph L. Love. Urbana: 1973.

Reeves Kennedy, Ruby J. "Single or Triple Melting Pot? Intermarriage Trends in New Haven, 1870-1940," *American Journal of Sociology* 49 (January 1944): 331-339.

Río, Manuel E. "Consideraciones históricas y sociológicas sobre la provincia de Córdoba." In *Córdoba: Su fisonomía, su misión. Escritos y discursos*. Córdoba: 1967, pp. 89-105.

_____. "Córdoba, 1810-1910," *Revista de la Junta Provincia de Historia de Córdoba* 1 (1960): 11-76.

_____. "Reseña histórica de la Universidad Nacional de Córdoba." In *Córdoba: Su fisonomía, su misión. Escritos y discursos.* Córdoba: 1967, pp. 257-258.

_____. "La Universidad de Córdoba." In *Córdoba: Su fisonomía, su misión. Escritos y discursos.* Córdoba: 1967, pp. 233-239.

Robinson, James H. and Charles A. Beard. "Preface." From *The Development of Modern Europe.* 2 vols. Boston: 1907. In *The Varieties of History: From Voltaire to the Present.* Ed. Fritz Stern. Cleveland: 1956.

Rodgers, Allan. "Migration and Industrial Development: The Southern Italian Experience," *Economic Geography* 46 (April 1970): 111-135.

Rodríguez Molas, Ricardo. "En los umbrales de *La Bolsa* de Julian Martel," *Anuario del Departamento de Historia* 1 (1963): 575-609.

Rogoff, Natalie. "Social Stratification in France and the United States," *American Journal of Sociology* 58 (January 1953): 347-357.

Romano Yalour de Tobar, Margot. "El proceso de socialización urbana." In *La urbanización en América Latina.* Ed. Jorge E. Hardoy and Carlos Tobar. Buenos Aires: 1969, pp. 235-256.

Romero, José L. "La ciudad latinoamericana y los movimientos políticos." In *La urbanización en América Latina.* Ed. Jorge E. Hardoy and Carlos Tobar. Buenos Aires: 1969, pp. 297-310.

Romero, Lilians Betty. "Córdoba en el decenio anterior a la Revolución del 90." In *Homenaje al Doctor Ceferino Garzón Maceda.* Córdoba: 1973, pp. 375-392.

Sánchez, Marta. "Movimientos de lucha y organización de la clase obrera en la ciudad de Córdoba, 1895-1905." In *Homenaje al Doctor Ceferino Garzón Maceda.* Córdoba: 1973, pp. 393-408.

Savorgnan, Franco. "Celibi e coniugati nella popolazione nativa e nella popolazione immigrata." In *Scritti Vari Dedicati al Prof. E. Masè-Dari.* Modena: 1935, pp. 36-40.

_____. "Matrimonial Selection and the Amalgamation of Heterogeneous Groups." In *Cultural Assimilation of Immigrants.* International Union for the Scientific Study of Population. London: 1950, pp. 59-67.

Scalabrini Ortíz, Raúl. "Historia del Ferrocarril Central Córdoba," *Cuadernos de F.O.R.J.A.* 2 (November 1938): 1-62.

Schermerhorn, Richard A. "Power in the Local Community." In *Structured Social Inequality: A Reader in Comparative Social Stratification.* Ed. Celia S. Heller. New York: 1970, pp. 168-175.

Schiff, Warren. "The Influence of the German Armed Forces and War Industry on Argentina, 1880-1914," *Hispanic American Historical Review* 52 (August 1972): 436-455.

Schnore, Leo F. and Peter R. Knights. "Residence and Social Structure: Boston in the Ante-Bellum Period." In *Nineteenth Century Cities: Essays in the New Urban History.* Ed. Stephan Thernstrom and Richard Sennett. New Haven: 1969, pp. 247-257.

Scobie, James R. "Buenos Aires as a Commercial-Bureaucratic City, 1880-1910:

Characteristics of a City's Orientation," *American Historical Review* 77 (October 1972): 1035-1073.

—————. "Changing Urban Patterns: The Porteño Case, 1880-1910." In *El proceso de urbanización en América desde sus orígenes hasta nuestros días.* Ed. Jorge E. Hardoy and Richard P. Schaedel. Buenos Aires: 1969, pp. 323-338.

—————. "Commentary on Urban Scales and Functions in Spanish America Toward the Year 1600: First Conclusions by Jorge E. Hardoy and Carmen Aranovich," *Latin American Research Review* 5 (Fall 1970): 100-105.

Scott, Joan W. "The Glassworkers of Carmaux, 1850-1900." In *Nineteenth Century Cities: Essays in the New Urban History.* Ed. Stephan Thernstrom and Richard Sennett. New Haven: 1969, pp. 3-48.

Sennett, Richard. "Middle-Class Families and Urban Violence: The Experience of a Chicago Community in the Nineteenth Century." In *Nineteenth Century Cities: Essays in the New Urban History.* Ed. Stephan Thernstrom and Richard Sennett. New Haven: 1969, pp. 386-420.

Smith, Peter H. "History." In *Quantitative Social Science Research on Latin America.* Ed. Robert S. Byars and Joseph L. Love. Urbana: 1973, pp. 14-61.

Soares, Glaucio A. D. "Economic Development and Class Structure." In *Class, Status and Power: Social Stratification in Comparative Perspective.* Ed. Reinhard Bendix and Seymour M. Lipset. 2nd ed. New York: 1966, pp. 190-199.

Sofer, Eugene F., and Mark Szuchman. "City and Society: Their Connection in Latin American Historical Research," *Latin American Research Review* 14 (1979): 113-129.

—————. "Educating Immigrants: Voluntary Associations in the Acculturation Process." In *Educational Alternatives in Latin America: Social Change and Social Stratification.* Ed. Thomas J. La Belle. Los Angeles: 1975, pp. 334-359.

Solberg, Carl. "Immigration and Urban Social Problems in Argentina and Chile, 1880-1914," *Hispanic American Historical Review* 49 (May 1969): 215-232.

Sopher, David. "Place and Location: Notes on the Spatial Patterning of Culture." In *The Idea of Culture in the Social Sciences.* Ed. Louis Schneider and Charles Bonjean. London: 1973.

Spalding, Hobart A., Jr. "Education in Argentina, 1890-1914: The Limits of Oligarchical Reform," *Journal of Interdisciplinary History* 3 (Summer 1972): 31-61.

Spalding, Karen. "Social Climbers: Changing Patterns of Mobility Among the Indians of Colonial Peru," *Hispanic American Historical Review* 50 (November 1970): 645-664.

Stout, Harry S. "University Men in New England, 1620-1660: A Demographic Analysis," *Journal of Interdisciplinary History* 4 (Winter 1974): 375-400.

Streuver, Nancy S. "The Study of Language and the Study of History,"

Journal of Interdisciplinary History 4 (Winter 1974): 401-415.

Suárez, Odilia E. "El diseño urbano en América Latina." In *La urbanización en América Latina*. Ed. Jorge E. Hardoy and Carlos Tobar. Buenos Aires: 1969, pp. 65-86.

Szuchman, Mark D. "The Limits of the Melting Pot in Urban Argentina: Marriage and Integration in Córdoba, 1869-1909," *Hispanic American Historical Review* 57 (February 1977): 24-50.

_____. "The State of Occupational Stratification Studies in Argentina: A Classificatory Scheme," *Latin American Research Review* 11 (Spring 1976): 159-171.

Thernstrom, Stephan. "Immigrants and WASPs: Ethnic Differences in Occupational Mobility in Boston, 1890-1940." In *Nineteenth Century Cities: Essays in the New Urban History*. Ed. Stephan Thernstrom and Richard Sennett. New Haven: 1969, pp. 125-164.

_____. "Notes on the Historical Study of Social Mobility," *Comparative Studies in Society and History* 10 (January 1968): 162-172.

_____. "Reflections on the New Urban History," *Daedalus* 100 (Spring 1971): 359-375.

_____. "Urbanization, Migration, and Social Mobility in Late Nineteenth Century America." In *Towards a New Past*. Ed. Barton J. Bernstein. New York: 1968, pp. 158-175.

Thernstrom, Stephan, and Peter R. Knights. "Men in Motion: Some Data and Speculations about Urban Population Mobility in Nineteenth Century America," *Journal of Interdisciplinary History* 1 (Autumn 1970): 7-35.

Torino, Damián M. "El problema del inmigrante y la cuestión agraria en la Argentina," *Atlántida* 4 (1912): 161-189.

Torrado, Susana. "Cambios en la estructura social de la provincia de Córdoba en el período de la inmigración masiva, 1870-1914." In *Jornadas de Historia y economía argentina en los siglos XVIII y XIX*. Buenos Aires-Rosario: 1964, pp. 205-219.

Tumin, Melvin M. "Some Principles of Stratification: A Critical Analysis," *American Sociological Review* 18 (August 1953): 387-393.

Turner, Ralph H. "Modes of Social Ascent Through Education: Sponsored and and Contest Mobility," *American Sociological Review* 25 (December 1960): 855-867.

Veblen, Thorstein. "The Theory of the Leisure Class." In *Class, Status and Power: Social Stratification in Comparative Perspective*. Ed. Reinhard Bendix and Seymour M. Lipset. 2nd ed. New York: 1966, pp. 36-42.

Verba, Sidney. "Cross-National Survey Research: The Problem of Credibility." In *Comparative Methods in Sociology: Essays on Trends and Applications*. Ed. Ivan Vallier. Berkeley: 1971.

Weber, Max. "Class, Status, Party." In *From Max Weber: Essays in Sociology*. Ed. Hans H. Gerth and C. Wright Mills. New York: 1969, pp. 180-195.

_____. "Religious Rejections of the World and Other Directions." In *From Max Weber: Essays in Sociology*. Ed. Hans H. Gerth and C. Wright Mills.

New York: 1969, pp. 323-359.

Welter, Barbara. "The Cult of True Womanhood: 1820-1860," *American Quarterly* 18, Part 1 (1966): 151-174.

Wirth, Louis, "Urbanism as a Way of Life," *American Journal of Sociology* 44 (July 1938): 1-24.

Yans-McLaughlin, Virginia. "A Flexible Tradition: South Italian Immigrants Confront a New York Experience," *Journal of Social History* 7 (Summer 1974): 429-445.

Yujnovsky, Oscar. "Estructura interna de la ciudad." In *La urbanización en América Latina.* Ed. Jorge E. Hardoy and Carlos Tobar. Buenos Aires: 1969, pp. 113-147.

Zavala, Mabel E. "Las fronteras del sur de Córdoba en los años 1844-1845," *Anuario del Departamento de Historia* 1 (1963): 629-650.

C. *Newspapers.*
La Carcajada, 1871-1905.
El Constitucional, 1875-1876.
El Eco de Córdoba, 1863-1878.
El Independiente, 1873.
La Libertad, 1891-1906.
El Oráculo, 1898.
La Patria, 1894-1906.
El Porvenir, 1886-1892.
Los Principios, 1894-1906.
El Progreso, 1875-1878.

D. *Unpublished Materials.*
Castro, Donald S. "The Development of Argentine Immigration Policy, 1862-1914." Doctoral dissertation. UCLA, 1968.

Celton, Dora Estela. "Censo de la ciudad de Córdoba del año 1840. Estudio demográfico." Thesis. Universidad Nacional de Córdoba, 1971.

Della Casa de Tauro, Azucena Perla. "Censo de la ciudad de Córdoba del año 1832. Estudio demográfico." Thesis. Universidad Nacional de Córdoba. 1972.

Galliari, Mabel and Marta Sánchez. "Aportaciones al estudio de la formación de la clase obrera en Córdoba en el período 1895-1905." Paper. Universidad Nacional de Córdoba, 1967.

Griswold del Castillo, Richard A. "La Raza Hispano Americana: The Emergence of an Urban Culture among the Spanish Speaking of Los Angeles." Doctoral dissertation. UCLA, 1974.

Hernando, Diana. *"Casa y familia:* Spatial Biographies in 19th Century Buenos Aires." Doctoral dissertation. UCLA, 1973.

Portes, Alejandro. "Assimilation of Latin American Minorities in the U.S." Mimeo. The University of Texas at Austin, 1972.

Rock, David. "Radicalism and Urban Working Class in Buenos Aires, 1916-1922."

Doctoral dissertation. Cambridge University, 1971.

Sofer, Eugene F. "From Pale to Pampa: Eastern European Jewish Social Mobility in Gran Buenos Aires, 1890-1945." Doctoral dissertation. UCLA, 1976.

_____. "Voluntary Associations and the Achievement of Bourgeois Norms: The Case of the Jews of Buenos Aires, 1890-1930." Paper presented at the Social Science History Association Meeting. October 1977.

Tulchin, Joseph. "Agricultural Credit and Politics in Argentina, 1910-1922." Mimeo, n.d.

Vaughan, Denton R. "Urbanization in Twentieth Century Latin America: A Working Bibliography." Mimeo. The University of Texas at Austin, 1969.

III. REFERENCE WORKS

Arkin, Herbert and Raymond R. Colton, comps. *Tables for Statisticians.* New York: 1963.

Arrazola, Roberto. *Diccionario de modismos argentinos.* Buenos Aires: 1943.

Boeri, Lelia I., ed. *Catálogo de estadísticas publicadas en la República Argentina.* 2 vols. 2nd ed. Buenos Aires: 1966.

Cáceres Freyre, Julián B. *Diccionario de regionalismos de la Provincia de La Rioja.* Buenos Aires: 1961.

Diccionario comercial e industrial de la República Argentina. Buenos Aires: 1942.

Fisher, Ronald A. and Frank Yates. *Tablas estadísticas.* Madrid: 1949.

Garzón, Tobías. *Diccionario argentino.* Barcelona: 1910.

Grenón, Pedro, S. J. and Emiliano Endrek. *Bibliografía Cordobesa (1850-1900).* Córdoba, n.d.

Nie, Norman H., Dale H. Bent, and C. Hadlai Hull. *SPSS: Statistical Package for the Social Sciences.* New York: 1970.

Universidad Nacional de Córdoba. *Catálogo de periódicos.* Córdoba: 1922.

Vázquez Presedo, Vicente. *Estadísticas históricas argentinas (comparadas). Primera parte, 1875-1914.* Buenos Aires: 1971.

Index